PRAISE FOR SYD FIELD

"[Syd Field is] the most sought-after screenwriting teacher in the world."—*Hollywood Reporter*

"Syd Field is the preeminent analyzer in the study of American screenplays."—JAMES L. BROOKS, Academy Award–winning writer, director, producer

"I based *Like Water for Chocolate* on what I learned in Syd's books. Before, I always felt structure imprisoned me, but what I learned was structure really freed me to focus on the story."—LAURA ESQUIVEL, writer, *Like Water for Chocolate*

"If I were writing screenplays . . . I would carry Syd Field around in my back pocket wherever I went."—STEVEN BOCHCO, writer/producer/director, *NYPD Blue*

"Syd Field's book[s] have been the Bible and Talmud for a generation of budding screenwriters."—Salon.com

THE SCREENWRITER'S WORKBOOK:
Exercises and Step-by-Step Instruction for Creating a Successful Screenplay

"One of the standards in the industry."—Amazon.com

SCREENPLAY:
The Foundations of Screenwriting

"*Screenplay* is one of the bibles of the film trade and has launched many a would-be screenwriter on the road to Hollywood."—*Library Journal*

"[Syd Field is the] guru of would-be screenwriters. . . . *Screenplay* is their bestselling bible."—*Los Angeles Herald Examiner*

"Full of common sense, an uncommon commodity."—*Esquire*

"Quite simply the *only* manual to be taken seriously by aspiring screenwriters."—TONY BILL, Academy Award–winning producer, director

"Impressive because of its rare combinations: a technical book, apparently mechanically sound, that's quite personable and lively and also seems to care about us, about our doing things right and making good. His easy-to-follow, step-by-step approaches are comforting and his emphasis on right attitude and motivation is uplifting."—*Los Angeles Times Book Review*

"A much-needed book."—Frank Pierson, Academy Award–winning screenwriter; president, Writers Guild of America, West

"The basics of the craft in terms simple enough to enable any beginner to develop an idea into a submittable script."—*American Cinematographer*

"A much-needed book... straightforward and informed... accurate and clear, and should be enormously helpful to novices."—*Fade-In*

"The complete primer, a step-by-step guide from the first glimmer of an idea to marketing the finished script."—*New West*

"Experienced advice on story development, creation and definition of characters, structure of action, and direction of participants. Easy-to-follow guidelines and a commonsense approach mark this highly useful manual."—*Video*

"Great advice for screenwriters. I always tell young writers to pick up *Screenplay* and read it right away—then either embrace it or rebel against it, but it'll certainly get your mind turning in the right ways."—David Koepp, award-winning writer, director, *Spider-Man, Secret Window, War of the Worlds*

SELLING A SCREENPLAY:
The Screenwriter's Guide to Hollywood

"A wonderful book that should be in every filmmaker's library." —Howard Kazanjian, producer, *Raiders of the Lost Ark, Return of the Jedi, Demolition Man*

"An informative, engaging look at the inside of the dream factory. This is a terrific aid for screenwriters who are trying to gain insight into the Hollywood system."—David Kirkpatrick, producer, former head of Paramount Pictures

FOUR SCREENPLAYS:
Studies in American Screenplay

"A book that writers will stand in line for and studio executives will Xerox."—JAMES L. BROOKS, Academy Award–winning writer, director, producer

"What does it take to write a great script? You'll find the answer here.... This is Field's masterpiece and a required purchase for all film collections."—*Library Journal*

"A first-rate analysis of why good screenplays work: a virtual must for aspiring screenwriters."—LINDA OBST, producer, *How to Lose a Guy in Ten Days, Sleepless in Seattle*

"A fascinating view into the most overlooked process of filmmaking." —MICHAEL BESMAN, producer, *About Schmidt*

"Theory comes alive with this hands-on approach to what makes four great screenplays tick."—DEBORAH JELIN NEWMYER, producer, executive vice president, Amblin Entertainment

"*Four Screenplays* is not only Syd Field's most instructive book... it's the most fun to read."—ANNA HAMILTON PHELAN, screenwriter, *Mask, Gorillas in the Mist*

"One of the very best books I have read on movies or screenplays. Syd writes both with passion and an astute understanding."—HANS ZIMMER, film composer, *The Da Vinci Code, Gladiator, The Last Samurai, Thelma & Louise*

THE SCREENWRITER'S PROBLEM SOLVER:
How to Recognize, Identify, and Define Screenwriting Problems

"Whatever your problem, screenwriting guru Syd Field can help." —Amazon.com

GOING TO THE MOVIES:
A Personal Journey Through Four Decades of Modern Film

"The master teacher of screenplay writing... reveals himself to be a true Hollywood character. No one sees films quite the way Field does.... An original thinker worth appreciating."—*Kirkus Reviews*

"Although cloaked in modesty, his illuminating, consistently entertaining memoir displays enough wit, intelligence and empathy to inspire a host of great films."—*Publishers Weekly*

"Syd Field knows movies inside and out, and this, his most personal book yet, is charming, warmhearted, and very wise. Grab some popcorn, sit back and share some big-screen magic with the master."—Ted Tally, Academy Award–winning screenwriter, *The Silence of the Lambs*

"What really makes this book is how well he conducts us on his journey... [and] his true love for the movies."—*Booklist*

"Those of us who've wondered why Syd would devote himself to raising the bar for screenwriting now learn why—a lifelong and passionate love for movies and filmmaking."—Marc Norman, Academy Award–winning screenwriter, *Shakespeare in Love*

"A fascinating journey through thirty years of moviegoing—asking the question we all ask: 'What makes a movie work?' and finding the answers."—Fay Kanin, former president, Academy of Motion Picture Arts and Sciences

"Field forges new pathways into understanding the transforming powers of the screenplay. In this insightful testament to film craft, Field's influence on generations of film devotees represents a climate of opinion, respected and imitated. Nothing is more rare."—James Ragan, director, Professional Writing Program, University of Southern California

"Field's passion for cinema shines throughout."—*Library Journal*

"Syd Field has spent a lifetime seeking answers to what makes a great movie. Now he shares his own remarkable story about the movies and the legendary filmmakers who inspired his extraordinary career."—*Variety*

Also by Syd Field

SCREENPLAY

GOING TO THE MOVIES

SELLING A SCREENPLAY

FOUR SCREENPLAYS

THE SCREENWRITER'S PROBLEM SOLVER

THE SCREEN WORK

SYD FIELD

THE SCREENWRITER'S WORKBOOK

REVISED EDITION

THE SCREENWRITER'S WORKBOOK
A Delta Book

PUBLISHING HISTORY
Dell trade paperback edition published July 1984
Delta Trade Paperback revised edition / November 2006

Published by Bantam Dell
A Division of Random House, Inc.
New York, New York

Cover design by Belina Huey

Library of Congress Cataloging-in-Publication Data
Field, Syd.
The screenwriter's workbook / Syd Field
p. cm.
ISBN-10: 0-385-33904-6
ISBN-13: 978-0-385-33904-9
1. Motion picture authorship. I. Title.
PN1996 .F44 2006 2006048458
808.2/3 22

Printed in the United States of America
Published simultaneously in Canada

www.bantamdell.com

BVG 10 9 8 7 6 5

To all those who went before
and to all those who follow...
and
To all the great Siddha Saints and Masters—
always in my heart, always in my mind...

A SPECIAL THANKS

To Jean Renoir for pointing out the path through the forest; to Michelangelo Antonioni and Sam Peckinpah who guided me along the path; and Tony Gilroy, an extraordinary screenwriter, for his generosity, insight, and creative spirit; and to my students, the world over, who taught me everything I needed to know.

Contents

Introduction

> "*Qu'est-ce que le cinéma?* What is film?"
> —Jean Renoir

"What is film?" Is it art? Literature?

That was the question my mentor Jean Renoir, the great French film director, often presented to us during the year he was Artist in Residence at the University of California, Berkeley. I met him after a performance of *Woyzeck,* the Georg Buchner expressionist drama, in which I was playing the lead role. I was told that Renoir was going to present the world premiere of his play *Carola,* and I was being asked to audition for the part.

A few days later, I read for Renoir, got the third lead in the play, playing the role of Campan, the French stage manager, and so began my mentorship with a man who would ultimately shape my attitude toward movies and my life. For the next year, I had a direct, close, and personal relationship with the great director. Not knowing much about film, what it was or what it could be, it was Renoir who opened up a treasure chest of knowledge and insight. He shared his personal view that movies "are a new form of printing—another form of the total transformation of the world through knowledge." He would refer to Lumière, inventor of the early French motion picture camera called the *Cinématographe,* as "another Gutenberg."

Renoir insisted that movies had the potential to be literature, but they should never be considered art. When I asked what he meant, he replied that art is the sole vision of one person, which in the scheme of the filmmaking process, is a contradiction. He explained that one person can't do everything that's required to make a movie. One person can write the screenplay, direct the film, photograph it, edit it, and score it—like Charlie Chaplin did—but, Renoir continued, the filmmaker cannot act all the parts, or record all the sound, or handle all the lighting requirements amid the myriad other details that are required to make a movie. "Art," he said, "should offer the viewer the chance of merging with the creator."

As young college students learning from the master, we would literally sit at his feet and ask questions, share our ideas, or discuss our opinions of life and art. He would answer everything. Every question, even the dumbest one, was received with interest and respect. When someone asked, "how can we be true to our art?" he shared his personal philosophy that "art is in the doing of it."

A simple answer, yet profound, relevant, and true. It's only during the process of working, he explained, whether directing a film, writing a song, writing a script, painting a picture, or whatever it may be, that one "creates art." Art, he proclaimed, is the process of actually sitting down and doing it. Not talking about doing it, not thinking or fantasizing about doing it, just doing it. Only after the work has been completed and exposed to public view will it be considered a work of "art" or not. If you think you're "an artist" just waiting for that one moment of inspiration to sit down and write, you'll be waiting forever.

Over the past twenty-five years, I've thought about Renoir's words as I've traveled the world conducting screenwriting seminars for professional and aspiring screenwriters. As I look back over the footprints of my life from the time I wrote the first edition of this book, some twenty-five years ago, to now, I see that screenwriting, both as an art and a craft, has evolved into an international language of engaging visual expression.

We're currently standing on the threshold of a new frontier in film, and there are no rules as to what we can or cannot do. It is a time of evolution/revolution, a time of transformation in which the theater of technology has embraced a new era of digital technology. *What we see* and *how we see it* have changed.

Story exposition is shown rather than told; characters are revealed through behavior, not dialogue; time present and past have merged into a compelling storytelling device. As said in Eastern philosophy, the inside and outside are one; the thoughts, feelings, and emotions that are inside our head are what creates the fabric of our experience. Basically, you are the baker of the bread you eat.

A screenplay is a special form; it is a story told in pictures, expressed in dialogue and description. The technological impact has facilitated a change in our classic traditional narrative; linear story lines like *Casablanca* and *The Godfather*, expressed in long expository scenes, have become more visually stylized presentations such as *Sideways*, *Magnolia*, and *Brokeback Mountain*. Nonlinear storytelling, almost a rarity during the last few decades, has now become part of a film lexicon that seems taken for granted: *The Bourne Supremacy*, *Memento*, and *The Constant Gardener*, are structured in bits and pieces from the shards and broken fragments of memory and have become part of the screenwriter's language.

The question Renoir posed so many years before, "*Qu'est-ce que le cinéma?*" is as relevant today as when I first heard it. How do we define the art of film? How do we analyze it? How do we craft our movies so they are more than mere flashing images on the screen, but become what Renoir referred to as "an art form that is larger than life."

We are now living in a time of visual storytelling. Whether you want to tell a story on the big screen or write a television show that can be downloaded onto an iPod, cell phone, or PDA; whether you want to create a video game or short film; a business plan or a PowerPoint presentation for any future delivery system, you have to know the tools and rules of visual storytelling. That's what *The Screenwriter's Workbook* is all about.

The Screenwriter's Workbook explores the process of writing a screenplay, which is visual storytelling. I call it a "what-to book," meaning that if you have an idea for a screenplay, but don't exactly know what to do to write it, this book will guide you through the screenwriting process. No matter whether it's a feature, a short film, a commercial, or other form of visual presentation, the book works.

Read a chapter, do the exercise at the end of the chapter, and by the end of the book you will have written a screenplay. The screenwriting process can be applied to any form of visual storytelling.

The Screenwriter's Workbook is based on the screenwriting workshops I have conducted around the world. I design and structure these seven-week workshops so students spend the first four weeks preparing to write, and the second three weeks writing. The goal of the class (and I'm very big on goals) is to write and complete the First Act, (anywhere from twenty to thirty pages) of the screenplay.

People come into a workshop with a short idea of their story. For example: "My story is about a woman executive on vacation in Hawaii, who meets and has an affair with a young man, then returns home only to learn the relationship doesn't work."

That simple.

In the first class we talk about the subject of the screenplay, the action and character—basically *what* happens and *whom* it happens to—and discuss the nature of dramatic structure. Their first assignment when they leave the class is to structure their idea, then write a four-page treatment focusing on the ending, the beginning, Plot Point I, and Plot Point II. I call this the "kick in the ass" exercise because the student is taking an unformed idea and trying to give it form; it very well may be the most difficult pages the participant writes.

The second week we talk about character, and how to give the main character a history by writing a character biography, the character's life from birth up until the time the story begins. They also outline the character's professional life, personal life, and private life. Their assignment for the next week is to write character biographies of their main character and one or two other major characters. The third week we structure the story line of Act I on 3 × 5 cards, and write up a back story, that is, what happens either a day, a week, or an hour before the story begins. The fourth week we write the first ten pages and the rest of the workshop is devoted to writing approximately ten pages a week. At the end of this seven-week session, the student will have completed the First Act of their screenplay, anywhere from twenty to thirty pages.

We take a short break and then continue into the Second Act Workshop. The goal of this seven-week course is to write and complete Act II of the screenplay. In the third seven-week workshop they complete Act III and rewrite the material.

By the end of the three sessions, almost 80 percent of my students complete their screenplays. Many have had tremendous success: Anna Hamilton Phelan wrote *Mask* in class, followed soon after with *Gorillas in the Mist;* John Singleton worked on *Boyz n the Hood,* followed by *Poetic Justice;* Michael Kane wrote *The Color of Money,* João Emanuel Carneiro worked on *Central Station* in the workshop I conducted in Rio de Janeiro; Janus Cercone wrote *Leap of Faith* in class; Randi Mayem Singer did *Mrs. Doubtfire;* Carmen Culver, *The Thorn Birds;* Laura Esquivel adapted her novel *Like Water for Chocolate* during my course in Mexico City; and in the same class Carlos Cuarón started exploring the idea of what would later become *Y Tu Mamá También.* There are others as well: Todd Graff *(Used People, Angie),* Kevin Williamson *(Scream),* Todd Robinson *(White Squall),* Humanitas Award winner Linda Elstad *(Divorce Wars),* and many others.

Several students have had their screenplays and teleplays optioned by producers and a few of my students have become production executives at film studios and production companies.

This book is designed and structured like my screenwriting workshops. Read a chapter, do the exercise at the end of the chapter, and by the end of the book you will have written a screenplay—at least in theory. *The Screenwriter's Workbook* is a step-by-step work plan for you to follow from the inception of the idea through completion; it is a map, a navigational guidance system to steer you through the screenwriting process. What's important to know is that the material works.

The exercises following each chapter are the tools that offer you the opportunity to expand and sharpen your understanding of the screenwriting process. I hope you view your journey through the screenwriting experience in this light. You won't learn anything unless you give yourself permission to make some mistakes, to try things that don't work, and do some plain old shitty writing.

Are you willing to do that? Are you willing to try something that doesn't work? Are you willing to write terrible pages? Are you willing to be lost in doubt and confusion, angry and concerned, not knowing whether your material is working or not?

This book is a learning experience. It is experiential. The more you do, the better you get, just like swimming or riding a bicycle.

Read the book, and when you're ready to start working on your screenplay, go through the book a chapter at a time. It is a step-by-step process; you may spend a week or a month on a single chapter, it really doesn't matter. Take as much time as you need to complete the material in each exercise.

The purpose of *The Screenwriter's Workbook* is to clarify, expand, and enlarge your knowledge, comprehension, and technique of the screenplay and the art and craft of screenwriting. *The Workbook* enables you to teach yourself the skills and craft required to write a professional screenplay.

Don't look for perfection. "Perfection," as Jean Renoir constantly pointed out, "exists only in the mind, not in reality."

Just tell your story.

ONE

PREPARATION

1

The Blank Page

```
The hardest thing about writing is knowing
what to write.
```

A short time ago, I was having dinner with a group of friends, and as is so often the case, the subject turned to movies. We talked about films we had seen, films we liked, films we didn't like, and what we liked or disliked about them, which covered a broad spectrum ranging from the acting performances to the editing and photography to the music, special effects, and so on. We talked about some of the great moments in films, lines of dialogue that still reside in our awareness, and while the conversation was intriguing and stimulating, what I really found so interesting was that nobody made any mention of the screenplay. It was as if the script didn't exist. When I mentioned that fact, the only response I got was, "Oh yeah, it was a great script," and that's about as far as it went.

I immediately noticed a short pause in the conversation, and then one of the other guests, an actress and television talk show host, mentioned she had written a book and several of her friends wanted her to turn it into a screenplay. She confessed she felt she needed a "partner" to help her take her novel, her own story, and write it as a screenplay.

When I asked why, she explained she was frightened of "confronting" the blank sheet of paper. But she had already written the novel, I replied, so how could she be frightened about turning it into a screenplay? Was it the form that challenged her? Or the visual description of images, the sparseness of dialogue, or the structure that frightened her? We discussed it for a while and as she was trying to explain her feelings, I realized many people have that same fear. Even though she was a published author, she was afraid of dealing with the blank page. She didn't know exactly what to do or how to go about doing it.

This is not such an unusual scenario. Many people have great ideas for a screenplay but when they actually sit down to write it they are seized by fear and insecurity because they don't know how to go about actually doing it.

Screenwriting is such a specific craft that unless you know where you're going, it's very easy to get lost within the maze of the blank page. The hardest thing about writing is knowing what to write. If *you* don't know what your story is about, who does? Throughout my many years of teaching screenwriting, both here and abroad, people approach me all the time and tell me they want to write a screenplay. They say they have a great idea, or a brilliant opening scene, or a fantastic ending, but when I ask them what their story is about, their eyes glaze over, they stare off into the distance and tell me it'll all come out in the story. Just like Miles when he tries to describe what his novel is about to Maya in *Sideways.* Great.

When you sit down and tell yourself that you're going to write a screenplay, where do you begin? With the dream of a heroic action like the Max Fischer character (Jason Schwartzman) in *Rushmore* (Wes Anderson and Owen Wilson)? With still photographs that show us the era in which your story takes place, like the Great Depression in *Seabiscuit* (Gary Ross)? In a darkened bedroom, with a clock ticking loudly and two people moaning in sexual passion, like *Shampoo* (Robert Towne and Warren Beatty)?

If you tell yourself you want to write a screenplay and then vow to commit weeks, months, or even years writing it, how do you confront the blank page? Where does the writer begin? It's a question I hear at workshops and seminars all the time.

Does the writer begin with a person, location, title, situation, or theme? Should he/she write a treatment, outline it, or write the book first and then the screenplay? Questions, questions, questions. All those questions really reflect *the* question: How do you take an unformed idea, a vague notion, or a gut feeling and transfer that into the roughly one hundred and twenty pages of words and pictures that make up a screenplay?

Writing a screenplay is a process—an organic, ever-changing, evolving stage of growth and development. Screenwriting is a craft that occasionally rises to the level of art. Like all literary arts, whether fiction or nonfiction, plays or short stories, there are definite stages a writer works through while fleshing out an idea. The creative process is the same no matter what you're writing.

When you sit down to write a screenplay and confront the blank page, you have to know what story you're writing. You only have a hundred and twenty pages to tell your story, and when you begin writing it's apparent very quickly that you don't have much room to work with. A screenplay is more like a poem than a novel or play in which you can feel your way through the story.

James Joyce, the great Irish writer, once wrote that the writing experience is like climbing a mountain. When you're scaling a mountain, all you can see is the rock directly in front of you and the rock directly behind you. You can't see where you're going or where you've come from. The same principle holds true when you're writing a screenplay; when you're writing all you can see is what's in front of you, that is, the page you're writing and the pages you've written. You can't see anything beyond that.

What do you want to write about? You know you have a great idea that will make an awesome movie, so where do you begin? Are you writing a challenging character study? Are you writing about a personal experience that impacted your life? Maybe you read a great magazine or newspaper article that you know will make a great movie.

One of my students in a recent screenwriting workshop was a published novelist and former editor of a major book publisher. She had never written a screenplay before and shared with me that she was somewhat nervous and insecure about writing the script.

When I asked why, she replied that she didn't know if her story was visual enough. She wanted to write a script about an active middle-aged woman who suffers a life-changing traumatic injury, and had doubts about the main character's confinement to a hospital bed during most of the second act. This raised another concern: would the main character be too passive? Could the interest in the character's plight be sustained with this limited sense of visual action? These were all valid, major considerations, requiring significant creative decisions.

During her preparation period we had several discussions, talked about the possibilities of opening it up, using the visual components found in the hospital: tests like EEGs, CAT scans, PET scans, and X-rays, and having the action broken up by the arrival of emergency cases and the various activities of the nurses on the floor. I wondered what would happen in the character's life while she was in the hospital. I suggested that she could show bits and pieces of the woman's former life, possibly through dreams and memories, and weave those flashbacks throughout. Because the main character was so static during the Second Act, she could add several more visuals to the story line about what the woman was thinking and feeling.

Feeling more secure, my student began preparing her material. She did her research, structured the First Act on cards, wrote up the back story, designed the opening sequences. As a novelist, she had always researched her ideas thoroughly and gradually, and it would be through the actual writing experience that she would find her story and characters. She told me she did not want to know "too much" because, in her experience, she wanted to let the story guide her to where it wants to go. I replied that you can do this when you're writing a novel or play, but not when you're writing a screenplay. A screenplay is a specific form; approximately one hundred twenty pages in length and knowing the end is always the first step in writing. You can "feel" your way through a four-hundred-fifty-page novel, or a one-hundred-page play, but not a screenplay.

A screenplay follows a definite, lean, tight, narrative line of action, with a definite beginning, middle, and end, though not necessarily in that order. A screenplay always moves forward toward the resolution, even if it is told in flashback like *The Bourne Supremacy* (Tony Gilroy), or *American Beauty* (Alan Ball.) A screenplay follows a singular line of action so every scene, every fragment of visual information, must be taking you somewhere, moving the narrative forward in terms of story development.

This was somewhat difficult for my student to understand because it was unlike her previous writing experience. But after she had done her preparation, when she knew her structure and had done some background character work, she was ready to start writing. She began writing the first act, the emphasis on the professional life of her main character, an active and dynamic woman responding to the challenges of the workplace with energy and integrity. As a professional woman, it was clear her character was active, likable, and well drawn.

But when the main character entered the hospital after the traumatic injury at the end of Act I, the *tone* of the story changed. The character was now confined to a hospital bed, weaving in and out of consciousness for several pages. Feeling the story becoming boring, my student became insecure and started looking for new cinematic areas to explore rather than focusing on the main character. One day she called to tell me she was writing new scenes with doctors and nurses, then told me she had a sudden inspiration to bring in the main character's daughter, an executive who always seemed to have trouble dealing with authoritarian male figures like doctors. I told her to go ahead and try it; after all, if it works, it works, and if it doesn't, it doesn't. All she would really lose was about three days of writing.

So she began writing this new character, the daughter, in Act II, and then another problem began to surface: the daughter was emerging as the dominant character. The mother, the main character, now seemed to be lost somewhere in a hospital room. By making the daughter the active force, or voice, in the story, my student had shifted the focus of the story line. The story was now about a daughter taking charge of the health and well-being of her mother.

That raised another issue. The story now hinged on the idea of "a durable power of attorney for a health issue," an interesting premise in medical therapy. The daughter was asked to choose the medical treatment for her incapacitated mother. The doctors told her there were two choices: electric shock treatments to jolt her mother out of her acute depression, or a regime of antidepressant drug therapy. And the doctors explained that both treatments could give rise to disastrous side effects. What should the daughter do? She was ambivalent about male authority figures, yet was now in a position where she had to make a life-altering decision about her mother. Seeking counsel and confronting her own feelings, the daughter decided to do nothing; she wanted to wait and see and possibly allow her mother to come out of it on her own. There were no shock treatments, no drugs, nothing; just patience, time, and understanding. At the end, the mother, through her own will, and the daughter's help, gradually steps back on the path to health and recovery.

That's the way my student completed the first words-on-paper draft. When I read this first draft, I saw immediately there were two separate stories. One story was the saga of the mother who recovers from her injury to take back control of her own life. The second story dealt with the woman's daughter who was forced, almost against her will, to take charge of the situation. And it's during this challenge that she overcomes her own deep-seated fear of male authority and resolves the formerly strained emotional relationship with her mother.

My student started out writing one story and ended up writing another. This happens quite often but the question remained: Was it the story of the mother or the daughter? Or both? Whose story do you tell?

My student didn't know. One of the things I've learned through the years is that when I'm uncertain about what course of action to take, I step back for a while. *When in doubt, do nothing* is my rule. So I suggested that she put the screenplay aside somewhere for a couple of weeks until she had a new perspective on the material. It's important to note that the issue here was not about the quality of writing, or dialogue, or character depth, or whether it worked or not; the issue was what story the writer wanted to tell. By moving into the daughter's domain, she changed her dramatic intention and changed the subject. I explained that it's not a question of good or bad, or right or wrong, but whether it was the story she wanted to tell.

She waited a short time, and then, in some doubt and uncertainty, she gave this first words-on-paper draft to a close friend of hers, a literary agent in Hollywood. Her friend saw that the script needed work, but liked the premise well enough to give it to one of her associates at the office. He read it and felt the script was "slow, dull, and boring." It should have more action: "It's the mother's story," he said. "Let's *see* her getting an electric shock treatment; maybe change the opening and have it start at the accident because that would make it more active."

My student came to me, angry and confused. She didn't know *what* to do. She kept talking about needing a more active, cinematic opening and I kept telling her that wasn't the problem; she had to know, creatively, which story she was writing. When she first sat down to face the blank page she wanted to tell the mother's story. She ended up telling the story of the daughter overcoming the constraints of her relationship with her mother focusing on the issue of "the durable power of attorney."

She kept asking me what to do, and I kept telling her she had to make a creative decision about which story she was writing. I suggested that before she began to rewrite anything, she rethink her idea from the beginning in order to find the focus and direction of her story. Who and what was her story about?

It's important to know that there is no "right" or "wrong" in this situation, no judgments about good or bad. The only issue is whether it works or not. So, I met her one day at a nearby Coffee Bean and while we sipped our white chocolate dream lattes, I suggested that she fashion her story into the relationship between the mother and the daughter and set it against the dramatic backdrop of her mother's injury, showing how this brings them together with a stronger bond of love and understanding.

She shook her head and told me this was not the story she'd planned to write. The story was about the mother. That's fine, I said. But if she set out to write the story she wanted to write, she had to focus on *that* story and integrate it into the relationship with her daughter. Ultimately, she left the Coffee Bean the same way she came in; lost, confused, and uncertain. She picked away at the script for several months, didn't feel she was making any progress with it, and finally shelved the project.

It happens all the time; to you, to me, to anyone.

What's the point of the story? Creative problems are part of the landscape of screenwriting. Either it's an opportunity to expand the limits of your craft or a way to give in to the fact that "it's just not working." My student couldn't let go of her original concept and while she had a very good story, valid and meaningful, she really didn't know which story she wanted to tell. Her mind told her one thing, her creative Self told her another.

What could she have done to solve the problem? Look at *The Sea Inside* (Alejandro Amenábar), a story that covers some of the same fertile, emotional, and thought-provoking ground. While the main character, Ramón (Javier Bardem) is confined to a hospital bed and room for some 30 years, fighting for his right to die, Amenábar opens up the smothering hospital room with soaring fantasies of Ramón walking and running, dreaming of love, so the story becomes a visual and eloquent testament of our imagination and how it can touch, move, and inspire others. It is possible that my student could have visually opened up her story in order to achieve her artistic intention, but didn't.

Most people would say *Million Dollar Baby* (Paul Haggis), which won the Academy Award for Best Picture, is a story about a woman determined to become a professional boxer who realizes her dream, only to become critically injured during a title fight. Other people would say this is a story framed by the female boxer but is really the story about an individual's right to die and the moral and legal issues of euthanasia.

In the case of *Million Dollar Baby,* both are true. But in my mind, the "true" story, the real subject of the screenplay, is the relationship between Frankie (Clint Eastwood) and Maggie (Hilary Swank). All the elements that make up this relationship—Maggie's determination, Frankie training Maggie, Frankie and Scrap (Morgan Freeman) bickering—lead to the ultimate moral premise of the screenplay:

Can Frankie, a tough, yet religious man, deliberately help another human being to die? Would that be labeled a criminal offense, or euthanasia? Is there a moral issue here? There are some who would call Frankie's act of injecting Maggie a murder and others an act of mercy. Call it what you will, it still is a story about the relationship between Frankie and Maggie.

Every screenplay is about something or someone and this subject becomes encased in the story you are telling. Can you define *what* you're writing about? *Who* are you writing about? There are approximately one hundred twenty sheets of blank paper to fill in a screenplay. As we all know, the blank page is intimidating, a tremendous and formidable challenge. When you first set out on this writing adventure, you'll probably only have a vague idea or an unformed notion about a character or incident running around in your head. You'll discover when you begin to formulate the idea into a workable description it may take several pages of free-association and terrible writing just to reduce your story into a general line of character and action. It may take several days of thinking and scribbling before you can even isolate the main components of your story. Don't worry about how long it takes. Just do it.

Before you can put one word on paper, you have to know what and who your story is about. What is the *subject* of your screenplay? For example: Your story may be about an attorney who meets and falls in love with a married woman, then kills her husband so they can be together. But he's been set up and ends up in prison, while the woman ends up with a fortune in a tropical paradise. That's the subject of Larry Kasdan's *Body Heat.* It could also be the subject of *Double Indemnity,* Billy Wilder's classic film noir. *A Beautiful Mind* (Akiva Goldsman) is the story of a physicist who loses touch with reality, overcomes his illness, and receives a Nobel prize for his scientific achievement. Action and character. The screenplay succeeds because there is a definite line of action.

The subject becomes a guideline for you to follow as you structure the action and the characters into a cohesive, dramatic story line. As a rule, you'll find that either the character drives the action or the action drives the character.

What's it about? is the most challenging question you'll ever be asked. In my experience, most aspiring writers seem to love the idea of writing a screenplay, but after talking with them I can tell they're unwilling to commit the time and effort to face the challenges they'll confront. Writing is hard work; make no mistake about it.

When I first began writing, I would confront the blank page with fear and insecurity. And when my mind clicked in and I knew that I had to fill up some one hundred twenty sheets of blank paper for a screenplay, I totally freaked. I couldn't deal with it. Only by dealing with, and confronting my fear, did I learn that for me, writing is a day-by-day job, five or six days a week, three or more hours a day, three or more pages a day. And some days are better than others. If I lose sight of writing the scene that is right in front of me and instead start thinking of what I should do later, it's a total washout.

The blank page. It's intimidating.

If you know your subject then you can create a step-by-step approach that will guide you through the process of writing a screenplay. If we take a look at what a screenplay is, its essential nature, then we can define it as a story told with pictures in dialogue and description and placed within the context of dramatic structure.

So, where does the writer begin? The answer is anywhere you want to. There are many ways to approach writing a screenplay. Sometimes you begin with character—a strong, three-dimensional character in an extraordinary situation that moves your story forward with skill and clarity. Character is a good, solid starting point.

You can also start with an idea; but an idea is only an idea unless it's executed properly. You've got to take that idea and expand it, clothe it, make it say what you want it to say. "I want to write a story about a man who has a near-death experience" is not enough. You've got to dramatize it. Legally, the law says: "You can't copyright an idea, only the *expression* of the idea." The "expression" means the specific characters, locations, structure, and action that make up the narrative throughline of the story.

Sometimes you may want to write a screenplay that deals with an incident, episode, or experience that happened to you or to someone you know. You can use this particular experience as the starting point in your story, but as you go through the preparation process, you'll find that you want to hold on to the "reality" of the experience; you want to be "true" to the situation or incident. Most people find it hard to let go of the experience. But often, you've got to let the "reality" go in order to dramatize it more effectively. I liken it to climbing a staircase: The first step is the actual experience, the second step is increasing the dramatic potential of the story, and the third step is integrating both of the previous steps to create a "dramatic reality." If you remain too true to "who did what" in the "real" order of the experience, it usually ends up as a thin story line with little or no dramatic impact. Do not feel "obligated" to remain "true" to reality. It doesn't work. The "reality" of the event may, and often does, get in the way of the dramatic needs of your story.

I tell my students over and over again to "let go" of the original source material and simply write what is needed for their story. I call it creating a dramatic reality and liken it to climbing the bottom three rungs of a staircase. The first rung is the reality, the way something really happened. But to turn it into effective drama, you might have to add some incidents or events that did not happen; I call it creating an "unreality." That brings you to the third rung, which I call the *dramatic reality.* This is where you take the first rung, the reality, add the unreality incidents or elements, and make it a dramatic reality.

It's like writing a historical screenplay. You always have to be true to the historical incidents of the time and place. Those are historical facts which you cannot change. The actual history of the event has to be maintained but you don't have to be true to the emotional, day-to-day events, leading up to the historical incident. Just look at *All the President's Men* (William Goldman), *Ray* (James L. White), *Erin Brockovich* (Susannah Grant), and *JFK* (Oliver Stone and Zachary Sklar). History is only the starting point, not the end point.

A student of mine was writing a screenplay based on a true story, and taken from the diary of a Hawaiian woman in the early 1800s whose husband contracted leprosy. When his disease was found out, the couple became outcasts, hunted down by a posse determined to eradicate them.

When my student started writing, she used exact scenes and dialogue from the diary, faithfully recording some of the authentic customs and traditions of the islanders. But it didn't work. It was dull and had no structure, therefore it was lacking in story line and direction.

She became frustrated. She didn't know what to do and what direction to take in the story. So, I suggested she make up some scenes that never happened but that would help the story flow. I call it *creative research*. She went back to the drawing board, and a week or so later she came back with several ideas for scenes. We selected a few, wove them into the story line in this second-page unit of action, and she went back to writing. Her new scenes may never have happened, but they did capture the integrity of the source material and the story blossomed.

The hardest thing about writing is knowing what to write.

If need be, let go of the reality of the person, incident, or event and fashion a creative reality based on the actual historical happening. Find the unreality, the theatricality of the event. This is a movie, remember. You must communicate the people, the story, and the events dramatically. Make up your scenes based on the needs of the story while honoring the integrity of the experience.

There have been times when I've started with a location and used it to weave a story line. But even if you start with a particular place, it's still not enough. You've got to create a character and action to build your story around.

Many people tell me they want to start with a title. That's cool, but what then? You need to create a plot, but a plot about what? Plot is what happens, and since you're sitting down in front of a blank sheet of paper, it should be the furthest thing from your mind. At this point, you don't know anything about the plot; forget plot. We'll deal with it when the time comes. First things first. What are you going to research? You've got to have a subject.

In my screenwriting workshops I always ask people, "What's

your story about?" Invariably, I hear answers like, "I'm writing a love story about two cousins." Or "I'm writing about an Irish family in Boston at the turn of the century." Or "I'm writing about a group of parents who build their own school when their neighborhood school is closed."

When I hear ideas or vague notions like this, I ask the writer to dig deeper and find a personal expression of the story he or she wants to write. And it's not easy. Most of the time I have to badger him or her to be more specific, but after a while he or she begins to focus on *who* the story is about and *what* the story is about. That's the starting point: the subject, where the writer begins.

Thelma & Louise emerged as Callie Khouri was driving on the freeway and the idea suddenly popped into her mind: Two women go on a crime spree. That was the original impulse of the script. So Callie sat down and had to ask and answer some essential questions: Who are the two women? What crime did they commit? What made them commit the crime? What happens to them at the end? The answers to these questions led her to the subject, which resulted in the story line for *Thelma & Louise.* It's an extraordinary movie and I use it as a teaching film all over the world. And it all came out of the idea "two women go on a crime spree."

Your subject can be as simple as two old friends taking a wine-tasting trip through Santa Barbara wine fields the week before one of them gets married. That's the subject of *Sideways.* Once we know the subject, we have enough material to start asking some questions: Who are these two old friends? How long have they known each other? What do they do for a living? What happens to them on their trip that expands or affects their lives? What happens to them at the end of the story? Are they changed, either emotionally, physically, mentally, or spiritually by their journey? What are the emotional or psychological forces working on them when the story begins? Why do they go on a wine-tasting trip in the first place? In this case, their journey gives them the opportunity to explore their lives, their friendship, their dreams, and possibly their loneliness too.

This is the power of the subject. It allows you to create a starting point to begin the creative process of clearly identifying and defining your story line. If you can't articulate your subject, who can?

Writing a screenplay is a step-by-step process, and it's important to prepare one step at a time. First, you generate the idea, then break down the idea into the subject, a character and action. Once you have the subject, you know enough to structure it by determining the ending, the beginning, and Plot Points I and II. Once that's done, you can build and expand your characters by writing character biographies, along with any other research you may need to do. Then you can structure the scenes and sequences, the content, of Act I on fourteen 3 × 5 cards. Next write up the back story, what happens a day, a week, or an hour before the story begins. Only after you've completed this preparation work can you begin writing the screenplay.

When you've completed this first words-on-paper draft, you'll do basic revisions to this second stage of this first draft, and any rewriting that's necessary to polish and hone your material until it's ready to be shown. Screenwriting is a process, a living thing that changes from day to day. As a result, what you write today may be out of date tomorrow. And what you write tomorrow may be out of date the next day or the day after that. You have to be clear every step of the way and know where you're going and what you're doing.

When you're writing an action movie or war film, you have to be very clear about your subject because there are so many different perspectives to explore. *Saving Private Ryan* (Robert Rodat), *Schindler's List* (Steven Zaillian), *Paths of Glory* (Stanley Kubrick), and *Apocalypse Now* (John Milius and Francis Ford Coppola) express interesting points of view on the cost of war. So does *Three Kings,* David O. Russell's extraordinary film about the Gulf War, a script that explores the nature of war by focusing more on the humanitarian aspect of what happens to both victors and losers alike. It's a story about the price of war and the physical loss of life and limb, as well as the emotional cost of shattered psyches, and the cultural uprooting of an entire way of life.

The action takes place the day after the war ends. Three soldiers (played by Mark Wahlberg, Ice Cube, and Spike Jonze) find a map on a captured Iraqi soldier. Their superior officer (George Clooney) joins them and they discover the map leads to a bunker filled with millions of dollars of Kuwaiti gold. And so, with the war over, the story line begins as the men embark on a treasure-finding mission. But what they find are Iraqi people in desperate need of assistance. This is the starting point of a film that explores the physical and emotional landscape of the effect of war upon the human spirit as well as the human body.

'Breaker' Morant (Jonathan Hardy, Bruce Beresford), an Australian film made in 1980, based on the play by Kenneth Ross, is the story of an Australian military lieutenant in the Boer War (1899–1902) who is court-martialed and executed for fighting the enemy in an "unorthodox and uncivilized" fashion, meaning using guerrilla tactics, or as it's now called, insurgent warfare. The subject questions what a soldier can and can't do in a combat situation. At that time, there was a certain "convention" of war, and it was determined by a military tribunal that 'Breaker' Morant's actions had broken the so-called code of organized warfare, which is a joke to begin with. The lieutenant is tried, convicted, and executed for political reasons, a pawn on the chessboard of international politics. His fighting tactics, issued under direct orders (later denied by his superiors, of course), had nothing to do with what he did or how he did it. The English army had to make clear to the world that they did not permit this sort of unorthodox or "uncivilized" fighting and this had to be dramatized on the world stage. They needed a political scapegoat, and 'Breaker' Morant was chosen to be the fall guy. Just look at the prison scandals in the Iraqi War; it's basically the same story told in a different time and a different place.

No matter what story you are telling, there is only one place where the writer begins—with the blank page.

If you set out on the arduous journey of writing a screenplay, no matter what genre—whether action movie, war movie, love story, romance, thriller, mystery, western, romantic comedy, or other—and you're unclear or unsure about what story you're telling, it's going to be reflected in the script. But once you frame the idea into a subject, you can take that action and character and structure it into a dramatic story line. And, that's the starting point.

Then you can structure it.

THE EXERCISE

Take your idea and begin to isolate the elements of the action and character of your proposed story line. Just throw down any thoughts or ideas on paper. You may need to free-associate the idea over several pages in order to see what you're really writing about. Don't be afraid to write three or more pages in order to gain more clarity on the story you want to tell. Then use your free-association essay to isolate the elements of action—what happens and the character to whom it happens.

Once you've done that, reduce it into three separate paragraphs, beginning, middle, and end. Start honing each paragraph by summarizing the beginning into a few sentences; specify the character and what happens to him or her during the course of the screenplay.

Reduce each paragraph to a sentence or two according to what happens in the action and then how it affects the character. If you want, start looking at the loglines of *TV Guide* to get an idea of what a subject looks like. That's what you're aiming for. Isolating your main character should present no problems, but defining the line of action may be a little more difficult. What's the resolution? Can you incorporate that into the subject line? Be general in your descriptions at this point and not specific in terms of action.

Remember, it may take you three or four pages of horrible writing to figure out what story you're telling. Just work in fragments, or notes. There's no need to try for complete sentences here. Trust the process. If you've written several pages, wandering here and there, go through the material and highlight things that help define the action or character. Take your time with this; you're taking a vague, general idea, and reducing it to a few sentences. Sometimes, it helps to give your character a name so you can become more specific. Read it out loud. Polish it some more. Do it until you are perfectly clear about your subject and can express it clearly and concisely in three or four sentences.

This is the first step in the screenwriting process.

2

About Structure

> "Screenwriting is like building furniture. It's a craft in which the pieces must fit, and it must function....The forms in screen-writing are far more limited and pre-prescribed. People talk about the three-act structure, that this is how you write a movie and it's got these elements. And, mastering the elements and making them seem natural and invisible is the trick to writing screenplays. You have to learn it and you have to unlearn it. Or, you have to learn it and disguise it so the audience never sees the machinery of the screenwriting itself."
>
> —Jose Rivera
> *The Motorcycle Diaries*

When I first started teaching about structure in the screenplay, many people thought I was talking about finding the "correct formula" for writing screenplays. You know, writing "by the numbers"—you write so many pages for this, so many pages for that, you hit this plot point on page 25, that plot point on page 80, and if you do it all, according to the numbers specified, you'll end up with a finished screenplay. I wish it were that easy. I used to get calls from students in the middle of the night whining that their Plot Point I was on page 35, and whimpering "what do I do now?" Wherever I went, people seemed to be discussing, arguing, or fighting about the importance of structure in the screenplay. People went on record either endorsing or dismissing this notion of screenwriting.

In one of my early screenwriting workshops in Paris where I was presenting structure as the foundation of screenwriting, I was literally booed off the stage. They referred to me as *le Diable* (the Devil) and claimed no one could write a screenplay using structure as the organizing principle of story. When I confronted them about how they built their own story lines, they replied in vague generalities and hazy abstractions, talking about the "mystery of structure," or the "ambiguity of the creative process," as if trying to describe the sun on an overcast day.

I've been teaching the craft of screenwriting for more than twenty-five years, and the more I talk about it, the more I understand how important structure is and how much more there is to learn.

When I first started out, I traveled to people's homes carrying a small white board under my arm. At that time, I can truly say I didn't understand the significance of building a visual story line, or constructing shots, scenes, and sequences, or formulating a character's arc and finding ways of documenting the emotional and physical changes in the character as he or she journeys through the landscape of narrative action.

Exploring the nature of structure has been a profound and insightful journey for me. I've always known that a thorough knowledge and understanding of structure was essential in the writing of a screenplay—I just didn't know *how* important it was. I still find screenwriters all over the world, both professional and amateur, who don't understand the intrinsic nature of structure and its relationship to the screenplay.

So what is structure?

According to *Webster's New World Dictionary,* there are two definitions of the word "structure." The root *struct,* means, "to put together," and the first definition is "to build something, like a building or a dam; or to put together." When we talk about structuring a screenplay, we're talking about building and putting together all the necessary ingredients that go into the making of a screenplay: the scenes, sequences, characters, action, and so forth. We are building, or constructing, the "content," or events, which lead us through the story line.

The second definition defines structure as the "relationship between the parts and the whole." A good illustration is a chess game. If you want to play a game of chess you need four things: first, you need a chessboard; it could be as big or as small as you want, as large as a football field or as small as a matchbox. Next, you need the pieces: the king, queen, pawns, bishops, knights, and rooks. The third thing you need are players, and fourth, you need to know the rules. Without the rules, it's not a chess game. Those four elements, the parts, make up the whole of the chess game. If you take away any one of these parts, there is no chess game. This is the relationship between the parts and the whole.

Not too long ago it was popular to say that the whole is nothing more than the sum of its parts. That's no longer true. Modern physics challenges that assumption with the General Systems Theory; a theory that states the whole is *greater* than the sum of its parts. There's an ancient Indian tale about three blind men and an elephant that illustrates this well. Three blind men are asked to describe an elephant. One man feels the trunk and says that an elephant is round, narrow, and flexible, like a snake. The second blind man feels the midsection and says the elephant is like a wall. The third feels the tail and says no, the elephant is like a piece of rope.

Who is right? The elephant is greater than the sum of its parts. That's the General Systems Theory.

What does this have to do with screenwriting? Everything. "A screenplay is structure," says the noted screenwriter William Goldman. "It is the spine you hang your story on." When you sit down to write a screenplay, you must approach your story as a whole. As mentioned, a story is composed of parts—characters, plot, action, dialogue, scenes, sequences, incidents, events—and you, as writer, must organize these parts into a whole, with a definite shape and form, complete with beginning, middle, and end.

Because a screenplay is such a unique form, you have to approach it from a different perspective. What is a screenplay? We define a screenplay as *a story told in pictures, in dialogue and description, and placed within the context of dramatic structure.*

It's different than a novel or play.

If you look at a novel and try to define its fundamental nature, you'll see that the dramatic action, the story line, often takes place inside the head of the main character. We see the story line unfold through the eyes of that character, through his or her point of view. We are privy to the character's thoughts, feelings, emotions, words, actions, memories, dreams, hopes, ambitions, opinions, and more. The character and reader experience the action together, sharing in the drama and emotion of the story. We know how they act or react, how they feel, and how they figure things out. If other characters are brought into the narrative, the story line may embrace their points of view, but the main thrust always returns to the main character, the one who the story is about. In a novel the action takes place *inside* the character's head, within the *mindscape* of dramatic action. Open any novel at random and read a chapter or two and you'll see what I mean.

In a play the action, or story line, occurs on stage, under the proscenium arch, so the audience becomes the fourth wall, eavesdropping on the lives of the characters, what they think and feel and say. They talk about their hopes and dreams, past and future plans, discuss their needs and desires, fears and conflicts. In this case, the action of the play occurs within the *language* of dramatic action; it is spoken in words that describe feelings, actions, and emotions. A play is told mostly in words. The characters are talking heads.

A screenplay is different because movies are different. Film is a visual medium that dramatizes a basic story line. It deals in pictures, images, bits and pieces of film: we *see* a clock ticking, ride inside a moving car, see and hear rain splattering against a windshield. We see a woman moving along a crowded street; a car slowly turning a corner, stopping in front of a large building; a man crossing the street; a woman entering an open doorway; an elevator door closing. These bits and pieces, these fragments of visual information joined together, allow us to grasp an incident or situation merely by looking at it. Just watch the opening of *The Lord of the Rings: The Fellowship of the Ring* (Peter Jackson, Philippa Boyens, and Fran Walsh), or *Close Encounters of the Third Kind* (Steven Spielberg), or

Andy Dufresne's escape from prison in *The Shawshank Redemption* (Frank Darabont). The essential nature of the screenplay deals in pictures.

That is its nature.

Jean-Luc Godard, the eminent French director, says that film is evolving into a visual language and it's up to us to learn how to read the pictures.

Several years ago, after I had conducted a European screenwriting workshop in Brussels, I went to visit Venice for the first time. While there, I visited the Accademia Museum, which displays a magnificent collection of early Venetian painting. In the Middle Ages, when monks in the monasteries were transcribing the Scriptures, they enlarged and elaborated the initial letter of a paragraph. (A similar convention is still followed today in which the first letter of a chapter is set in large type.) It wasn't long before the monks were illustrating their manuscripts with scenes from the Bible, and soon they were decorating their walls with illustrations similar to Roman frescoes; then these scenes were put on wood panels which leaned against the wall, and this gave way to painting on canvas which then hung on the wall. The Accademia Museum displays a marvelous collection of this early Italian painting.

As I wandered around the museum, I was struck by one painting in particular: it was composed of twelve individual wood panels depicting scenes in the life of Christ: one panel showed his birth, another the Sermon on the Mount, another the Last Supper, and then the Crucifixion, and so on. Something about this painting grabbed me and held my interest, and I didn't know why. I stared at that painting for a long time, thinking about it, then moved away, and found myself coming back to it, intrigued. What made this painting different from all the others? The answer came immediately: it wasn't just one painting. It was a series of twelve paintings mounted together to tell the story of the life and death of Christ. It was a story told in pictures.

It was a profound experience. The interaction between the story and picture in each panel was the same as the visual relationship between the story and character in a screenplay.

I stared at those panels, suddenly seeing the connection between painting and film. It was a stunning, awesome moment. Everything exists in relationship to something else and I remembered one afternoon when I was taking a walk with Jean Renoir after a rehearsal of his play *Carola.* It had just rained and as we strolled through the sloping landscape of the Berkeley Hills, he stopped and looked at a wildflower growing in the middle of a rock. "Nothing is as strong as nature," he observed. "The force of nature is what drives that little wildflower right through the rock." Then, as we continued walking he said, "learning is being able to see the relationship, the connections, between things."

I understood what he meant. The force of nature, like the force of creative expression, is like the tiny seed of the wildflower driving its way up through the rock. "The force that through the green fuse drives the flower" is the way the great poet Dylan Thomas expresses it.

When you write a screenplay, you are describing what happens, which is why screenplays are written in the present tense. The reader sees what the camera sees, a description of the action placed within the context of dramatic structure. When you write a scene or sequence, you are describing what your characters say and do—the incidents and events that tell your story.

Structure is a context; it "holds" the bits and pieces and fragments of images that tell your story in place. Context is really *a space* that holds things inside. A suitcase is a context—no matter what shape or form or fabric or size, the space inside holds clothes, shoes, toiletries, or anything else you may want to pack. A suitcase can be any size, fabric, or shape. But the space inside doesn't change; it's the same no matter how big or small the space is. Space is space. The same thing with an empty glass; an empty glass has space inside that holds the *content* in place. You can put anything you want inside that empty glass and the space, the context, does not change. You can put in coffee, tea, milk, juice, water, or whatever and the space does not change. You could also put in grapes, trail mix, nuts, anything that fits and the space, the context, always holds the content in place. In the same way, structure holds your story in place whether told in a linear or nonlinear way. It is the skeleton, the spine of your story.

Dramatic structure is defined as "a linear arrangement of related incidents, episodes, and events leading to a dramatic resolution."

It is a starting point in the process of writing.

Structure is a context; it is like the natural force of gravity; it holds everything in place. Not only does gravity influence every single element in the cosmos, from subatomic particles to the dark forces of antimatter, it affects the very life functions of every living species on Earth. Without the natural force of gravity, human beings would not be able to stand upright; nor would the trees and plants climb toward the sun; nor would the earth remain in stable orbit around our sun; nor would the sun remain in secure orbit in the Milky Way. In short, structure in the screenplay is like gravity because it *holds* everything together, everything in place.

Screenplay structure is so integral to your story, so closely intertwined with the action and characters, that most of the time we don't even see it. Most of the time, good structure remains the spine, the foundation, the invisible glue, of your screenplay. It "holds" the story in place, just the way anchor screws hold a painting on the wall. Every good screenplay has a strong and solid structural foundation whether it's a linear film like *Sideways* (Alexander Payne and Jim Taylor), *The New World* (Terrence Malick), and *The Godfather* (Francis Ford Coppola and Mario Puzo), or a nonlinear film like *The Hours* (David Hare), *The Bourne Supremacy* (Tony Gilroy), *The English Patient* (Anthony Minghella), or *The Usual Suspects* (Christopher McQuarrie).

What is so interesting about structure is that it's as simple as it is complex. I liken it to the relationship between an ice cube and water. An ice cube has a definite crystalline structure, and water, a definite molecular structure. But when an ice cube melts in water, you can't tell the difference between which molecules were the ice cubes and which molecules were the water. They are indistinguishable from each other. When we talk about structure, we are talking about an intrinsic part of the story. They are part and parcel of the same thing.

Whether the story is told in a straight line or fragmented or circular doesn't matter. What we see and how we see it is evolving right before our eyes. You can see it in the new emerging technologies: the rapid growth of computer technology and the dramatic influence of computer-graphic imagery, along with the expanded impact of MTV, reality TV, Xbox, PlayStation, and all the new wireless LAN technology, have powerfully impacted every phase of visual communication. We may not be aware of it, but we're in the middle of an evolution/revolution of screenwriting.

I first became aware of this shift in visual storytelling in 1995. I had been teaching the nature of structure in workshops all over the world for almost twenty years when I saw three films that radically changed my perception. The first was *Pulp Fiction* (Quentin Tarantino), and though I thought it was a "B" movie in terms of content, I saw immediately it was a new departure in storytelling. Everywhere I went in the world, people wanted to talk about *Pulp Fiction.* In many of my workshops, the participants asked if the film represented a new structure, and wanted to hear my opinion. People "dared" me to analyze it in terms of my structural paradigm; everybody, it seemed, thought *Pulp Fiction* was *it;* innovative in thought, concept, and execution, everything a revolutionary film should be.

A few months later, I was in Mexico City conducting a screenwriting workshop for the Mexican government when I was invited to see a new film by the noted Mexican director, Jorge Fons, called *El Callejón de los Milagros* (Midaq Alley) featuring Salma Hayek in one of her first major film roles. The film seemed more novelistic than cinematic to me. There were four stories in the film, each one revolving around four or five different characters, all living, working, and loving on the same street, but linked by a key incident that shatters the relationship between the two main characters, a father and son. The incident affects all the characters in some way, and is woven into the structure as characters and events sometimes fold back on themselves in flashbacks of memories almost like a novel. The film, though high in melodrama, is unique, striking in terms of concept and execution.

The more I thought about it, the more it seemed these two films were a kind of an indicator, or marker, influencing a possible future form of the screenplay. As I studied these two films, I understood once again what Jean Renoir called the "relationship between things." Somehow, I sensed, there was a connection between the way a story is laid out in linear progression, and the way it's laid out in a nonlinear presentation.

Shortly after I returned, I was invited to a screening of *The English Patient* (Anthony Minghella). I loved it. The way the past and present are fused into one organic story line captivated me. What do these three films all have in common? I asked myself.

I started from the obvious: even though they are all nonlinear in their stylistic approach, all have a beginning, middle, and end, though not necessarily in that order. I remembered a line from the great Russian playwright Anton Chekhov's play *Three Sisters* that has always stayed with me: "The principle thing in life is its form. That which loses its form, ends itself, and it's the same with our everyday existence." Everything in life has a form. Every twenty-four-hour period is exactly the same, but different. The day begins in the morning, goes into the afternoon, and is followed by night. You can make further distinctions with that of course: early morning, later afternoon, late night, and so on. It's the same with the twelve-month period we label a year; it's always the same, but different. The same with our seasons: there is spring, summer, fall, and winter. It never changes. It's always the same, but different. Remember the riddle that Sophocles presented for Oedipus: he asks what walks on four legs in the morning, two legs in the afternoon, and three legs at night? The answer: A human being.

All these questions led me to believe that there was something in these films that I needed to explore. I started with *Pulp Fiction.* I got a copy of the screenplay. When I read the title page, it said that *Pulp Fiction* was really "three stories . . . about one story." I turned the page and read two dictionary definitions of *pulp:* "a soft, moist, shapeless mass of matter," and "a magazine or book containing lurid subject matter and being characteristically printed on rough, unfinished paper." That's certainly an accurate description of the film. But on the third page, I was surprised to find a Table of Contents. I thought that was rather odd; who writes a Table of Contents for a screenplay? Then I saw the film was broken down into five individual parts: Part I, the Prologue; Part II, Vincent Vega and Marsellus Wallace's Wife; Part III, The Gold Watch; Part IV, The Bonnie Situation; and Part V, the Epilogue.

As I studied the script, I saw that all three stories bounce off the key incident of Jules and Vincent Vega retrieving Marsellus Wallace's briefcase from the four guys. This one incident became the hub of all three stories, and each story is structured as a whole, in linear fashion; it starts at the beginning of the action, goes into the middle, and then proceeds to the end. Each section is like a short story, presented from a different character's point of view.

If this key incident is the hub of the story, as I now understood it, then all the actions, reactions, thoughts, memories, or flashbacks, are tethered to this one incident. The entire film is structured around this one event, and then branches off in three different directions.

Suddenly, it all made sense. Understanding "three stories about one story" allowed me to see the film as one unified whole. *Pulp Fiction* is three stories surrounded by a prologue and epilogue, what screenwriters call a "bookend" technique: *The English Patient* uses that same device. So do *The Bridges of Madison County* (Richard LaGravenese), *Sunset Boulevard* (Billy Wilder and Charles Brackett), and *Saving Private Ryan* (Robert Rodat).

Now I began to see how *Pulp Fiction* was put together. The Prologue sets up the two characters, Pumpkin and Honey Bunny (Tim Roth and Amanda Plummer), in a coffee shop discussing various types of robbery. When they finish their meals, they pull their guns and rob the place. The film freezes and we cut to the main titles. Then we cut into the middle of a conversation between Jules (Samuel L. Jackson) and Vincent (John Travolta), driving and having an enlightening discussion about the relative merits of a Big Mac both here and abroad.

Part I sets up the entire film and tells us everything we need to know; the two men are killers working for Marsellus Wallace; their job, their dramatic need, is to retrieve the briefcase. That's the true beginning of the story, and by this reckoning, in Part I, Jules and Vincent arrive, state their position, kill the three guys, and only by the grace of God do they leave alive with Marvin. That's the key incident of the story. They report back to Marsellus Wallace (Ving Rhames). Vinnie takes Mia (Uma Thurman) out to dinner, and after she accidentally overdoses on some heroin, he revives her and they say good night, promising not to share what happened with anyone. Part II is about Butch (Bruce Willis) and his gold watch and what happens when he wins the fight, killing the other fighter, instead of losing it like he had agreed with Marsellus Wallace in Part I. Part III deals with cleaning up Marvin's remains, which are splattered all over the car—a continuation of Part I. That's followed by the Epilogue where Jules talks about his transformation and the significance of Divine Intervention in their lives, and then Pumpkin and Honey Bunny resume the holdup that began the film in the Prologue.

Seeing that connection in *Pulp Fiction*, comparing it with *El Callejón de los Milagros* and *The English Patient* started me thinking about the changes occurring in the screenplay due to the impact of technology. In each case they shared something in common; besides the way the stories are laid out, besides the special effects and intriguing subject matter, all three films created an emotional response. At that moment, I realized that no matter how a film may be structured, the language of the cinema speaks directly to the heart, as Ingmar Bergman used to say. It doesn't matter whether the story is told in a linear or nonlinear form; it doesn't matter whether the story is told with ingenious special effects, or branded with the visual brilliance of the director or the great acting of the actors or the broad sweep of the photography or the poetry of the editing. When you really get right down to it, there's only one thing that holds the whole thing together.

And that's the story.

Movies are all about story. "Nothing can be made out of nothing," King Lear muses in the clarity of his madness. No matter what the framework, ideas, concepts, jargon, or analytical comments are, whether the movie proceeds in a straight line or circle, or is fractured and splintered into little pieces, it doesn't make a bit of difference. No matter who we are, or where we live, or what generation we may belong to, the singular aspects of storytelling remain the same. It's been that way since Plato created stories out of shadows on the wall. The art of telling a story with pictures exists beyond time, culture, and language. Walk into the Elmira caves in Spain and look at the rock paintings, or into the world of Hieronymus Bosch and the early Flemish Primitives, or walk through the gallery of the Accademia Museum in Venice, and gaze upon those magnificent panels, and you enter a grand view of visual storytelling.

No matter how evolved or revolutionary or fractured or fragmented the story might be, regardless of incredible computer graphics or technological innovations, all screenplays reside within the context of structure; that is its essential form, its foundation. Just look at *Terminator 2: Judgment Day* (James Cameron and William Wisher, Jr.), *Spider-Man 2* (Alvin Sargent), *The Incredibles* (Brad Bird), *The Bourne Supremacy* (Tony Gilroy), *Eternal Sunshine of the Spotless Mind* (Charlie Kaufman), or *The Manchurian Candidate* (Daniel Pyne and Dean Georgaris); they are all told within the paradigm of dramatic structure.

I wondered how I would go about writing a nonlinear film. Many of the scripts being written today seem to be employing certain novelistic techniques—stream of consciousness, flashbacks, memories, and voiceover commentary—in order to get closer to the main character, to get inside their heads. As different as all these films are, the one common bond they all share is a strong and solid sense of structure; they all have a beginning, middle, and end, and the story revolves around a key incident which anchors the storylines together. *Courage Under Fire* (Patrick Duncan), *The Usual Suspects* (Christopher McQuarrie), *Lone Star* (John Sayles), *Magnolia* (Paul Thomas Anderson), *American Beauty* (Alan Ball), *Memento* (Christopher Nolan), and *Groundhog Day* (Danny Rubin and Harold Ramis) are good examples and if you study them you'll see they all revolve around one key incident. The key incident is the hub of the story line, the engine that powers the story forward and reveals to us what the story is about.

The Bourne Supremacy revolves around the key incident that Jason Bourne (Matt Damon) is trying to remember, the incident that happened in Berlin, where he killed the politician and his wife. The key incident in *Eternal Sunshine of the Spotless Mind* is when Clementine (Kate Winslet) ends the relationship by erasing all memories of Joel (Jim Carrey). This incident sets up the entire story and we experience what's happening at the same time as the main character. What happened during those three missing days in *The Manchurian Candidate* is what the whole movie is about. It is the key incident in the story line.

In *The English Patient,* there are two story lines: one in the present, in which Almásy (Ralph Fiennes) has been found burned almost beyond recognition, his body swathed in bandages. As he journeys to the hospital, he begins his relationship with his nurse Hana (Juliette Binoche). He muses about the past and his relationship with the married Katharine (Kristin Scott Thomas) and we flash back and forth between time past and time present, seeing both relationships develop. Anthony Minghella structured the present story from beginning to end, and structured Almásy and Katharine's story from beginning to end, and then inserted various parts of the relationship wherever it was applicable to move the story forward. It works very effectively.

What happens if the structure doesn't work? Basically, a screenplay without structure has no direction. It wanders around, like a series of episodes searching for itself. A film like *21 Grams* (Guillermo Arriaga), for example, while a dynamic, interesting attempt depicting the effect of a key incident (the car accident) on the lives of several characters, doesn't work in my mind because there's no structural unity in the film as the story unfolds, only a series of sequences slapped together in a seemingly haphazard, nonlinear way. There's no cohesiveness to the story. Robert Altman's *A Wedding,* or *American Hot Wax* (Floyd Mutrux), while interesting ideas, do not seem to have any clear-cut line of dramatic action or development, so whatever structural aspects there are only seem to highlight a dramatic situation, not a story line. The throughline of narrative action in these films are like two parallel lines that never meet.

A good screenplay has a strong line of dramatic action; it goes somewhere, moves forward, step-by-step, toward its resolution. It has direction, defined as a line of development. If you're going on a vacation or trip, you don't plan it by going to the airport, finding parking, walking to the closest terminal, seeing what flights are available, and then figuring out where you're going, do you? When you take a trip, you're going somewhere. You have a destination. You start *here* and end *there.*

That's what structure is all about. It's a tool that lets you shape your screenplay with maximum dramatic value (MDV). As stated earlier, structure is what *holds* everything together; all the action, characters, plot, incidents, episodes, and events that make up your screenplay.

The late Richard Feynman, the Nobel prize-winning physicist from Caltech, has pointed out that the laws of nature are so simple it's hard to see them. In order to do so, we have to rise above our level of complexity and understanding. For example, human beings had been observing natural phenomena for almost 400 years before Newton understood that "for every action there is an equal and opposite reaction." That's Newton's Third Law of Motion.

What could be simpler than that?

THE EXERCISE

This is a workbook that provides you with the opportunity of improving your screenwriting abilities. Try this little exercise on structure. Choose two of these movies: *Sideways, The Hours, Thelma & Louise, The English Patient, Ordinary People, Collateral,* and *The Bourne Supremacy.* See if you can analyze the structure of each film.

Take a sheet of paper and, by free-association, see if you can break each film down into a beginning, middle, and end. Just write it all down. Don't worry about whether you're right or not, just jot down your thoughts, words, and ideas about the flow of the story. No one's going to read this but you and it will give you good insight into the direction of the story.

Then, off the top of your head, just write down any idea that you might like to work on as a screenplay. See if you can structure it into a beginning, middle, and end. It doesn't matter whether it's a linear or nonlinear idea. Just lay it down in a couple of pages. Don't worry about grammar, spelling, or punctuation. Do it, then put it away and forget about it.

The *Workbook* is experiential; the more you put in, the more you get out.

3

The Paradigm

"Form follows structure; structure doesn't follow form."

—I. M. Pei
Architect

A screenplay is unique: as a story told in pictures, utilizing both dialogue and description to move the story forward, the narrative line is held together within the context of a dramatic structure that anchors the story line in place. There is a beginning, middle, and end. We spoke about context as being "the space" that holds something in place, that something being the content—all those scenes, sequences, action, dialogue, characters, and more, that make up the story line. Context doesn't change. Content changes.

Structure is form.

"A screenplay," as William Goldman says, "is structure, structure, structure." To illustrate the context of structure—what it looks like—we build a model, just like an architect builds a model to scale so we can "see" what a building looks like. We build the context of dramatic structure by illustrating it with the paradigm. A paradigm is defined as "a model, an example, or a conceptual scheme." It is really a tool or guideline, a roadmap through the story of the screenwriting process.

The more I learn about the paradigm, the more amazed I am at how important it really is. I conceived the paradigm after writing nine original screenplays and reading in excess of two thousand screenplays and more than a hundred novels looking for material during my stint as head of the story department at Cinemobile Systems. Most of what I read was not very good; as a matter of fact, I only found forty out of two thousand screenplays to submit to our financial partners. Since then, I have read, analyzed, and worked with screenwriters on thousands and thousands of screenplays in several different languages.

The one thing that all good screenplays have in common is structure. Structure is like a system; in science, systems are referred to as either being open or closed. A closed system is like a rock—it takes nothing from its environment and gives nothing back. There is no interchange between the rock and whatever its surroundings may be.

An open system is like a city: it interacts with its environment, and there exists a natural interchange between them. The city depends on the earth of the surrounding areas for food and raw materials, and people in those areas depend upon the city for jobs, trade, and other services. There is a give-and-take exchange between the city and its surroundings.

Writing a screenplay is very much an open system. You plan what you're going to write—for example, "Grace leaves Bill's apartment and takes a long walk through the city"—but sometimes it doesn't work out that way. Grace "tells" you she doesn't want to go on a long walk through the city—she wants to listen to music, go dancing, have an apple martini, and be around people. And if that ever happens, you better listen. That spark of spontaneity that jolts an unexpected image or thought or sequence or line of dialogue is what makes the creative process an open system. But you've got to be open to receive the new ideas and allow the process to emerge from your creative self. You can't let any preconceived notions or ideas hamper you from taking another direction in the screenwriting process. The writing experience should always be an adventure, and we're never really quite sure how the creative process is going to reveal itself to us.

That's what teaching is all about. It, too, is an open system. The teacher presents the material to the students; they listen, question, doubt, argue, and assimilate whatever connects with them. The way they listen can create a possible breakthrough in the understanding of craft, or an expansion of the original material, which in turn could evolve into the story taking a new direction. If we're open to the process, the story may take an unseen "twist," expanding the story line or characters, even adding new characters and subplots. The structure of the story may even change.

Over the years, I've defined the paradigm in many ways. If we could hang a screenplay on the wall like a painting, we could "see" what it looks like. For example, if you wanted to illustrate the paradigm of a table how would you define it? What is a table? A top with four legs. But that covers a lot of ground; there are many different types of tables: a short table, long table, high table, low table, or narrow table. There can also be a square table, round table, rectangular table, or octagonal table. You could also have a chrome table, wrought-iron table, wood table, glass table, plastic table, and so on. As you can see, the paradigm of a table does not change; it is "a top with four legs." That is its nature; that's the model of a table.

If you're building a new house, or remodeling an old one, you hire an architect or designer to draw blueprints, preliminary plans, and working plans. But if you're like I am, you may have trouble visualizing what the house is going to look like when it's finished based only on a blueprint. Lines on paper do not really show you the walls, doors, and ceilings. Some of us need to see a model before we can make any kind of aesthetic decision. It doesn't matter whether it's a house, office building, swimming pool, tennis court, car, bus, or boat, sometimes we just need to see it. In other words, we need a model.

In the same way, the paradigm is a model, an example, a conceptual scheme of what a screenplay looks like. If we could hang it on the wall like a painting, and see it in its wholeness, this it what it would look like:

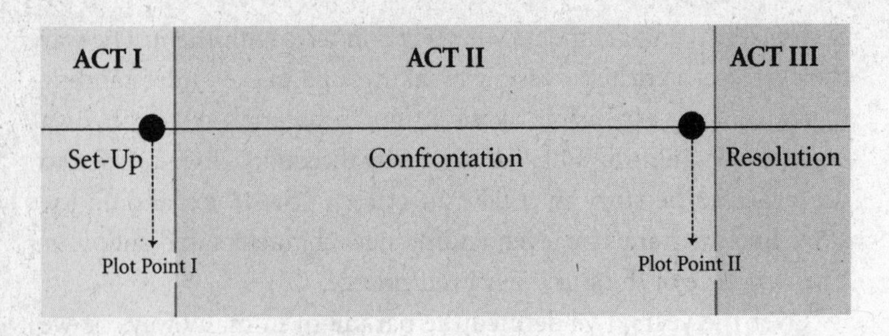

Let's explore the context of the paradigm. Here's how it works: If a screenplay is "a story told with pictures, in dialogue and description, and placed within the context of dramatic structure," what is a story? And what do all stories have in common?

A beginning, middle, and end—though as mentioned, not always in that order. Because we're dealing with a dramatic medium, the beginning corresponds to Act I, the middle to Act II, the end to Act III.

The average length of a film is about two hours long. Since one page of screenplay equals approximately one minute of screen time, the average screenplay is about one hundred and twenty pages long. Some are longer, some shorter, but most are close to this length. The contracts being written by most major Hollywood studios and production companies today usually stipulate that movies in production cannot be longer than two hours, eight minutes. That means approximately one hundred and twenty-eight pages. And you are not the exception.

You may want to check this out. Read a screenplay, then see the movie and determine if it's true or not! Check your watch. You should be reading as many screenplays as you can to familiarize yourself with the visual presentation of the story. If you're seriously interested in writing a screenplay, you should be reading all the scripts you can get your hands on, and seeing all the movies you can afford—in a movie theater, if possible. If not, then rent or buy the DVD.

If you don't have access to any screenplays, go online and search the Web. There are many Web sites devoted to the screenplay.

At some sites, you can download scripts free of charge—sites like *simplyscripts.com* or *Drew's Script-O-Rama.com* or *dailyscript.com.* Or, do a Google or Yahoo search for "screenplays" and see what comes up. There are many, many sites and many, many screenplays you can download.

It breaks down this way: Aristotle states there are three unities of action—time, place, and action. Act I is a unit of dramatic (or comedic) action. It begins at the beginning, page one, with the opening shot or sequence, and goes through to the end of Plot Point I. It is approximately twenty to thirty pages long and is held together by the dramatic context known as the *Set-Up.*

Act II is a unit of dramatic action that begins at the end of Plot Point I and extends through the end of Plot Point II, and it is approximately fifty or sixty pages long. It is held together by the dramatic context known as *Confrontation.* Act II is all about conflict and obstacles confronted and overcome. All drama is conflict; without conflict, you have no action, and without action, you have no character. Without character, you have no story, and without story, you ain't got no screenplay. If you know your character's dramatic need—that is, what he or she wants to win, gain, get, or achieve during the course of your screenplay—then you can create obstacles to that need and your story becomes your character overcoming obstacle after obstacle to achieve his or her dramatic need.

Act III is also a unit of dramatic or comedic action; it goes from the end of Plot Point II, approximately page eighty or ninety, to the end of the screenplay, roughly page one hundred and twenty. It, too, is roughly twenty to thirty pages long and is held together with the dramatic context known as *Resolution.* It's important to remember that resolution means solution and in this unit of action your story is resolved. Not necessarily wrapped up neatly, but complete in whatever way you choose. In this, the preparation, or preplanning stage of writing the screenplay, what you need to know about the resolution of your story is basically what happens to your character at the end of the story.

Does your character live or die, succeed or fail, win the race or not, return safely home or not, get married or divorced? Resolution means solution and Act III is all about how your story is resolved. If you don't know how to resolve your story, ask yourself how *you would like it* to be resolved, regardless of how effective it is, or whether "they"—those unknown film executives who live in your head—would like it. It's your story so you get to choose how it's going to end. And that will be your starting point.

When Stuart Beattie was preparing his script of *Collateral,* he knew that Max (Jamie Foxx) had to stand up to the hired killer to save his life as well as to redeem himself; otherwise, he would just be another murder statistic on the streets of L.A. That's the character arc that Max had to go through in order to realize that his "someday dream" would never happen unless he made it happen. Beattie structured the evolution of the character just like he did the story and it's a good illustration of using the paradigm as a structural template.

In many films, like *American Beauty* (Alan Ball), or *The Bourne Supremacy* (Tony Gilroy), Act I is anywhere from eighteen to twenty-two pages long. We're not talking numbers here, we're talking *form:* beginning, middle, and end. Act II can be anywhere from fifty to sixty pages, plus or minus a few pages, and there are times when Act III is fifteen to twenty pages long. The paradigm, remember, is only a model, an example or conceptual scheme. It's not something that's laid down in concrete. As a matter of fact, the great thing about structure is that it's fluid; like a tree in the wind, it bends, but doesn't break.

Act I is a unit of dramatic action that sets up your story. In the first twenty to thirty pages of screenplay, you must set up your story. You must introduce your main characters, establish your dramatic premise (what the story is about), create the dramatic situation (the circumstances surrounding the action), and set up the relationships between your character's professional life, his or her personal life (relationships), and his or her private life (private time and hobbies). Most, if not all, of these elements need to be established in this first unit of dramatic action.

Everything in Act I focuses on setting up your story. You don't have time for cheap tricks or clever scenes or cute dialogue if they don't move the story forward, establish the relationships between the characters, or reveal information about the characters. You've got to set up your story immediately, from page one, word one. The purpose of each scene is either to move the story forward or reveal information about the character. Anything that does not serve these two functions should be dropped. Act I sets up the story and holds each scene and sequence in place. Context, remember, is the space that *holds* the content in place; all those scenes, dialogue, description, shots, and special effects that make up a screenplay. Everything in this unit of action sets up everything that will follow.

A perfect example is *Lord of the Rings: The Fellowship of the Ring* (Peter Jackson, Philippa Boyens, and Fran Walsh). After the brief prologue establishing the history of the Ring, we follow Gandalf as he enters the Shire. There, we meet Frodo, Bilbo Baggins, Sam, Merry, and Pippin, and see the Hobbit's life in the Shire. We learn that Bilbo found the Ring, wants to leave the Shire to write his book, and uses the Ring to disappear from his birthday party. That causes Gandalf to research the history of the Ring, and soon realizes the danger that the Ring brings with it. Already, the dark horsemen of Sauron are searching the Shire for it. Frodo reluctantly inherits the Ring when Bilbo vanishes and Gandalf convinces Frodo of the need to leave the Shire. So Frodo and Sam set out on their journey—their mission: to travel to Mordor, land of the enemy, and destroy the Ring in the fires of Mount Doom, where it was forged. The act of Frodo and Sam leaving the relative safety of the Shire now takes us into Act II where they encounter obstacle after obstacle before they reach their journey's end. (As a side note, the context of Part II, *The Two Towers,* is all about confrontation and the overcoming of obstacles.) Everything is set up in this first unit of dramatic action. We establish relationships between the main characters: we know who the main character is (Frodo), what the story is about (destroying the Ring in the fire), and what the dramatic situation is (Sauron, rallying the forces of evil to destroy Middle Earth).

THE STORY: *The Lord of the Rings: The Fellowship of the Ring*

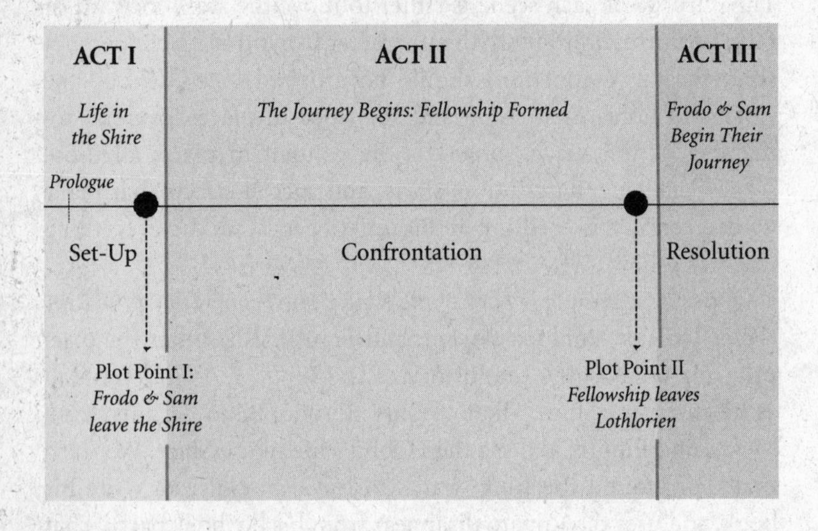

In Act I of *The Shawshank Redemption* (Frank Darabont), the opening sequence sets up the three threads of visual action: we see Andy Dufresne (Tim Robbins) sitting in his car, drunk. He pulls out a gun and sloppily inserts the bullets. Then we intercut to his trial where he is charged with the murder of his wife and her lover, then see his wife and her lover preparing to have sex. Together, these three visual threads of dramatic action set up the entire story line: Andy's wife and lover are murdered, Andy is convicted of the murders, and he enters prison to serve "two life sentences." We enter Shawshank Penitentiary as Andy Dufresne enters. We meet another convicted murderer, Red (Morgan Freeman), and he explains in voiceover who he is and how he met Andy. We are with Andy when the warden sets forth the rules of Shawshank. We watch as Andy is hosed down, deloused, and enters his cell. The doors slam shut. Welcome to Shawshank.

Night comes, the fat man breaks down, and is beaten and taken to the infirmary. Andy is assigned to the laundry room, is hustled by "the girls"—the deadly gang of gay men—and we see him gradually adjust to prison life. At the end of Act I, he's in the yard, meets up with Red ("I hear you're a man who can get things done."), and they establish their relationship. The whole story is set up in Act I.

Which then brings us to the next question: how do we get from Act I, the Set-Up, into Act II, the Confrontation? And how do we get from Act II, the Confrontation, into Act III, the Resolution? The answer: to create a Plot Point at the end of Act I and Act II. A Plot Point is defined as *any incident, episode or event that "hooks" into the action and spins it around into another direction,* in this case, into either Act II or Act III. Direction, of course, is a "line of development." We are moving the story forward, from Act I, the Set-Up, into Act II, the Confrontation, and then into Act III, the Resolution.

Over the years, I've heard many questions about the Plot Point. Does it have to be a major event or dramatic incident? Can it be a scene or sequence? The answer is yes to both questions. A Plot Point can be anything you want it to be; it is a story progression point. It can be as simple as an action: John Dunbar (Kevin Costner) arriving at the deserted fort in *Dances With Wolves* (Michael Blake). It can be a line of dialogue, or short scene done completely in silence like Plot Point I in *Witness* (Earl Wallace and Bill Kelly): The ten-year-old Amish boy who sees a murder take place pointing out the killer to John Book (Harrison Ford) in the police station. It can be an action sequence: Jason Bourne (Matt Damon) escaping from the customs agent in Naples in *The Bourne Supremacy*. It can be a dramatic sequence as in *Thelma & Louise:* Thelma and Louise are driving to the mountains for the weekend, but a brief stop at a bar turns into an attempted rape and results in a murder, setting the two women on the run.

In *An Unmarried Woman,* one of my favorite teaching films, written and directed by Paul Mazursky, Act I establishes the marriage of Erica (Jill Clayburgh). We see her jogging with her husband,

Martin (Michael Murphy), sending their daughter off to school, then enjoying a "quickie" with her husband. She goes to her part-time job in an art gallery, gets hustled by Charlie the painter (Cliff Gorman), meets her best friends for lunch. During their conversation, we learn that most of them are divorced, unhappy, and bitter about men and declare their envy of Erica's seventeen-year marriage. Mazursky sets up Erica's character in the first act, doing it with visual bits and pieces of information about who she is and what she wants.

From the outside, Erica's marriage looks fine. Then, about twenty or twenty-five minutes into the film, her husband suddenly breaks down and bursts into tears.

"What is it?" Erica asks, concerned. "What's wrong?"

Martin turns to her and tells her that he's met another woman, fallen in love, and wants a divorce. One scene, one line of dialogue, and the entire story shifts into another direction. No longer is she married; now she is divorced, an unmarried woman. It is the true beginning of the story.

That's an illustration of a Plot Point—an incident, episode, or event that "hooks" into the action and spins it around into another direction, in this case, Act II. It moves the story forward. Act I sets her up as the married woman, Act II reveals her as an unmarried woman and shows how she copes with that, and Act III dramatizes her life as a single person, able to live life on her own terms without leaning or depending on a man.

Here's what it looks like on the paradigm.

THE STORY: *An Unmarried Woman*

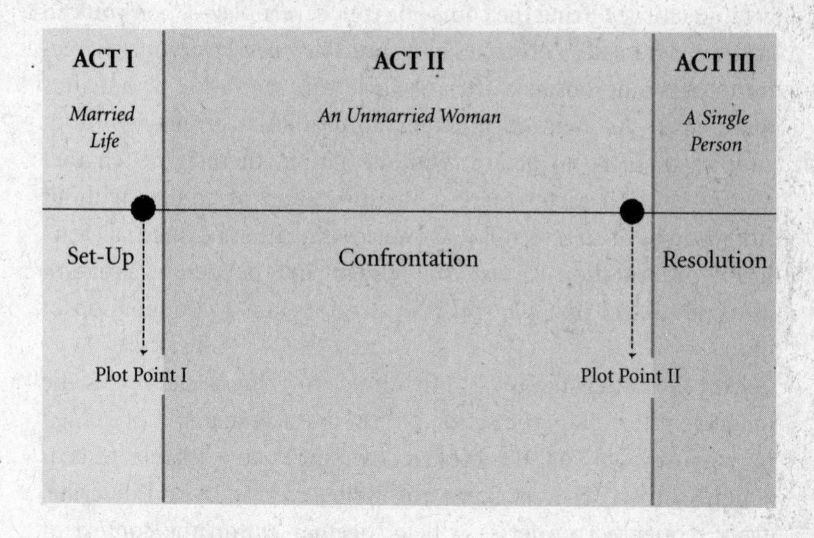

Plot Point I is the true beginning of your story. A Plot Point can be anything you want it to be as long as it moves the action forward. It is a function of character, leading us from Act I into Act II or from Act II into Act III. It should be noted here that there can be many Plot Points in your screenplay but at this stage in the writing process, the preparation, we are only focusing on Plot Points I and II; they are the anchor points that hold the elements of your story line in place.

Before you can write one word on paper, you must know four things: your ending, your beginning, Plot Point I, and Plot Point II. Only when you know these four elements can you start to "build" or structure your story line.

Act II is also a unit of dramatic or comedic action, held together by the context known as Confrontation. Act II goes from the Plot Point at the end of Act I to the end of Plot Point II and is approximately fifty to sixty pages long. During this section of your screenplay, your character will be challenged by numerous obstacles to achieve his or her dramatic need. If you know your character's dramatic need—what your character wants to win, gain, get, or achieve during the course of your screenplay—then you can create the necessary obstacles and your story becomes your character overcoming obstacle after obstacle to achieve his or her dramatic need. As mentioned earlier, all drama is conflict—without conflict there is no action; without action, there is no character; without character there is no story; and of course, without story, you have no screenplay. Obstacles can either be internal (fearing a confrontation) or external (caught in a dangerous situation like Jamie Foxx in *Collateral*). Mostly, they are a combination of both.

Act II is often the most difficult act to write because it is the longest unit of dramatic action. (With the new material presented in this workbook, Act II is broken down into two workable units of action.) In Act II, every scene you write, every shot you describe, every sequence you devise is held together within the context of Confrontation. In *Thelma & Louise*, the two women run from the crime they committed because they panic and don't know what else to do. Once on the run, they encounter obstacle after obstacle: they've run from the scene of a crime, don't have enough money, have very little gas, and are scared. They encounter all kinds of obstacles, either internal (fear and uncertainty of what they've done and what's going to happen to them) or external (the police want them for questioning).

Act II of *An Unmarried Woman* deals with Erica as an unmarried woman after being in what she thought was a "good" marriage for seventeen years. She must learn how to adapt and deal with her new life. She feels betrayed, abandoned, angry, and bitter. It's an enormous change for her, and she finds adjusting difficult. She enters therapy, learns how to be a single parent, overcomes her anger at men in general (focusing it instead on her husband, where it belongs), and begins to experiment sexually.

Near the end of Act II she meets Saul (Alan Bates), an artist, at the art gallery where she works and has sex with him, but refuses to see him again, saying she's still experimenting and doesn't want to enter into any kind of relationship, especially a serious one. "Nothing personal," she adds. A few nights later she meets him again at a party. They talk, enjoy each other's company, and decide to leave the party together. Despite what she had said at the end of their sexual encounter, she likes him and he likes her, and soon she feels comfortable enough to spend more time with him. The Plot Point at the end of Act II is when they decide to leave the party together; it occurs about eighty or ninety minutes into the film and is the incident that "spins the action around into another direction"—in this case, Act III. The third act focuses on Erica's new relationship with Saul. This is the way it looks on the paradigm:

THE STORY: *An Unmarried Woman*

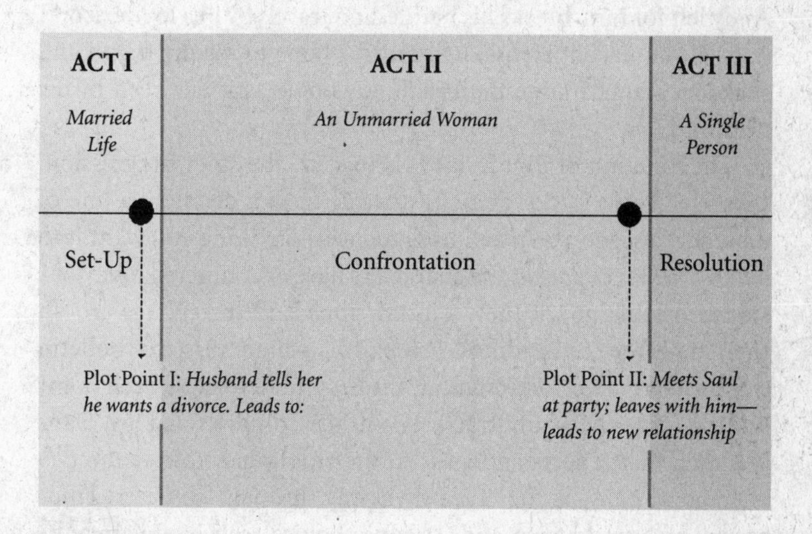

The Plot Point at the end of Act II "spins the story around" into Act III. It is that incident, episode, or event that "hooks" into the action and leads the action into Act III, the Resolution.

In *The Shawshank Redemption,* Andy Dufresne has learned who actually murdered his wife and her lover, a crime for which he has been convicted and served time. He wants the warden to help him get a new trial; he's served some nineteen years for a crime he didn't commit. The Warden has his own reasons for keeping Andy in prison, and to make sure, he has the young man who gave Andy the new information murdered. Andy knows now that he's not going to get out; he's going to spend the rest of his life in Shawshank unless he does something about it. He is guilty, yes—not of murder but of being a bad husband, and that's all. He has served his time. If *The Shawshank Redemption* is about anything, it's about hope.

So Andy chooses a time and escapes—something, we learn, he'd been planning for years. The escape sequence is a brilliant moment of filmmaking and is the Plot Point at the end of Act II. After he escapes, we have to resolve the story. Red gets his parole, finds the rock Andy left for him, breaks his parole, and travels by bus to Mexico. "I hope I can make it across the border. I hope to see my friend and shake his hand. I hope the Pacific is as blue as it has been in my dreams. I *hope.*"

The function of Plot Point II is to serve the story progression. Like Plot Point I, Plot Point II can either be a decision, a line of dialogue, a scene, or an action sequence—anything you want it to be. In *Thelma & Louise,* the characters have encountered many obstacles by this point: they've been ripped off, the police are on their trail, they're heading for Mexico with an all-states bulletin out for their arrest. Throughout the Second Act, we've been bombarded with the soundtrack, beautifully orchestrated by Hans Zimmer, that reflects and adds to the emotional state of the two characters. Now, as they race their way through the desert landscapes of New Mexico and Arizona, Louise realizes this may be their last night alive on this Earth. She knows that her act of killing Harlan at the end of Act I will probably cost the two women their lives.

Overcome by this knowledge, Louise is driving through the vast, magnificent landscape of Monument Valley in Utah. It is a gorgeous night; the moon is full, the high plateaus silhouetted in light and shadow. Louise pulls off the road to stare at this beautiful sight, probably the last time she will ever pass this way again. The music stops and on the soundtrack there is only the silence of the landscape, the whisper of a slight wind, accompanied by the night sounds of the valley. The silence speaks volumes and is extremely effective.

Louise gets out of the car, takes a few steps off the road, and stares in beauty and wonder at the magnificent sight in front of her. And, as she says in a later scene, she now understands that killing Harlan may be the actual cause of their death.

Thelma steps up behind her. "What's goin' on?" she asks, breaking the moment of silence. "Nothing," Louise replies.

This one moment, brief, silent, devoid of dialogue or music, is a glimpse into their sure and immediate future. This moment is Plot Point II. From then on to the end of the screenplay, Thelma and Louise are racing against time and circumstance. They don't make it to Mexico; they only get as far as the edge of the Grand Canyon. It is here that they realize their destiny. With the Grand Canyon in front of them, and the elite Arizona SWAT team behind them, the two women know they don't want to spend the rest of their natural lives in prison, or be gunned down. Given their choice, they prefer to take their own lives. They grasp their hands together, Louise bears down on the gas pedal, and they leap into the chasm of the Grand Canyon together.

On the paradigm it looks like this:

THE STORY: *Thelma & Louise*

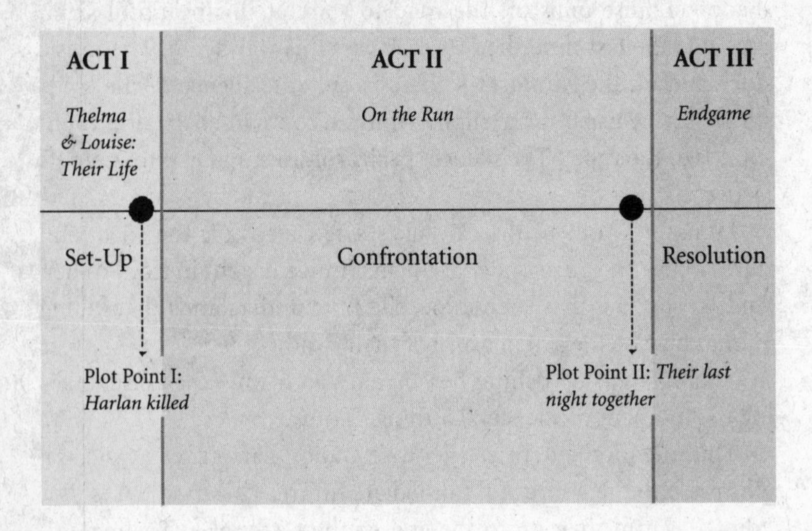

Do all films have Plot Points? Films that "work" have a strong, organic structure with their Plot Points clearly woven and defined within the context of their story.

Which brings us to Act III. Act III is a unit of dramatic action that is approximately thirty pages long and goes from the Plot Point at the end of Act II to the end of the screenplay. Act III deals with the dramatic context of *Resolution.* What is the solution to your story? Does your character live or die, succeed or fail, go on a trip or not, get the promotion or not, get married or divorced, survive the test or not, get away safely or not? You must know what the resolution of your story line is. I don't necessarily mean the specific scene or sequence at the end of the screenplay but what happens to resolve the dramatic conflict. If you don't know the ending of your story, who does?

I recently had the opportunity of working with some of the space scientists from JPL and NASA, and I observed that designing a mission follows the same principles as structuring a screenplay. In a scientific mission the first thing they do is declare what the undertaking is; they state their intention, clearly defining what they want to accomplish or achieve. For example, they want to send a manned exposition to Mars and take soil density readings and return, or to explore the atmospheric components of Io, one of the moons of Jupiter. Each project begins with a destination and a purpose. In the same way, you need to know how your story ends, the Resolution. That's where you're going; that is your destination.

When you reach Plot Point II, there are usually two or three things left unresolved in your story. What are they? Can you define and articulate them? What's going to happen to the main character? In *Thelma & Louise,* two things need to be resolved: one, do they escape safely to Mexico or not, and two, do they live or die? Act III shows us, scene by scene, how their time runs out and how they choose to end their lives together. In *The Shawshank Redemption,* when Andy escapes at Plot Point II, we need to know what happens to him—does he get away safely? When Red receives the postcard from Mexico, we know Andy has accomplished that. But what's going to happen to Red? Those two story points are resolved in Act III. In *An Unmarried Woman,* Erica learns to be a single person and create her own identity.

Structure, as you can see, dramatically establishes the relationship between the parts and the whole. Each part is a separate and complete unit of dramatic action. Act I is a whole as well as a part. It is a whole because it has a beginning, middle, and an end. It begins at the beginning and ends at the Plot Point at the end of Act I. Act II is a whole as well as a part and begins at the end of Plot Point I and goes through the end of Plot Point II. Act III is a whole as well as a part, beginning at the end of Plot Point II and going to the end of your screenplay. *Set-Up, Confrontation, Resolution* is the context that holds your story together. It is the structural foundation of your screenplay, "a linear arrangement of related incidents, episodes, and events, leading to a dramatic resolution."

THE EXERCISE

Before you can express your story dramatically, you must know four things: 1) the ending, 2) the beginning, 3) Plot Point I, and 4) Plot Point II. These four elements are the structural foundation of your screenplay. You "hang" your entire story around these four elements.

Here's how it works. Suppose you take an idea and sculpt it into a subject. For example: *A YOUNG WOMAN, a painter, in an unhappy marriage, enrolls in an art class and has an affair with her teacher. Against her will, she falls in love with him, then learns she is pregnant. Torn between her husband and lover, she decides to leave both and raise her child by herself.*

The first thing to do with your subject—the action and character—is to structure it. What's the ending of your story? Where the young woman goes off to have her child by herself, leaving both her husband and lover, much like Nora in Ibsen's play *A Doll's House.* That's the end.

What about the beginning? We want the audience to know that the young woman is in an unhappy marriage, so we must show this. What kind of scene or sequence would reveal an unhappy marriage? Is the woman's husband unable to communicate with her? Does he take her for granted? Is he distant and weak? Is he flirting with other women? Having affairs? What kind of scene would communicate that to the audience? When they're in bed? At a party? Preparing for an evening out? The great Italian director, Michelangelo Antonioni opened his great film *L'Eclisse* in a living room at dawn. The room is a mess, the curtains are drawn, ashtrays are overflowing, dirty glasses sit on the table, and there's a fan in the foreground that whirs incessantly. It's the only sound in the room. Vittoria (Monica Vitti) and her lover Riccardo (Francisco Rabal) stare at each other in silence. They have nothing left to say to each other; everything has been said that could have been said. We see immediately their relationship is over.

Find a way to open with a scene that will illustrate, or reveal, your dramatic premise. Think about it. Try out several different ways and see what works the best. Does it take place during the day or at night? At work or at home?

What happens at Plot Point I? If Act I sets up the marriage, the Plot Point at the end of Act I might be the woman enrolling in the art class, leading to the relationship with her art teacher; it is the Plot Point that "spins" the story into another direction. It is the true beginning of your story.

What about Plot Point II? If Plot Point I is the beginning of the relationship, Plot Point II might be where she learns she's pregnant. This discovery precipitates the action that leads to the resolution, the "solution" of the story: she resolves her dilemma by leaving both husband and lover.

Once you know these four elements—ending, beginning, Plot Point I, and Plot Point II—draw the paradigm:

THE STORY: *A young woman, a painter, in an unhappy marriage, enrolls in an art class and has an affair with her teacher. Against her will, she falls in love with him, then learns she is pregnant. Torn between her husband and lover, she decides to leave both and raise her child by herself.*

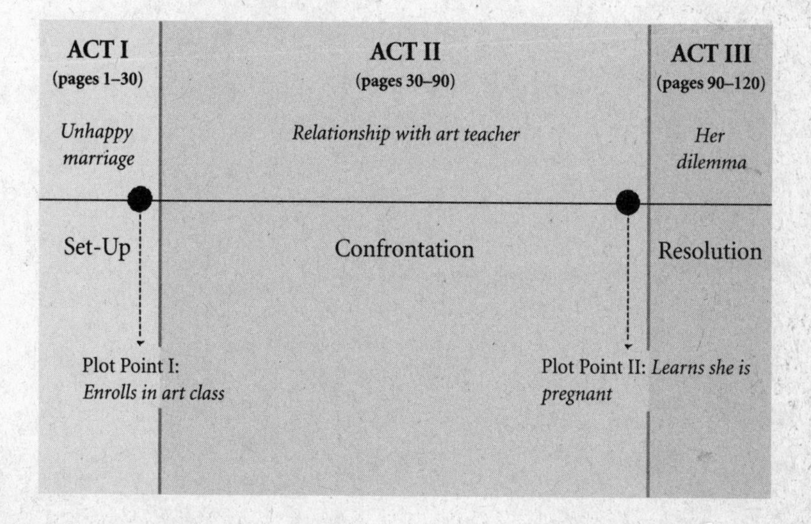

This is what your idea might "look like" when it is structured. The paradigm, remember, is a conceptual tool, enabling you to "see" your story line clearly. It gives you an overview.

You don't have to be too specific; just lay it out in broad, general strokes. You can fill in the details later.

The exercise is designed to prepare you to structure your own idea so you can move into the next stage in the screenwriting process.

It is the first step in preparing your screenplay.

4

Four Pages

"It is good to have an end to journey towards; but it is the journey that matters in the end."

—Ursula K. LeGuin
Author

Not too long ago, I was taking a yoga class with a well-known television actor. We started talking and after a while the subject, as always, turned to the movies, then to screenwriting. He told me that he had a great idea for a screenplay.

"What's it about?" I asked.

"Well," he began, "it's about this guy in the Sahara Desert. We open at sunrise with a long shot of dust rising out of the desert. Then we see a Jeep racing across the sand. Suddenly, the engine sputters, coughs, and finally dies. The man climbs out of the Jeep, looks around, and jerks open the hood. Then we hear strange noises coming from behind a distant dune. Suddenly, several racing camels sweep down over the hill. They see him and stop. They look at each other surrounded by the silence."

He looked at me, enthused. "Isn't that a great idea?"

"It's a great opening," I replied. "What happens next?"

"I haven't figured it out yet. But it'll all come out later, in the plot."

Sure. How many times have you heard that before? What plot?

I nodded in understanding. Yeah. Sure.

I can't tell you how many times I've heard that same scenario from aspiring screenwriters. Of course, they can't tell you any more about the story because they don't know any more about it. They haven't defined it to themselves yet.

What's it about? Briefly, in terms of describing the story line, *what's* your story about, and *who* is it about? Can you define it, articulate it in a few sentences? It's something I emphasize over and over again in my workshops and seminars:

"If you don't know your story, who does?"

Writing a screenplay is more about the journey than the destination. It is an ongoing, evolving process that changes day to day. You prepare the material in stages or steps. First, you need an idea, which is broken down into a subject, the action and character. Then, when you have your subject, you can structure it on the *paradigm* with the four anchoring points that hold your story together: the ending, beginning, Plot Points I and II. You really can't write anything with any degree of certainty until you know those four things; they are the foundation of your story line, the glue that holds your story together.

Only when you know these four elements can you begin to tell your story in a narrative fashion. In fact, the word "narrative" means an arrangement, or sequence of events or happenings, factual or imagined, and implies a sense of direction. The story progresses from beginning to end. And direction, remember, is a line of development.

Putting your story down on paper is essential because it's a necessary stage in fleshing out and developing your idea. How accurate it will be in terms of the finished screenplay five or six months from now, or how good or bad it is, is totally irrelevant.

That's why I think it's necessary to write a short, four-page treatment. A treatment is defined as a narrative synopsis of your story line. Some dialogue can be included if it helps to shed light upon the lives of your characters. I have my students write four-page treatments because it helps articulate and define the structural events that hold the story together.

Why is this necessary? Because it allows you to take those unformed, fragmented ideas that are running around your head and put them down on paper. It sharpens the details of your story and clarifies the relationships you've been thinking about.

I call this a "kick in the ass" exercise, because you're taking this amorphous idea, or notion, and trying to give it form. It's an important step in the screenwriting process.

It should be mentioned that in Hollywood, a treatment, any kind of a treatment, is only a writer's tool; it's just part of the ongoing journey of writing a screenplay. Writing a treatment and hoping it will sell, is only a pipe dream. A treatment is not a screenplay. Don't expect the treatment you write to be sold, or optioned, especially if you're a new or aspiring screenwriter. In television, it's a different story; there, treatments, or beat sheets, or outlines, may be developed in conjunction with the production executive and the network. But we're talking about screenplays here, and in Hollywood only a finished screenplay can be sent out to studios and production companies.

It's also a different story in Europe and in some Latin American countries. In Europe, for example, a treatment is often sold or optioned by members of the Film Commission or Ministry of Culture, and then the writer is given a nominal sum of money to develop the treatment into a screenplay. What happens to the screenplay after it's written, of course, is anybody's guess. Sometimes, the treatment is optioned, a screenplay written, and then it simply sits on a shelf somewhere gathering dust for whatever reason—a director is not available or doesn't like the material or the budget is too high or there's been a change in the policy or members of the Film Commission. Whatever. I hear this over and over and over again from European and Latin American screenwriters. The stories are legion.

Writing a four-page treatment is not something you have to do, but if you take the time to prepare your material correctly, it pays off during the actual writing process.

I learned this the hard way. When I was making documentaries for David L. Wolper, I was a staff writer and wrote, produced, researched, directed, or was associated with more than 125 television network documentaries. After four and a half years, I felt it was time for a change. I left Wolper Productions and went looking for a job in feature film production, actively seeking a job as a production executive. But nothing was available at the time. Things were tight. Then, after several months, I was asked to rewrite a documentary feature, called *Spree,* directed by Walon Green, whom I had worked with at Wolper Productions. Now the Executive Producer of TV's *Law & Order,* Walon had co-written *The Wild Bunch* with Sam Peckinpah, the writer–director who was a mentor to me and who had been so instrumental in my understanding of the screenplay.

After writing *Spree,* I realized I could possibly earn a living as a writer while waiting for some kind of a production job. So, I became a screenwriter living the life of a freelancer—a job here, a job there, just enough to make ends meet. It went on like this for the next seven years, during which time I wrote nine original screenplays. Two were produced. The next four scripts I wrote were optioned, meaning a producer paid me a certain sum of money so he or she had the exclusive right to produce the movie for a certain length of time, usually two years. At the end of that period, the rights reverted back to me. The three others I wrote went nowhere. Everybody told me how much they liked them, but nothing happened with them and they still sit on my shelf. "Hollywood," said novelist Dorothy Parker, "is the only place where you can die from encouragement."

The way I worked was simple. I would get an idea and research it—get books from the library and talk to people about it until I felt comfortable with the material. Then I would do my character work, write character biographies, talk to more people, look at pictures, read any first-hand accounts from diaries of that period. Next I would sit down and start writing. I used to call it "hitting my head against the typewriter." I always came up with a script, but the cost, both physically and emotionally, was very high. It was a slow and painful process, and after years of working this way, I began to look at screenwriting as something I *had* to do rather than something I *wanted* to do. There's a big difference between the two; one is a negative experience, the other positive. While it's important to see both sides, writing is too hard a job, too demanding a task, to color it with a negative or painful experience.

One of the scripts I wrote during this time was a painful, but ultimately beneficial experience. It was a western about a man named Balinger who rode with Butch Cassidy and the Sundance Kid, an "unchanged man in a changing time," as Peckinpah used to say. But when Butch and Sundance left for South America in 1902, my character, Balinger, refused to believe the times were changing. He stayed behind, pulled a couple of holdups, was caught, sentenced to prison, escaped, and continued to do the only thing he knew how to do: rob banks.

Balinger was a character who was at odds with the times. On one hand, he was born ten years too late; on the other, he was born ten years too early. That was the basic idea. He was a character who didn't belong.

In the back story, Balinger robs a bank, gets caught, and is sentenced to prison. I wanted to open the script with an exciting sequence of Balinger escaping from prison, having served four years of a ten-year sentence. After he escapes, he teams up with his old partner, adds a few young members to his gang, and begins to pursue his old way of life. But of course, times have changed. Banks have started using checks, stocks and bonds are negotiable securities, and with something called the telephone you could call from Denver to San Francisco. Balinger couldn't understand that. After planning a robbery, his expectations are thwarted because nothing works. In one job he gets a bundle of checks, along with a thousand dollar bill he can't cash. Another job nets only a few hundred dollars in coins and some stock certificates.

At this point, he doesn't know what to do or where to go, and the Pinkerton detectives chasing him are closing in. Balinger knows his time is at an end and talks about joining Butch and Sundance in Bolivia. One last job—a big one, he thinks—will do it. So, the motley group rides to a town in Washington State, on the banks of Puget

Sound. They pull the job, but in the ensuing shoot-out, the money is left behind and Balinger chooses to end his own life by deliberately colliding with the Coast Guard cutter chasing him. His last words were something like, "Maybe Butch and Sundance had the right idea."

That's about all I knew when I sat down in "the pit" and started writing. But this time, "hitting my head against the typewriter" didn't work. Or, I should say, it worked for about thirty pages, and after that I went into a state of confusion. I didn't know what happened or what to do or where to go, and after struggling with the story line for several weeks, I plunged into the infamous writer's block.

It was awful. To help me, I started doing a lot of drugs, but instead of finding my story I simply got further and further away from it. I became angry, despondent, and frustrated, then surrendered to a deep depression. It went on for several weeks, until I became frightened, and stopped taking everything. Cold turkey.

A few days later a friend of mine, then the story editor for a major production company, called and we went out to dinner. During the course of the meal I shared the problem with him and he asked a very simple question: "What's your story about?"

I looked at him dumbfounded. In all my despair and pain and depression over my "writing block," I had forgotten all about my story. It was the first time I had been asked to tell the story, to describe it out loud.

I stammered awhile, trying to remember what it was about, and finally managed to blurt out the basic idea. He listened, asked some pertinent questions, made some suggestions, and told me he wanted to see something in writing.

I agreed, and when I returned that night, I sat down and wrote a short treatment. I couldn't believe what happened—as soon as I knew my story, my writer's block vanished. That's when I suddenly understood: "*The hardest thing about writing is knowing what to write.*"

That experience taught me how important it is to know your story. In all my screenwriting workshops and seminars across the

United States, Canada, Europe, Mexico, and South America, I continually stress the fact that you must know your story before you can write anything. And it all starts when you're able to take the four elements, the ending, beginning, Plot Point I, and Plot Point II, and structure them into a dramatic story line.

Why a four-page treatment and not ten or twenty pages?

Because at this stage you really don't know much about your story. You only have a general idea of an action and character, and a general basis for your plot, as well as the four anchoring points: ending, beginning, Plot Points I and II. That's all you know about your story at this point. You don't know what the purpose of a particular scene is or what part it plays in the story line. You probably don't even know whether it moves the story forward or reveals information about the character. Most of us don't have the answers to these kinds of questions at this stage. We have to frame in the story line, anchor it in the foundation of narrative.

The treatment helps set you up for the actual writing of the screenplay. So, when you're writing this short, four-page treatment, don't get carried away with excessive detail. Adding in too much detail now does not serve your best interests.

You'll always be able to be more specific later on, adding individual characterization, what kind of a car he or she drives, how his or her apartment looks, the paintings on the wall, and why he or she goes by train and not plane. You don't need to know that right now. Later on, yes.

That's why a four-page treatment is a good length at this stage for organizing your story line. It is not your story, it's just an outline of the story, a start point in the screenwriting process. So put all your expectations, your hopes and dreams away in a drawer somewhere where they're out of sight, and simply sit down and write the treatment.

Here's the assignment: you're going to write a four-page treatment, a narrative synopsis, of your story line. In the preceding chapters, we talked about isolating the idea and putting it into a subject. Basically, it describes *what* your story's about and *who* it's about. Then we took the subject and broke it down on the paradigm so we knew the ending, the beginning, Plot Point I, and Plot Point II. The *paradigm* becomes your structural anchor.

Now take the subject of your story line—the action and character—and lay it out in dramatic structure on the paradigm. Choose your ending first, then determine your beginning, then choose Plot Point I and Plot Point II. Do it the same way you did the structure exercise in the previous chapter.

As Aristotle says, we begin at the beginning. What's your opening scene or sequence? We're going into some brief detail here. Where does it take place? With your character arriving at the airport, like Vincent arriving in Los Angeles in *Collateral*? Or does it take place on a deserted road, in a car, in the back country? Does your script open in a dream, or flashback, as in *The Bourne Supremacy*? Or do you open on a crowded city street, or an empty elevator, or in a bedroom with an erotic sex scene like *Basic Instinct* (Joe Eszterhas)? At this moment you don't have to be too specific or precise; you don't have to know everything yet. Just deal with your story line in broad strokes. The details will come later.

If your opening scene or sequence takes place at the office, what is your character doing? Arriving at work on Monday morning? Leaving on Friday afternoon? Sketch it in, knowing you can change it all later. Remember that the purpose of this exercise is to define and synopsize your story line in four pages. It should either be double-spaced, or a space and a half.

Not eight pages, not five pages—*four* pages.

Once you've decided on what your opening scene or sequence is, we're going to break the treatment down into two distinct categories. The first category I call the *dramatic recreation* of the scene or sequence. It visually describes the action. For example: "Night. A car slowly weaves though the streets. It turns a corner, pulls over to the side. Stops. The lights go out. The car sits in front of a large house. Waits. Silence. In the distance, a dog BARKS. JOE sits behind the wheel, silently, a radio transmitter on the seat next to him. He slips on a pair of earphones, slowly turns the dial to pick up police calls. Then he listens. And waits."

I call that a *dramatic recreation* because it's a visually specific description of the action. Remember, we're setting up the opening scene or sequence here. Describe the action of the opening in about half a page. Use a few lines of dialogue if you need to.

Remember, this is not your screenplay; it's only a treatment, a narrative synopsis of your story.

The second category I call the *narrative synopsis*, and that's where you summarize the action in broad, general strokes. If your story is about the relationship between a recently divorced mother and her teenage son who wants to live with his father in another state, you want to *summarize* what happens during the rest of Act I. If your opening scene or sequence starts with a dream of the mother waking up to an empty house, the rest of Act I deals with setting up and establishing their relationship. For example, "the mother tries to communicate with her son but he continues to disrupt life by performing poorly in school, becoming defiant and disrespectful of his teachers. He criticizes her constantly, complaining of her physical inability to do 'guy' things like throwing footballs and lifting weights. It seems clear that the mother feels she's losing him. She vows to spend more time with him and puts him before her work and her own well-being. But her determination does little to gain his respect or appreciation. The mother doesn't know what to do anymore or what it will take to win back his affection."

The *narrative synopsis* is a general description, a summary of the action that takes place during the rest of Act I. If you contrast this type of writing with the opening, the dramatic recreation, you'll see that the opening is specific, whereas the narrative synopsis is general. That's the tone we want to achieve in this four-page treatment. You want it to look like there's a full story, but the truth is there are only four points of the story line which are specific. It leads us directly into the next step, a *dramatic recreation* of Plot Point I.

What is the incident, episode, or event that is the Plot Point at the end of Act I? Is it an action sequence or a dialogue sequence? Where does it take place? What's the purpose of the scene or sequence? Remember, a plot point is always a function of character. Does it reveal character or move the story forward?

Next, in about half a page, in a *dramatic recreation,* write the Plot Point at the end of Act I. If you're writing an action film, and your character is setting out on a mission to avenge a wrong, wanting to discover who's after him and why by traveling to another location, it could be as simple as this: "He sits on motorcycle facing east. Packed for travel. Revving up the carbon. Dropping into gear. The waiting is finally over. It's time. The warrior is returning to do battle." Remember, a plot point can be as simple as a change of locale or as complex as an escape from a prison. It's anything you want it to be.

Something else to take into account: if your character's dramatic need changes at Plot Point I, be clear on what the new dramatic need is. In *Thelma & Louise,* the two women start out for a weekend holiday, but after killing the would-be rapist, their dramatic need changes. Now, they are two women wanted for questioning who are running from the police.

With just three dramatic elements, the opening, Act I, and Plot Point I, you're up to a page and a half of a four-page treatment. Not bad for just two scenes or sequences.

We've completed Act I so now you're ready to move on into Act II. Act II is a unit of dramatic action that is approximately sixty pages long. It begins at the end of Plot Point I and goes to the end of Plot Point II. It is held together with the dramatic context known as *Confrontation.* If you know your character's dramatic need—what he or she wants to win, gain, get, or achieve during the course of the screenplay—you can create obstacles to that need and then your story becomes your character overcoming obstacle after obstacle (or not overcoming them) to achieve his or her dramatic need.

Remember, all drama is conflict. Without conflict you have no action. Without action, you have no character. Without character, you have no story, and without story you have no screenplay.

So think about Act II for a moment. Your character is going to be encountering conflict. Conflict means "in opposition to," so what does your character encounter? It's important to note that there are two types of conflict: External conflict, where a force is working against the dramatic need of the characters, like being pursued or pursuing someone, being captured by an enemy, trying to survive during a natural disaster, overcoming a physical injury, and so on. Then there's internal conflict, such as fear, whether it's fear of failure, fear of success, or fear of intimacy or commitment. An internal conflict can become an impediment to the character's action. It is an emotional force within the character that interferes with his or her dramatic need.

Cold Mountain (Anthony Minghella) is a good example. Inman, the Jude Law character, is wounded during the Civil War and taken to a hospital behind the lines. In flashback and voiceover narration, we see and hear about his relationship with Ada (Nicole Kidman). She wants him to "come back to me," so Inman deserts the Confederate Army and starts his physical and emotional journey back to Cold Mountain. The community of Cold Mountain is not only a physical town, but also an emotional place in the heart. Inman has to overcome all kinds of obstacles, including weather, enemy soldiers, capture, and being hunted by the Confederate Police to serve his dramatic need: returning to Cold Mountain and Ada. The obstacles he confronts during Act II are both internal and external, and bring drama and tension as he attempts to survive the journey home.

Ada's conflict is also both internal and external. She has been raised with the skills and qualities of a "lady"—she can play the piano, be a premiere hostess at church gatherings, read, and be a personable companion. But, she doesn't know the first thing about surviving on the farm after her father dies. She must deal with the internal frustration of not knowing what she has to do to survive, mending fences or planting crops or just fending for herself.

Most of the time we encounter both internal and external conflicts. So, as you prepare to describe the action that takes place in

Act II, it's a good idea to sketch out some of the obstacles your character may confront.

First, take a separate sheet of paper, and list four obstacles your character confronts during Act II. Do you know what they are? Can you define and articulate them? Are they internal obstacles or external? Think about it and when you're ready, just list them. Ask yourself whether these four obstacles generate a sense of dramatic conflict within the progression of your story. If your story is about a botanist in the Grand Canyon, possible obstacles might include the dangers of running the white-water rapids; succumbing to the tremendous heat; or a physical hardship, such as a severe ankle strain or a broken bone. It could be the raft overturning, losing supplies, or friction between the other characters. Select four conflicts, either internal or external, or some combination of both, but always making sure they are obstacles that confront your character and that move the story forward to the Plot Point at the end of Act II.

When that's complete, go back to your treatment. In a *narrative synopsis,* summarize the action of Act II in a page, using these four conflicts as the anchoring points of the story line. Just follow your character as he or she confronts each obstacle, and then summarize the obstacle in about a quarter of a page. It's important to generate a dramatic flow to the material at this point. Focus on your character confronting and overcoming these obstacles and simply describe the action—that is, what happens—in broad strokes. As mentioned, you'll find that if you spend too much time on the specific details of the action, you'll wind up with something like eight pages, not four. So, keep the material general; at this stage, too much detail is the enemy.

When you finish, you should have written about two and a half pages, and you're ready to write the Plot Point at the end of Act II. What is Plot Point II? Can you describe it? Dramatize it? In a *dramatic recreation,* write Plot Point II in about half a page. If you want, use a few lines of dialogue if necessary. How does the Plot Point at the end of Act II "spin" the action around into Act III? Keep the story flowing smoothly without regard to the specifics of the narrative. Again, your tendency will probably be to add detail, so watch for it and don't get caught up in it. You'll know when you're starting to overthink it because you'll find yourself spending time trying to decide exactly *how* it happens, what the character's specific motivation is, what kind of car he's driving, or which job or location to use. Just let it go. You don't need too much character motivation for this exercise.

This now takes you into Act III, the Resolution. What happens in Act III? Does your character live or die, succeed or fail, win the race or not, get married or not, get divorced or not, kill the bad guy or not? What is the solution of your story? Do you know what has to happen to resolve the story line? What is the solution? Not the specifics, only the generalities. In about half a page, write up the *narrative synopsis* of what happens in Act III. Describe the resolution simply.

Now we're at the ending. You know what the resolution is, so in half a page, write the *dramatic recreation* of the ending. It could be an action sequence, like a rescue, or an emotional scene, like a wedding. It doesn't have to be perfect, and feel free to change anything you want to regarding the ending at a later time. The end scene or sequence is only a dramatic choice at this point and can be changed, heightened, or exaggerated during the actual writing process. When you complete the exercise, you'll have your story line written up and dramatized in four pages:

To recap:

In half a page—write a *dramatic recreation* of the opening scene or sequence;

In half a page—write a *narrative synopsis* of the action summarizing what happens during the rest of Act I;

In half a page—write a *dramatic recreation* of the Plot Point at the end of Act I;

Then, on a separate sheet of paper, write four obstacles—either internal or external, or some combination of both—that your character confronts during Act II. Then:

In a page—write a *narrative synopsis,* summarizing the action of Act II by focusing on four conflicts that confront your character. It could be as simple as a couple of sentences describing each obstacle. Then, write:

In half a page—a *dramatic recreation* of the Plot Point at the end of Act II;

In half a page—a *narrative synopsis* of the action in Act III, the Resolution;

Then, in half a page—write a *dramatic recreation* of the ending scene or sequence of the screenplay.

That's a four-page treatment. It looks like a story, reads like a story, but it's only a treatment of what your story line is about. It's something you can register at the Writers Guild of America, West or East, and it is the "proof of authorship." You can register it online at www.wga.org and click on registration. As of this writing, it costs $20 for a nonmember and $10 for a member. Registering the treatment allows you to claim authorship of your story as of the date it's registered. It's not necessary to copyright your material. If you want, you can also send the four-page treatment to yourself, certified, with a return receipt requested, but do not open the envelope when you receive it.

Writing these four pages is what I call "the kick in the ass" exercise; they may be the toughest pages you'll write during the entire screenplay. You are taking an unformed and undefined idea, arbitrarily choosing an ending, and structuring it in terms of beginning, middle, and end. It's tough, because you really don't have too much material to work with. Your characters are not defined, and there's no room for specific detail. If you do put in too much detail, you may end up getting lost or confused. It may take two or three times to write up your story line and edit it down to four pages. Your first effort may be eight pages long, which you'll reduce to five, then finally cut to four.

You might experience all kinds of internal resistance when writing the treatment; you might get angry or bored, and the chances are that you'll probably make a lot of judgments and evaluations about what you're writing. Your critical voice may tell you "this is the most boring story in the world!" Or "I hate it! It's simple and stupid." Or "I've heard it all before." Or "Why did I think I could write this?"

You may be right. At this stage, the chances are that your story may actually be boring.

So what? It's only a four-page treatment. It's only a first words-on-paper exercise, nothing more. You can't lose sight of the fact that you're just writing four pages. It is what it is. These pages are not going to be carved in stone or written in gold. Just write the treatment. It's okay that it's not perfect.

Bear in mind that this four-page treatment may have little or nothing to do with the way your final screenplay turns out. It's only a start point, not the finished product. Your story is going to change and evolve and grow during the writing experience, so don't expect these pages to be flawless. Forget your expectations. You don't need to make too many critical evaluations. Save them for later! Writing is experiential—the more you do, the easier it gets.

One last note of caution: when you complete the treatment, the chances are that you'll be uncertain about whether it works, or whether it's good or bad. Your tendency may be to get feedback, some kind of affirmation about what you're writing.

Don't.

Don't let your wife, husband, lover, girlfriend, boyfriend, brother, or sister read it. They'll want to, I'm sure. They may even beg and plead to read your four pages. Don't let them. And here's why: I've had many students show these pages to the significant people in their lives looking for feedback and affirmation. One woman, in particular, was insecure and showed her treatment to her husband, who happened to be in the movie business. Out of his love for her, out of his concern to "really be honest" with her, and because he cared so much, he told her what he truly thought about it. His "truth" was that the material was dull, the characters weren't fleshed out, plus as an afterthought he mentioned that there might have been a similar film made several years earlier. Needless to say, she was devastated. Not only did she put the treatment in a drawer and bury it, but what's worse, she never went back to writing again. She had a wonderful sense of comic potential but she chose to listen to her husband because she thought he knew more than she did, and she never recovered.

I've seen this happen over and over again. It's why you have to understand that this is only a four-page treatment. It's not your screenplay. It's only a starting point exercise, not an end point.

Don't write these four pages thinking you can sell it, either. This is an exercise to clarify your story in your own mind. Just do the exercise and tell the story. Don't get caught up trying to sell the treatment or thinking about how much money you're going to make when the movie is made.

Focus on getting your story line down to four pages and don't worry about what happens after it's written.

The way the ancient Sanskrit text, the *Bhagavad Gita,* puts it: "Don't be attached to the fruits of your actions."

THE EXERCISE:

1. Structure your four story points on the *paradigm.*
2. In half a page, dramatize the scene in a *dramatic recreation.*
3. In half a page, write a *narrative synopsis* of what happens in Act 1.
4. In half a page, write a *dramatic recreation* of Plot Point I, like you did in the opening scene or sequence.
5. On a separate sheet of paper, list four obstacles your character confronts in Act II. These obstacles can be internal or external or any variation thereof.
6. In one page, in *narrative synopsis,* summarize the four obstacles the character confronts.

7. In half a page, in *dramatic recreation,* write what happens at Plot Point II.

8. In half a page, in *narrative synopsis,* write what happens in Act III.

9. In half a page, in *dramatic recreation,* write the ending scene or sequence of the story.

10. Draw the paradigm. This is the way it should look.

THE PARADIGM STRUCTURED

THE STORY: ______________________

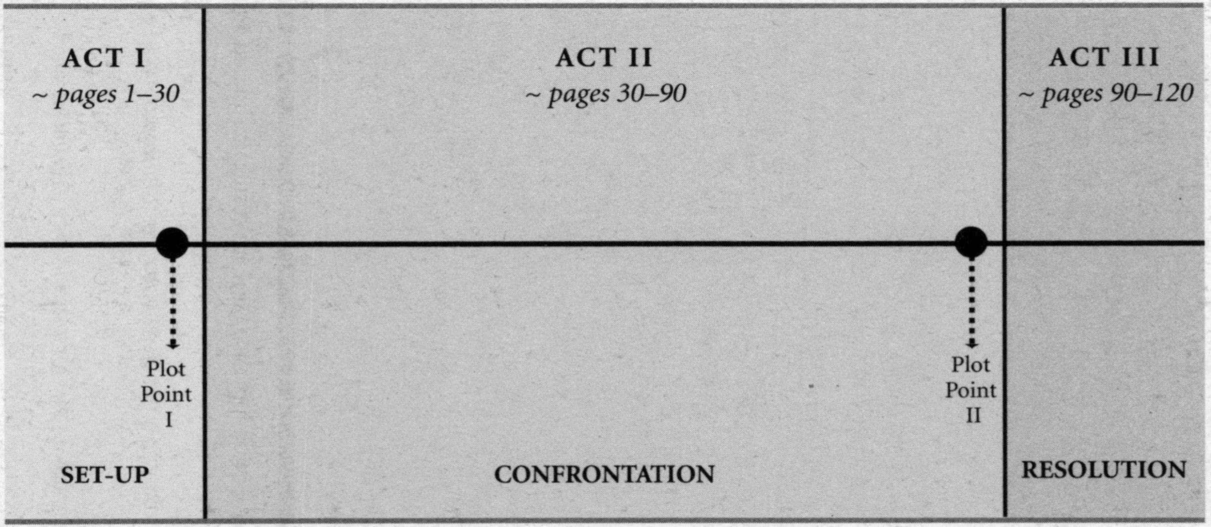

ACT I ~ *pages 1–30*	ACT II ~ *pages 30–90*	ACT III ~ *pages 90–120*
Plot Point I		
	Plot Point II	
SET-UP	CONFRONTATION	RESOLUTION

5

What Makes Good Character?

Wolf: "Just because you *are* a character doesn't mean you *have* character."
—Quentin Tarantino and Roger Avary
Pulp Fiction

Many years ago, while traveling with some friends in Italy, I went to visit the little town of Assisi, the home of St. Francis of Assisi. We took a bus up the long and winding road to the little church and monastery high on the hill where St. Francis lived, worked and studied. I didn't know too much about him; I knew he started the Holy Order of the Franciscans and I knew he wrote sublime poetry, essays, and philosophy. The paintings and images I had seen had always showed him being surrounded by birds and other animals. It was said that he could talk to the animals, and his poetry and writings are filled with the harmony and union of nature and that all life is connected by divine consciousness. All living things are related, he said, the birds, the trees, the rocks, the rivers, the streams and oceans, we are all manifestations of the one consciousness, and as living beings we express the life force that flows through us. Call it God, or Nature, or whatever you want, it doesn't matter. It is what it is.

As we toured the tiny, sparse rooms of the church and monastery and climbed the steep paths that wandered along the wooded hills, walking through shadows and sunlight, I noticed the birds were everywhere, chirping and singing in a cacophony of sound. I stood observing this symphony of sound and movement, thought about walking on the same path as St. Francis, and I became aware that my breathing had become calm and even, my mind still, and I felt like I was in a meditative state. I looked around the beautiful landscape and wondered whether I was experiencing this feeling because of the harmony of the landscape, or whether the land and trees and birds had absorbed St. Francis' state and I was just immersed in the energy or vibration of the place itself. I wondered whether this divine state, mind calm but senses totally alert, was the same state that St. Francis referred to in his poetry and writings.

I speculated as to whether we, as human beings, have this same potential to transcend our ordinary reality and enter this state of transcendence. It was like I had merged into the environment. I don't know how long I stood on that footpath, absorbed in this energy. It could have been a few minutes or an hour. When I looked around, I saw a large number of birds resting on tree limbs nearby, and I knew deep down inside, they were watching me, like they were tuning into my thought waves. It was an extraordinary experience.

I roused myself and started down the path leading to the monastery. As I made my way down the hill, I found myself wondering what kind of a person St. Francis was. Was he such a radiant and powerful being that he could transcend his identity as a man and merge into this living energy, or vibration, to became one with the spirit of the birds and animals of Assisi? What kind of a person was he that he could rise above his human limitations and become one with this divine energy? In other words, what qualities did St. Francis possess that made him so unique as a person?

And that brought up the question of character. It was a question I've asked myself many times, both as a teacher and a student, when writing and teaching about the qualities of character.

What makes good character?

Is it the character's purpose or motivation? Is it the dialogue that he or she speaks? Is it what the character wants to achieve during the course of the screenplay? Is it his insights or cleverness or credibility or believability? His integrity? Is it the action he goes through to achieve his dramatic purpose? What qualities must a character possess to keep us interested in him or her as he or she moves through the landscape of the screenplay?

Philosophers talk about a man's life as being measured by the sum total of his actions; our lives are "measured" by what we accomplish, or do not accomplish, in our lifetime. "Life consists in action," Aristotle said, "and its end is a mode of action, not a quality."

What is character?

Action is character—a person is defined by what he does, not what he says.

In a screenplay, either the character drives the action, or the action drives the character. For example, in *The Bourne Supremacy,* Jason Bourne sets out on a personal journey to avenge the death of his girlfriend Marie, and to find out who is after him and why. It could be a story of revenge, but instead becomes a story of discovery and redemption. In this case, the character drives the action. He learns that his fingerprints were found in Berlin where two CIA agents were killed, while he was several thousand miles away, in Goa, India. Who is after him? And why? Midway through the film, he discovers that he was responsible for killing a Russian politician and his wife several years earlier. Now he must accept the responsibility for his actions and find the daughter of the two people he killed. It is his actions that determine his character.

In *Batman Begins* (Chris Nolan and David Goyer), the action drives the character. Bruce Wayne sets out to avenge the murder of his father and mother. But first, he must overcome his fear of bats. If anything, *Batman Begins* is a story of the caped crusader overcoming his own fears to bring justice and order to Gotham City. These two elements become the narrative thrusts that drive the story forward to its dynamic resolution.

In the classic film *The Hustler,* written by Sidney Carroll and Robert Rossen, from the book by Walter Tevis, Fast Eddie Felson (Paul Newman) is a smooth-talking, fast-shooting pool player from Oakland. Fast Eddie comes to town to take on the "king of straight pool," Minnesota Fats (Jackie Gleason). Though Fast Eddie may be a better pool player, his attitude and his action make him, in Bert

Gordon's (George C. Scott) terms, "a loser." During the story, Fast Eddie goes from being a loser to being a winner. That is his action, his character arc.

Good characters are the heart and soul and nervous system of your screenplay. The story is told through your characters and this engages the audience to experience the universal emotions that transcend our ordinary reality. The purpose of creating good characters is to capture our unique sense of humanness, to touch, move, and inspire the audience.

"When you create characters," the great English playwright and screenwriter, Harold Pinter says, "they observe you, their writer, warily. It may sound absurd but I've suffered two kinds of pain from my characters. I have witnessed their pain when I'm in the act of distorting or falsifying them, and I've suffered pain when I've been unable to get to the quick of them, when they willfully elude me, when they withdraw into the shadows.

"There's no question a conflict takes place between the writer and his characters. On the whole I would say the characters are the winners, and that is as it should be. When a writer sets out a blueprint for his characters and keeps them rigidly to it, where they do not at any time upset his applecart, when he has mastered them he has also killed or rather terminated their births."

F. Scott Fitzgerald wrote in one of his journals that "when you begin with an individual, you create a type." His first novel, *This Side of Paradise*, written when he was twenty-two or twenty-three, portrayed a dazzling heroine modeled after his wife Zelda. The book quickly became a best-seller, and it wasn't long before the "type" created by Fitzgerald was celebrated in the movies, in the likes of Clara Bow, who would soon become known as the "It" girl. Women all over the country imitated her, dressed like her, styled their hair like hers, and acted and talked like her. She typified "the flapper," truly a phenomenon of the twenties.

The flapper is really a type. In the same way, James Dean was a type because he inspired others to look and act like him. The flower child of the sixties was a type, as were The Beatles and Bob Dylan.

These performers influenced an entire generation. Long hair became the fashion, antiwar demonstrations became commonplace, and hippies were everywhere. Madonna is a type because she inspires a new way of thinking and dressing. Michael Jordan is a type—not only was he a great and celebrated basketball player, but an athlete who shaved his head and influenced others to do the same for more than a decade.

Creating good characters is essential to the success of your screenplay. That means you want to create "a type." As mentioned earlier, all drama is conflict; without conflict, you have no action; without action, you have no character; without character, you have no story; and without story, you have no screenplay.

When you set out to create your characters, you must know them inside and out; you need to know their hopes and dreams and fears, their likes and dislikes, their background and mannerisms. In other words, they have to have a personal history.

Creating a character is part of the mystery of the creative process. It is an ongoing, never-ending practice. In order to really solve the problem of *character*, it's essential to build the foundations and fabric of his or her life, then add ingredients that will heighten and expand his or her individual portrait.

What makes good characters? Is it their purpose? Their motivation? The way they overcome, or fail to overcome, the conflict they must deal with? Is it their dialogue? Ask yourself what qualities your characters exemplify during the course of the screenplay. In order to create a character we must first establish the *context* of character, the qualities of behavior, that makes him or her unique, someone we can root for and identify with. Once we establish this, we can add his or her characterization, coloring and shading the various traits and mannerisms of his or her character.

Action is character. It's important to note that your character must be an active force in your screenplay, not a passive one. So many times, I read screenplays where the character only reacts to incidents, episodes, or events. He or she doesn't cause anything to happen; things merely happen *to* the character. If your main character is too passive, then he or she often disappears off the page and a minor character will leap forward to draw attention away from the main character.

I've read and evaluated thousands upon thousands of screenplays during the course of my career. And in all that reading and analyzing, I have come to understand there are four things that go into the making of a good character: one, the character has a strong and defined *dramatic need;* two, he or she has an individual *point of view;* three, the character personifies an *attitude,* and four, the character often goes through some kind of *change,* or *transformation.*

These four elements, these four essential qualities, are the anchors for what makes good characters in a screenplay. Every major character has a strong dramatic need. *Dramatic need* is defined as *what your main character wants to win, gain, get, or achieve during the course of your screenplay.* The *dramatic need* is his purpose, his mission, his motivation, the force that drives him through the narrative action of the story line.

In most cases, you can express the dramatic need in a sentence or two. It's usually simple and can be stated in a line of dialogue or through the character's actions. Regardless of how you express it, you, as writer, *must know* your character's dramatic need. If you don't know it, who does?

In *Cinderella Man* (Cliff Hollingsworth and Akiva Goldsman), James Braddock's dramatic need is to provide for his family. How he does this is what the movie is about. As he is rocked and socked by the Depression, his dramatic need stabilizes him and becomes the driving force keeping him going so he does not give up. Ironically, the injury he suffers to his left wrist before the Depression becomes the tool he uses to strengthen his left hand. Working as a dock worker, he lifts cargo with his left hand and when he is given a second chance to fight, his dramatic need provides him with the courage and will to win the Heavyweight Championship of the World against Max Baer.

In *Thelma & Louise,* the characters' dramatic need is to escape safely to Mexico; that's what drives these two characters through the story line. In *Cold Mountain,* Inman's dramatic need is to return home to his love Ada, and Ada's dramatic need is to survive and adapt to the conditions around her. In *The Lord of the Rings,* Frodo's dramatic need is to carry the ring to Mount Doom and destroy it in the fires that created it.

There are times when the dramatic need of your character changes during the course of the screenplay. If your character's dramatic need does change, it usually occurs at Plot Point I, the true beginning of your story. In *American Beauty* (Alan Ball), Lester's (Kevin Spacey) dramatic need is to regain his life. When the story begins he feels like a dead man and it takes meeting Angela (Mena Suvari), the young friend of his daughter, to bring him back to life. The rest of the film deals with Lester learning to live again, in joy, freedom, and full self-expression.

The dramatic need is the engine that powers your character through the story line. What is your character's dramatic need? Can you define it in a few words? State it simply and clearly? Knowing your character's dramatic need is essential. In a conversation with Waldo Salt, the Academy Award-winning screenwriter of *Midnight Cowboy* and *Coming Home,* he told me when he creates a character, he starts with the character's dramatic need; it becomes the force that drives the story's structure.

The key to a successful screenplay, Salt emphasized, was preparing the material. If you know your character's dramatic need, he said, dialogue becomes "perishable," because the actor can always improvise lines to make it work. But, he added forcefully, the character's dramatic need is sacrosanct. That cannot be changed because it holds the entire story in place. Putting words down on paper, he said, was the easiest part of the screenwriting process; it was the visual conception of the story that took so long. And he quoted Picasso: "Art is the elimination of the unnecessary."

The second thing that makes a good character is *point of view.* Point of view is defined as "the way a person sees, or views, the world." Every person has an individual point of view. Point of view is a belief system, and as we know, what we believe to be true, is true for us. There's an ancient Hindu scripture titled the *Yoga Vasistha,* which states that "the World is as you see it." That means that what's inside our heads—our thoughts, feelings, emotions, memories—are reflected outside, in our everyday experience. It is our minds, how we *see* the world, that determines our experience. "You are the baker of the bread you eat," is the way one Great Being puts it.

Point of view shades and colors the way *we see* the world. Have you ever heard or reacted to phrases like: "Life is unfair," "You can't fight City Hall," "All life is a game of chance," "You can't teach an old dog new tricks," "You make your own luck," or "Success is based on who you know"? These are all points of view. Since a point of view is a belief system, we act and react as if they are true. That's why every person has a definite and distinct point of view, singular and unique. For it is our experience that determines our point of view.

Is your character an environmentalist? A humanist? A racist? Someone who believes in fate, destiny, and astrology? Or does your character believe in voodoo, witchcraft, or that the future can be revealed through a medium or psychic? Does your character believe that the limitations we confront are self-imposed, like Neo in *The Matrix*? Does your character put his faith in doctors, lawyers, the *Wall Street Journal*, and the *New York Times*? Is your character a believer in popular culture, an advocate of *Time, People, Newsweek*, CNN, and the network evening news?

Point of view is an individual and independent belief system. "I believe in God" is a point of view. So is "I don't believe in God." Or, "I don't know whether there is a God or not." These are three separate and distinct points of view. Each is true within the individual's fabric of experience. What's important to note here is that there is no right or wrong here, no good or bad, no judgment, justification, or evaluation. Point of view is as singular and distinctive as a rose on a rose bush. No two leaves, no two flowers, no two people are ever the same.

Your character's point of view may be that the indiscriminate slaughtering of dolphins and whales is morally wrong because they are two of the most intelligent species on the planet, maybe smarter than man. Your character supports that point of view by participating in demonstrations and wearing T-shirts with *Save the whales and dolphins* on them. That's an aspect of characterization.

Everyone has an individual point of view. A friend of mine is a vegetarian; that expresses her point of view. Another friend marches against the war in the Middle East, and she spends time and money supporting the cause. That expresses a point of view. Imagine a confrontation between pro-choice and pro-life supporters. Two opposing points of view generate conflict.

In *The Shawshank Redemption,* there's a short scene between Andy and Red that reveals the differences in their points of view. After almost twenty years in Shawshank Prison, Red is cynical because, in his eyes, *hope* is simply a four-letter word. His spirit has been so crushed by the prison system that he angrily declares to Andy, "Hope is a dangerous thing. Drives a man insane. It's got no place here. Better get used to the idea." But Red's emotional journey leads him to the understanding that "hope is a good thing." The film ends on a note of hope, with Red breaking his parole and riding the bus to meet Andy in Mexico: "I hope I can make it across the border. I hope to see my friend and shake his hand. I hope the Pacific is as blue as it has been in my dreams... I *hope.*"

Andy has a different point of view; he believes that "there are things in this world not carved out of gray stone. That there's a small place inside of us they can never lock away. Hope." That's what keeps Andy going in prison, that's what makes him sacrifice one week of his life in solitary, "the hole," just so he can listen once again to an aria from a Mozart opera. Hope is a forceful dynamic in Andy Dufresne's character.

The third thing that makes good character is *attitude. Attitude* is defined as a "manner or opinion," and reflects a person's personal opinion determined by an intellectual decision. An attitude, differentiated from a point of view, is determined by a personal judgment—this is right, this is wrong, this is good, this is bad, this is positive or negative, angry or happy, cynical or naive, superior or inferior, liberal or conservative, optimistic or pessimistic.

Attitude encompasses a person's behavior. Do you know someone who is "always right," about everything? That's an attitude. Being socially or morally superior is also an attitude; so is being "macho." A political opinion expresses an attitude, as does complaining about what is wrong with the world. In professional sports, trash-talking has become a way of life. That's an attitude, as are most of the lyrics in rap music.

By the same token, have you wanted to buy something and found yourself dealing with a salesperson who does not want to be there, has negative energy, and thinks he or she is superior to you? That's attitude. Have you ever attended a function and been overdressed or underdressed, literally not wearing the "right" clothes? And some people may invariably give the impression that they are morally superior to you. That sense of righteous behavior mirrors a person's attitude. They are convinced they're right and you're wrong. Judgments, opinions, and evaluations all stem from attitude. It's an *intellectual* decision they make. "I would never belong to a club that would have someone like me as a member," is the way Alvy Singer puts it in Woody Allen's *Annie Hall.*

Understanding your character's attitude allows you to show who she or he is by their actions and dialogue. Is he or she enthusiastic or unhappy about his or her life and job? People express different parts of themselves through their attitude—someone, for example, who feels the world owes them a living, or attributes their lack of success to "who you know."

Sometimes, you can build a whole scene around a person's attitude. *Collateral* is a case in point. At Plot Point II, the first time Max really stands up to Vincent, most of the scene is driven by the attitudes of the two characters. Angry and upset, Max asks Vincent why "you didn't kill me and find another cab?" Vincent replies that the two of them are connected. "You know, fates intertwined. Cosmic coincidence. All that crap." Max says, "You're full of shit." Vincent, somewhat defensive, wants to justify that "all I'm doing is taking out the garbage. Killing bad people."

The whole exchange is one of attitude. Both characters are expressing their opinions by defending their actions. Max asks Vincent why he kills people and Vincent tells him that there is "no why. . . . There is no good reason. No bad reason. To live or to die." Vincent says he's totally "indifferent" to the lives he takes. "C'mon, man. Get with it. Millions of galaxies of hundreds of millions of stars and a speck on one. In a blink... that's us. Lost in space. The universe don't care about you. The cop, you, me? Who notices?" Max looks at him, aghast, suddenly understanding that there will be no end to this nightmare until Max stands up for himself and takes the action that may save his life.

The exchange also *reveals character*, as Vincent probes and bursts Max's dream balloon. Up until now, Vincent says, Max has lived in a dream, in a "someday" state: someday he's going to fulfill his dream of starting his own limousine company, someday he's going to meet the woman of his dreams, someday he'll have it all and be fulfilled as a person. It's a pretty big "someday." Vincent points out that there is only now, only today, this present moment, this point in time. "Someday" has become only an excuse for not going after what he truly wants.

In *Annie Hall*, Alvy Singer (Woody Allen) presents his attitude in the opening lines when he expresses "how I feel about life. A lot of suffering, pain, anxiety and problems—and it's all over much too quickly. That's the key joke of my adult life in terms of my relationships with women." That's what the movie is about: his relationships with women. The film illustrates his attitude.

Sometimes it's difficult to separate *point of view* from *attitude*. Many of my students struggle to define these two qualities, but I tell them it really doesn't matter. When you're creating the basic core of your character, you're taking one large ball of wax, the character, and pulling it apart into four separate pieces. The parts and the whole, right? Who cares whether one part is *point of view* and another is *attitude*? It doesn't make any difference; the parts and the whole are really the same thing. So if you're unsure about whether a particular character trait is a *point of view* or an *attitude*, don't worry about it. Just separate the concepts in your own mind.

The fourth quality that makes up good character is *change* or *transformation*. Does your character change during the course of your screenplay? If so, what is the change? Can you define it? Articulate it? Can you trace the emotional arc of the character from the beginning to the end? In *The Truth About Cats & Dogs* (Audrey Wells), both characters undergo a change that brings about a new awareness of who they are. Abby's final acceptance that she is really loved *for who she is* completes the character arc of the change.

From the beginning of *Collateral,* Max has been portrayed as being weak, a wimp, a man afraid to stand up to the cab dispatcher, a man who lives his "someday" dream pictured in the postcard. In short, this scene, set amid the fury and confusion of the speeding cab, allows us to watch Max's internal transformation from weakness to strength and ultimately leads to the film's conclusion. Max has completed his character arc.

Having a character change during the course of the screenplay is not a requirement if it doesn't fit your character. But transformation, change, seems to be universal—especially at this time in our culture. I think we're all a little like the Melvin character (Jack Nicholson) in *As Good As It Gets* (Mark Andrus and James L. Brooks). Melvin may be complex and fastidious as a person, but his dramatic need is expressed at the very end when he says, "When I'm with you I want to be a better person." I think we all want that. Change, transformation, is a constant in our lives and if you can impel some kind of emotional change within your character, it creates an arc of behavior and adds another dimension to who he or she is. If you're unclear about the character's change, take the time to write an essay in a page or so, charting his or her emotional arc.

In *The Hustler,* Fast Eddie's dramatic need is to beat Minnesota Fats and win ten thousand dollars in one night. And the entire screenplay is woven around this dramatic action. When Fast Eddie plays Minnesota Fats the first time around, he loses. Pride, overconfidence, and a "losing" attitude—he drinks too much during the game—bring about his defeat. He is forced to accept the fact that he is, indeed, a loser. When he realizes this, he signs with Bert Gordon (George C. Scott) because "twenty-five percent of something is better than a hundred percent of nothing." His realization and acceptance of who he is enables him to become a winner. Fast Eddie challenges Minnesota Fats and this time defeats him easily. His character arc goes from being a loser to being a winner. That is his change, his transformation.

Seabiscuit (Gary Ross) is another good example of change. Based on a true story, we see who the characters are and what they want to become. Charles Howard (Jeff Bridges) comes to San Francisco, with a few dollars in his pocket, to create his fortune. He is a man who believes in the future. But then his young son is killed in an auto accident, his wife leaves him, and Howard sinks into deep depression. He meets a young woman, marries her, and acquires an interest in horses and horse racing. But deep down, he continues to mourn for the loss of his son.

Red Pollard (Tobey Maguire) is raised in an affluent middle-class home, filled with books and intellectual discussions. But Red has a gift for riding horses. When the Depression strikes, his family is forced out of their house and into the basic struggle for survival. At about the age of fifteen, Red enters some horse races and is successful—so successful, in fact, that his father gives him away to the owner of a racing stable because he cannot provide for his son. Red feels worthless, unwanted, and his sense of self-destructive behavior soon becomes evident as he ekes out a living on the racing circuit.

Tom Smith (Chris Cooper) also has an uncanny gift of communicating with animals. The one thing that drives his life is his pursuit of freedom. In a marvelous little scene at the beginning of the film, Tom Smith is riding his horse on the open plains when he reaches a spot which is blocked by barbed wire. As he examines the fence, we hear Charles Howard talking about the future in voiceover.

Setting up these three characters is an illustration of showing what they have lost in their lives: Howard has lost his son; Pollard, his family; and Tom Smith his freedom. In addition, if you contemplate the life of the horse, Seabiscuit, he's taken away from his mother at six months, trained, punished, and ridiculed by various horse trainers. Soon, he becomes an outlaw, a defiant animal who has "forgotten what's it's like to be a horse," as Smith observes.

These four characters are joined together in a journey, and through their efforts and teamwork, they form a rallying cry for an entire country. Howard looks upon his team as family; Red looks up to him as a father figure. Tom Smith sleeps outside under the stars. And it's through the heroic antics of Seabiscuit that they are all joined together. As Red Pollard observes in the last scene of the movie: "You know, everybody thinks we found this broken-down horse and fixed him, but we didn't. . . . He fixed us. Every one of us. And, I guess in a way, we kind of fixed each other, too."

All four characters—Howard, Pollard, Smith, and Seabiscuit—have gone through a change, a transformation, and in the process, they have engaged our sensibilities in a way that touches, moves, and inspires us.

Ordinary People, written by Alvin Sargent from the novel by Judith Guest, shows Conrad Jarrett (Timothy Hutton) undergoing a major change. In the beginning of the film, he is closed off and emotionally damaged by his brother's death and his parents' withdrawal. By the end, he's able to open up and express himself, he's able to understand the emotional dynamics of his brother's death and let go of his painful burden of guilt, he is able to reach out and ask for help from both his father and his psychiatrist, and he finds a girl he can confide in and be comfortable with.

His father, played by Donald Sutherland, also undergoes change. He begins as conventional and complacent, but he learns to listen to his son, becomes tolerant and understanding, and soon questions himself, his attitudes, and his marriage. He even seeks help from his son's psychiatrist, played by Judd Hirsch. In short, he learns to question his own values, needs, and wants.

The only major character who does not change is Conrad's mother, played by Mary Tyler Moore. Described in the opening stage directions as being "graceful and controlled," she is like her refrigerator: "well stocked, and perfectly organized, with nothing out of place." She is the kind of person who believes that appearance is everything. Her house is immaculate, the closets are clean, and I'll bet anything that if you open any drawer in the entire house everything is laid out meticulously. That's the kind of person she is. She always seems to be firmly in control, unbending in attitudes and beliefs, convinced she is right. By the end of the film, father and son have changed but she has not, and the family splinters. In the last scene, father and son are sitting on the porch after the mother has left. Her leaving brings father and son closer together.

See if you can have your character go through some kind of change, either emotional or physical, as it will broaden and deepen the character in terms of a universal recognition that transcends language, color, culture, or geographic location.

If you know and can define these four elements of character—dramatic need, point of view, change, and attitude—you'll have the tools to create good characters. Sometimes they will overlap, like an attitude emerging as a point of view, or the dramatic need will bring about change, and change will affect your character's attitude. If that happens, don't worry about it. Sometimes it's necessary to take something apart in order to put it back together.

THE EXERCISE

Determine your main character. What is his or her *dramatic need*? What does your character want to win, gain, get, or achieve during the course of your screenplay? What is the emotional or physical force that drives your character through the screenplay from beginning to end? Define it, articulate it. Write it down in a sentence or two. Define it clearly and succinctly.

Do the same with your character's *point of view*. How does your character *see* the world? Through rose-colored glasses, like a dreamer or idealist, like the opening scene of Wes Anderson's brilliant *Rushmore*? Or, through jaded and cynical eyes, like Lester Burnham in *American Beauty*? Remember, it's a belief system. Know your character's point of view. Write it down. Define it.

Do the same with your character's *attitude*. What is your character's manner or opinion? Write it down. Define it.

What about *change*? Does your character go through any change during the screenplay? What is it? Write it down. Define it.

You should be able to define these four qualities in a few

sentences. The thinking time is more relevant here than the writing time. As I've said before, the hardest thing about writing is knowing what to write. Think about the qualities that go into making a good character and see how they apply to your characters.

6

The Tools of Character

> Narrator: "Royal Tenenbaum bought the house on Archer Avenue in the winter of his thirty-fifth year. Over the next decade, he and his wife had three children, and then they separated."
>
> —Wes Anderson and Owen Wilson
> *The Royal Tenenbaums*

As mentioned in Chapter 1, the action of a novel takes place within the mindscape of dramatic action, a play's action unfolds through dialogue, and a screenplay is a story told with pictures, in dialogue and description and placed within the context of dramatic structure. Three different forms, three different ways of approaching a story line.

Film is behavior. We know a lot about characters by how they act, or react, in certain situations. Pictures, or images, can reveal different aspects of the character. In *Thelma & Louise,* for example, the two women approach packing their suitcases differently: Thelma stands in front of her closet, unsure, so she takes everything. Louise, on the other hand, takes a pair of shoes, wrapped in plastic, two sweaters, two bras, three pairs of underwear, two pairs of socks, then, as an afterthought, throws in another pair of socks just to be on the safe side. Then she washes and dries the single glass that is on the sink, puts it away, and walks out the door. What do their actions reveal about their characters? Thelma could be called ditzy or an airhead, whereas Louise seems focused and organized. Film is behavior.

Seabiscuit is another example of this. Tom Smith is looking for a rider for Seabiscuit and he watches as four grooms try to wrestle the defiant horse to a standstill while a jockey attempts to mount him. The horse fights back in a terrific struggle. Unable to mount the animal, the jockey stomps off, muttering angrily to himself. Smith shakes his head and starts walking away when he sees Red Pollard engaged in a fistfight with four stable hands. The jockey boldly challenges the other men and continues to fight back. Smith looks at Red fighting, then at Seabiscuit fighting; back and forth he watches and we can see his mind working. He sees what we see: Seabiscuit and Red are kindred spirits. No dialogue, no explanation. The next thing we know, Red is the horse's jockey.

Character reveals the deep-seated nature of *who a person is,* in terms of his values, actions, and beliefs. Characters illuminate themselves by their actions, reactions, and by the creative choices they make. *Characterization,* on the other hand, is expressed in the details of their lives, the way they live, the car they drive, the pictures they hang on the wall, their likes and dislikes, what they eat, and other forms of character expression. Characterization expresses an individual's taste and how he presents himself to the world.

Creating character is a process that will be with you from the beginning to the end, from fade in to fade out. It is an ongoing educational progression, an experience that continues expanding as you go deeper and deeper into your characters' lives.

There are many ways to approach writing character. Some writers mull over their characters for a long period of time and then, when they feel they "know" them, jump in and start writing. Others create an elaborate list of characterizations. Some writers list the major elements of their character's life on 3 × 5 cards. Some write extensive outlines or draw diagrams of behavior. Some use pictures from magazines and newspapers to help them *see* what their characters look like. "That's my character," they say. They may tack the pictures above their work area so they can "be with" their characters during their work time. Some use well-known actors and actresses as models for characters.

Anything that makes it easier for you to create your character is a good tool. Choose your own way. You can use some, all, or none of the tools mentioned here. If it works, use it; if it doesn't, don't. Find your own way, your own style in creating character. The important thing is that it's got to work for you.

One of the most insightful character tools is writing a *character biography.* The character biography is a free-association, automatic-writing exercise that reveals your character's history from birth up until the time your story begins. It captures and defines the forces, both physical and emotional, internal and external, working on your character during those formative years that fashion his or her behavior. It is a process that reveals character.

Start at the beginning. Is your character male or female? How old is he or she when the story begins? Where does he live? What city or country? Where was he born? Was he an only child, or did he have any brothers and sisters? What kind of relationship did he have with his brothers and sisters? Was it good, bad, confiding, adventurous? What kind of childhood would you say your character had? Would you consider it happy? Or sad? Was it physically or medically challenging, with illness or physical problems? What about his relationship to his parents? Was it good or bad? Was he a mischievous child getting into a lot of trouble or was he quiet and withdrawn, preferring his own inner life instead of a social one? Was he stubborn and willful, and did he have a problem with authority? Do you think he was socially active, made friends easily, and got along well with relatives and other children? What kind of a child would you say he was? Good or bad? Was he outgoing and extroverted or a shy and studious introvert? Let your imagination guide you.

When you begin formulating your character from birth, you see your character grow and expand in body, shape, and form. This is a process, remember, that *forms* character.

What do her parents do for a living? Are they poor, middle class, or upper-middle class? Were her parents divorced? Was your character raised by a single parent, either mother or father? Did that impact her? Were her parents abusive, either physically or verbally? What about the grandparents? Aunts and uncles? Was your character streetwise or sheltered? Did her parents work full-time? If so, how did that impact your character? Was it difficult for her parent(s) to make financial ends meet? What kind of sacrifices did they have to make?

Most of the time, I'll break my character biography down into the first ten years of my character's life, the second ten years, the third ten years, and beyond, if need be. You'll want to explore these first ten years thoroughly because that's when behavioral patterns are formed. Imagine their pre-school years, then follow them into their lives in grade school. See if you can sketch in relationships with friends, family, and teachers.

Consider the second ten years of your character's life, ages ten to twenty. That means middle school and high school. What kind of influences did your character have while growing up? Who were his or her friends? What kind of interests did he or she have? Did your character take an interest in extra-curricular events, like debating or history clubs? Did he or she participate in after-school athletics, social or political activities? What about sexual experiences? Who was his or her first love? What about relationships with other students? Did your character work part-time during high school? What about sibling relationships? Any envy or hostility present, and did this manifest in your character's behavior in some way? What kind of relationship did your character have with his or her parents during these years?

What was his or her high school like? What about his or her relationships with teachers? Did your character have a mentor, and if so, who was it? And what was the benefit of their guidance? Did any major traumatic events happen that may have emotionally impacted your character? Did he or she feel like an outsider? Take a look at *Mean Girls* (Tina Fey). The whole film is built around this situation. You want as much information as you can get about your character as he or she is growing up.

Go into the third ten years of your character's life. Did he or she go to college? If so, which one? What did he or she major in? What were his or her dreams, hopes, and aspirations? Was he or she a good student or did he or she party all the time? What was his or her grade point average? Did his or her focus or interest change during the years at the university? What about love affairs? Many or just a few? Did he or she become active in the political scene on campus? Did he or she work full- or part-time during his or her time in college?

What happened after he or she graduated? Did he or she find a job easily? Did he or she marry and settle down? Did he or she feel lost and confused about his/her direction in life? This is a good period of their life to focus on as individual dreams often collide with reality; sometimes you can build an entire story around this premise. Keep exploring your character's life up until the time the story begins.

How powerful can the character biography be? It is a tremendous tool, revealing deep and profound insights about the main character, and is a marvelous source for generating conflict.

While the character biography is a tool only for you, there are times when you might want to incorporate some, part, or all of the biographical material in your screenplay. In *The Royal Tenenbaums,* the first few pages of the screenplay set up the characters as the narrator tells us the family history in what I term a novelistic approach to screenwriting: "Royal Tenenbaum bought the house on Archer Avenue in the winter of his thirty-fifth year," the narrator begins. "Over the next decade, he and his wife had three children, and then they separated. . . ." As the narrator gives us this information, we see the three children growing up. It sets the tone for the entire film, establishing the familiar Anderson themes of family, failure, and forgiveness.

In *Annie Hall,* Woody Allen shows us Alvy Singer's character biography in the first ten pages of screenplay. "I was a reasonably happy kid, I guess. I was brought up in Brooklyn during World War II." And then we *see* his early years growing up and how it impacted him in his relationship with women. "My analyst says I exaggerate my childhood memories, but I swear I was brought up underneath the roller coaster in the Coney Island section of Brooklyn. Maybe that accounts for my personality, which is a little nervous, I think."

A character is the sum total of his or her experience. Actors and actresses also use the character biography to build and form character. One of my students, an actress, auditioned for a Martin Scorsese film. To prepare for her audition, she approached her part by doing a character biography, then structured the audition scene that she was given into an emotional beginning, middle, and end. When she auditioned, Scorsese liked her and commented on how good her preparation was. He called her back three times after that, twice to audition with Robert De Niro. They both liked her, even if she didn't get the part. They decided to go with a "different look." That's show biz. But it was her preparation that got her that far.

You need to do the same kind of preparation so you can really know your character. How long should it be? I tell my students that a character biography, written in free-association, should be about five to seven pages, or longer. That's just a rule of thumb. I also tell them that when I write a character biography, I'll sometimes write about twenty-five pages. I'll begin with my character's grandparents, on both sides, then progress to my character's parents, on both sides, and then do my character's life from birth up until the story begins. I might even do past-life biographies, ending with the character's astrological chart. I'll write as many pages as I can in free-association. It doesn't matter how many pages I write—whether it's fifteen or twenty pages, I'll do whatever I need to do to know my character.

If you're having trouble getting inside your character, try writing the character biography in the first person. For example: "My name is David Hollister. I was born in Boston on the fifth of July. My father was a maritime attorney and always seemed to be angry. I wasn't sure why, but I always thought I had something to do with it. He wanted me to be a professional person, but I was more interested in music."

What's so great about the character biography is that when you've finished, you have a feeling that you really know your character.

When you've finished the biography, you can take the pages you've written and put them in a drawer somewhere. You've gotten all those random, dissociated thoughts, feelings, and emotions out of your head and onto the paper. When you face the blank sheet of paper, your character work will help you find the voice of your character.

Since the character biography delves into your character's life from birth up until the time the story begins, what about your character's life during the time the screenplay takes place, from fade in to fade out? This is where we define the *professional, personal,* and *private* aspects of your character.

First, your character's professional life: What does your main character do for a living? What is his or her relationship with his boss or supervisor? Good? Bad? Feeling neglected? Taken advantage of? Underpaid? How long has your character worked at his or her present job? What is your character's relationship with his or her associates? Does he or she socialize with them? Where and when did he or she begin his or her career? In the mailroom? At an executive training program? Was he or she hired right from college?

Is there something going on between the supervisor and your character that causes an emotional tension? Perhaps the loss of a client? In *American Beauty,* Lester has been with his employer for some fourteen years, and when the story begins, the company has hired an efficiency expert to evaluate the business. And Lester doesn't like it. His wife, Carolyn, is a realtor and though we only see that in a couple of scenes, how rich it makes her character.

It's important to know these facts about your character. In *The Bourne Supremacy,* Jason Bourne is a victim of amnesia, and must overcome all kinds of obstacles to find out who he is and what his past history is. Write a two- or three-page free-association essay tracing your character's professional life. Describe and explore your character's life, focusing on his or her relationships in the workplace, whatever they might be.

Once you've established and defined your character's professional life, delve into your character's *personal life.* Is your character single, married, widowed, divorced, or separated when the story begins? Maybe your character has just separated from a partner before the story begins. Or, perhaps the relationship is rocky and will splinter soon. Suppose your character is married; how long has he or she been married, and to whom? Where did they meet? Blind date? Chance? Business meeting? Is it a good marriage? A marriage where they take each other for granted? The marriage of Jim Braddock (Russell Crowe) and his wife Mae (Renée Zellweger) in *Cinderella Man* is a good example. Their marriage is tested all the way though the film, and their commitment to each other and their children adds another dimension to the character. In the same way, the relationship between Frankie Dunn (Clint Eastwood) and his unseen daughter in *Million Dollar Baby* (Paul Haggis)—captured only by the letters he writes her, which are all returned—gives us a deeper insight into Frankie's relationship with Maggie (Hilary Swank). What happened between Frankie and his daughter that caused the rift? Why is there such enmity there? And even though it's only alluded to, it adds a strong motivational device in Frankie's relationship with his protégé.

The *private life* is what your character does when he or she is alone. What hobbies or interests does he or she have? Jogging? Exercise class? Hatha Yoga? Taking university extension courses? Cooking, woodworking classes, fixing up a house, painting, writing, gardening? Defining your character's private life is a great way to add depth and dimension to your character.

In one of director John Frankenheimer's films, the main character, a detective, takes a gourmet French cooking class one night a week. The detective's dream is to learn how to make a special soufflé. He's hunting a serial killer and when he tracks him down, it happens to be on the same night they were preparing the soufflé. It's a great little touch. In The *Shawshank Redemption,* Andy Dufresne's hobby is carving chess pieces out of rocks. Later, we'll learn that this same interest leads to tunneling his way out of the Shawshank Penitentiary.

Write about your character's professional, personal, and private life in about two or three pages each. Use free-association; just let it come out. Define it, articulate it, but don't censor it. As you go through the exercise, remember you're engaging in a process that *reveals* character. It's just one of the tools of creating character.

Another tool that you can use to expand your ability to create characters is *Research*. There are two kinds of research, *live* research and *textual* research.

In *live* research, you interview people for ideas, thoughts, feelings, experience, and background material. Suppose you're writing a story about an auto body shop that specializes in customizing cars and you want to know how it functions and operates. Find out if there are any shops like this in your area. If need be, do a Google search on it, or check the Yellow Pages. If you can talk to the people in management, or the designers, and the people who work in the garage, you'll get an insight into the people and the environment.

Write out a list of questions you want to ask, and take a small audio recorder to record your subjects and a notebook to write your impressions. (A cautionary note: you should always ask permission to record them, whether by phone or in person. Most of the time they'll say yes, especially if you tell them you're writing a screenplay or teleplay. If they ask for you for money to pay for their time, or some kind of fee up front, look for someone else.) Most people will share their expertise. Besides, if you write the script, sell it, and it goes into production, the producer may ask your subject to be some kind of consultant on the movie.

If you read a newspaper story and you want to talk to the subject(s) of the article, call the paper, ask for the reporter who wrote the story, and see if you can get in touch with them. Call them and explain your interest and ask if you can interview them. See what you can learn. A friend of mine, a well-known studio executive turned writer, wrote a story about a professional assassin. He finished the first draft and told me he wasn't satisfied with it and asked me to read it. I did, and while the subject was good, the story was superficial, lacking in depth and dimension. I asked how much research he had done and was surprised when he replied, "Just a little." I told him it showed, and he should think about researching his main character before he began the rewrite.

I happened to recall that *Rolling Stone* had published an in-depth interview with a professional assassin a few months earlier, and I mentioned it to my friend. He called *Rolling Stone,* talked to the reporter who had done the piece, located the assassin, and arranged to interview him over the phone. My friend learned more about the world of the assassin than he ever conceived. (In the same way, one of the reasons that the Vincent character in *Collateral* was so well drawn was because of the extensive research the screenwriter, Stuart Beattie, did to prepare.) After my friend talked with the assassin, he rewrote his script and made an agreement that if the film was ever made, the writer would ask that the assassin be hired as a special consultant at a very good salary. He couldn't promise that, of course, but he could request it of the producer or director. Later, the script was optioned by a producer, and a few months after that it was sold to a studio and became a "go" project; the assassin was asked to be an advisor on the film.

Recently, I was writing a futuristic science-fiction screenplay and needed information about a powerful cosmic phenomenon that would impact the earth. I called the Jet Propulsion Laboratory, spoke to the public relations person and told her what I was looking for, and she guided me to two scientists who worked in the area of gamma ray bursts. I set up an appointment with them, took my tape recorder with me, and recorded their thoughts and ideas on the topic. I even used some of their ideas when I wrote the screenplay. That's the value of *live research.*

Textual research is where you go to the library, museum, or institution and get information from books, periodicals, microfiche, or old newspapers. When I was making documentaries at David L. Wolper Productions, my first assignment was doing research, and I became quite adept at "finding" things. I found the very first modeling stills of a seventeen-year-old Grace Kelly. I uncovered the original footage taken on one of the boats during the infamous Bay of Pigs invasion and was then questioned by officials from the State Department and FBI who wanted to know how and where I found it. I uncovered the very first filmed acting job (a short industrial film for the Union 76 Gas Company) by a young actress who would later be known as Marilyn Monroe.

If you're looking for information about your subject matter, either a character or event, search the library for any books or magazines written on the subject. If you find something that looks appealing, search through the table of contents. Does it seem interesting? Does it apply to the area you're interested in? Look through a couple of chapters. Is it easy to read? Does it have enough facts and detail to help illuminate your subject? Three or four books should provide you with enough material to keep you busy for a few weeks. If necessary, you can always go back and get other books later. You don't want to be overloaded with too much information that may not even be necessary.

A few years ago, I was researching a project about an archeologist in the field and I wanted to get some background information. I called the archeology department at UCLA and arranged to interview a graduate student who had just come back from a field trip. Then I called the Museum of Northern Arizona, where the story took place, and spoke to the reference librarian, who sent me a complete catalogue of books, articles, films, and names of people I could talk to. It was an invaluable tool.

Check out magazines and newspapers. Refer to *Readers' Guide to Periodical Literature* and *The New York Times Index*. If you need help finding books or periodicals, go to the reference desk of the library. The librarians are usually extremely helpful. Also check the bibliography in the back of any books you may find. I start every project that way, whether it's an original screenplay or a documentary film. That way I know what's been written on the subject.

Research is a wonderful tool to expand and broaden both characters and story. *Seabiscuit* is a good example of how research can effectively broaden the historical perspectives of the story line, not only in the plot but also in pictures and the newsreels of the time. It is a wonderful tool that can capture a time and place as well as inspire incidents or events that you can draw upon for your story.

What about dialogue? Dialogue is a tool of character. It's also a *function of character*. It's true that some writers have a better ear for writing dialogue than others, but if you know your character well enough, if you feel comfortable inside his or her skin, the dialogue will be individual and appropriate enough to capture the "essence" of that character. You can say things, show things, or explain things in order to reveal character.

One of the questions I continually get asked is, "How can I improve my dialogue?" When I ask what's wrong with it, the writer's response is usually "it's weak, stilted, awkward, phony, and all sounds the same." They might be right.

People get hung up on dialogue because they don't understand what it is, or what it does. They put too much importance on it. They say good dialogue is "everything" in a script, and when they start writing and their dialogue doesn't match their expectations, they become concerned, insecure, or sometimes angry and depressed. Soon after, they'll find themselves censoring their work, judging and evaluating it and becoming supercritical. If they continue in this manner, they'll probably stop writing altogether because they don't feel their dialogue is good enough.

So what? Dialogue is experiential. The more you do the easier it gets. When you sit down to write, you'll probably end up writing 50 to 60 pages of shitty dialogue. Let it be terrible! It doesn't matter at this stage. You're going to rewrite it later, so let yourself be willing to write some awful dialogue. Most words-on-paper drafts will probably be this way. Nobody can write perfect dialogue in the first words-on-paper draft. Writing good dialogue is a skill, like playing the piano, swimming, or riding a bike. *The more you do it the easier it gets.* Never mind how good or how bad it is. Trust the process. It's larger than you are. Let your characters speak for themselves. Just keep writing. Be aware of any judgments or evaluations you're making, and don't let them influence you. Easier said than done, of course. Just be willing to write some shitty dialogue. Don't get locked into the trap of wanting to write perfect dialogue from page one, word one.

What's the purpose of dialogue? It serves two functions: it either moves the story forward or it reveals character. The next time you watch a film, preferably at home on a DVD where you can study the film, listen to the dialogue. Take a piece of paper and mark down what the dialogue accomplishes in each scene. If you want, you can literally chart each scene into some aspect of these two functions. Try it and see if I'm right.

Just know that if you're willing to write 50 or 60 pages of terrible dialogue, most of the time it will clear up in the natural process of writing. You'll find certain little phrases or expressions, particular cadences or rhythms of their dialogue that will tend to individualize your character. By the end of the first words-on-paper draft, you'll be amazed at the change. When you rewrite those pages, your dialogue will improve tremendously. For some people, writing dialogue is a gift they're born with. But for most of us, it's something we can develop.

There are tools you can use to help you write more effective dialogue. One is using a cassette or digital recorder to record a conversation with a friend or acquaintance. Play it back and listen to it. Notice how fragmented it is, how quickly thoughts come and go. If you want to see what "real" dialogue looks like, type it up in screenplay form. Listen for mannerisms and inflections; find the *style* of speech, the phrasing. Then think about your character speaking in those "rhythms," or in that "language."

One of my students, a well-known journalist, was writing a screenplay she had been thinking about for years. Her writing style was elegant and readable. Her dialogue was beautiful. That is, it *read* beautifully on the page—every sentence was clear and concise, every idea complete in thought and execution. The language and punctuation were perfect.

But when you read it aloud, it didn't work at all. People don't speak in skilled and elegant prose. Real people talk in fragments, run-on sentences, and incomplete thoughts, and they change mood and subject with the blink of an eye. Just listen to people speaking; you'll get a whole new perception of how people talk. Dialogue is not spoken in beautiful prose or iambic pentameter. We're not doing Shakespeare here.

A screenplay is a reading experience before it becomes a visual one. As mentioned, one of the main functions of dialogue is to move the story forward. In that regard, it must communicate necessary facts and information to the reader so he or she knows what is happening as the story line progresses.

Moving the story forward means providing the *exposition* needed so the reader and the character knows what's going on. Exposition is defined as the necessary information to move the story forward or reveal information about a character. Exposition is usually, but not always, achieved through dialogue; characters talk about what happened in order to establish the next direction in the story line. Too much exposition becomes trite, mundane, and boring. You really don't need much of it; you just need to set things up.

A good example is *The Shawshank Redemption.* When Andy Dufresne enters prison, the first scene shows the new prisoners walking into a large admitting area. The warden introduces himself and lays down the rules of the prison. "I am Mr. Norton, the warden. You are sinners and scum, that's why they sent you to me. Rule number one: no blaspheming. I'll not have the Lord's name taken in vain in my prison. The other rules you'll figure out as you go along."

Simple. Plain. Just enough to set up the story and an indication of what's going to happen next. When one of the prisoners asks, "When do we eat?" we *see* him severely beaten for speaking out of turn. Those are the "rules." You can also provide exposition visually, as in *American Beauty.* The opening shots show the city, the street, and the house where Lester lives. In voiceover we hear Lester say: "My name is Lester Burnham. I'm forty-two years old. In less than a year, I'll be dead... that's my wife Carolyn. See the way the handle on those pruning shears matches her gardening clogs? That's not an accident."

The second function of dialogue is to reveal character. That can be accomplished in many ways. Sometimes you'll be direct, as in exposition, and other times you'll want to be indirect, that is, playing *against the grain of the scene,* meaning in an unobvious or unexpected way. Things may look great, and the conversational dialogue may be warm, friendly, and open, but what the characters are talking about may be harsh and loaded with venom. The dining room scene in *American Beauty* is a good example of this. Lester, his wife Carolyn, and their daughter Jane are sitting at the dining room table having dinner. There are candles on the table, a beautiful flower arrangement, chilled wine, and soft music playing in the background. It looks absolutely great, an American family having their evening meal together.

But the subject of the scene is all about complaints: "Mom, do we always have to listen to this elevator music?" daughter Jane whines. And Carolyn replies: "No. We don't. As soon as you've prepared a nutritious yet flavorful meal that I'm about to eat, you can listen to whatever you like." And it goes downhill from there, ending in anger, silence, and guilt.

Another way to reveal character is to have other people shed light upon the character through dialogue. Henry James had a theory he called *The Theory of Illumination,* where he put forth the idea that the main character of the story occupies the center of a circle, and on the periphery of the circle are all the other characters in the story. Each time a character interacts with the main character, he or she "illuminates" a different aspect of the main character, like walking into a darkened room and turning on floor lamps in each corner of the room. In the same way, dialogue illuminates and *reveals* something about the character.

Sometimes, you can play a scene using the tool of *subtext.* Subtext is *what is not said* during the scene. A friend of mine, an actor who had roles in several television series, was out of work and needed a job. A dear friend of his had just gotten hired to direct a big movie. It had been a while since they had seen each other, so they set up a time to get together. The need of my friend, of course, was to see if there would be a part for him in the film. The director's need was to be noncommittal. So, they got together and during the meal, what was the one thing they didn't talk about? That my friend needed a job. That's subtext.

There's a great little scene in *Annie Hall* that captures this. Alvy Singer has just met Annie Hall and they go back to her place for a drink. They walk out on the balcony and as they talk to each other, subtitles flash on the screen about what they're really thinking, which totally contradict what they're saying to each other. It's a great scene to illustrate the depth and dimension we can achieve by using subtext.

The drama of confrontation is another way of writing effective dialogue. Since you want to create conflict in your scenes, either from an exterior force or from within the character, you can create a verbal confrontation. In *Sideways,* Miles (Paul Giamatti) and Jack (Thomas Haden Church) are constantly confronting each other because they want different things. Miles wants to enjoy the winetasting experience and Jack wants to get laid. Two characters having opposing points of view allow you to create dialogue that generates conflict to keep the story moving forward and illustrate character.

Dialogue is also a good transition device. A word or visual transition connects one scene to another, scene A with scene B. You might end a scene with one character saying something, then cut into a new scene with another character continuing the same dialogue. For example, you can end one scene with a character asking a question and then open the next scene with another character answering that question. This is effectively done in *The Silence of the Lambs* (Ted Tally) and *Julia* (Alvin Sargent). You can write a montage sequence—a visual series of scenes, connected by one single idea, with a definite beginning, middle, and end. *American Beauty* illustrates this beautifully in the real estate sequence. Carolyn wants to sell a house and shows it to several different people. The dialogue is continuous as it plays over each scene with different characters in various locations in the house, but the whole sequence could really be one scene. It's a way to condense time, place, and action.

These are the tools of character. Creating full and dimensional characters and writing effective dialogue illuminates and reveals character.

And that's what it's all about.

THE EXERCISE

Write character biographies for two or three of your main characters in about seven to ten pages, or more if necessary. Focus on their early years. Where was the character born? What did his or her father and mother do for a living? What is his relationship with his parents? Does he or she have any brothers or sisters? What's the relationship—friendly and supportive or angry and combative?

Define the other relationships the character has in his or her second and third decade and see how these relationships formed his or her character. Remember Henry James' *Theory of Illumination:* every character sheds light on your main character.

Before you begin writing your biography, think about your character(s) for a few days, then set aside a time where you can work for two or three hours without interruption. No phone calls, no TV, no email, video games, or visits from friends. It may help to lower the lights or turn on some soft music, maybe drink half a glass of wine to take the edge off. Anything more and you'll be writing to get drunk. Then start "throwing down" thoughts, words, and ideas about the character. Just let it come out. Don't worry about grammar, punctuation, spelling, or bad writing. Just get your thoughts down on paper, and don't worry about anything else. You're not going to show these pages to anyone; it's only a tool for you to use while you discover and get to know your characters. If you want to include parts of your character biography in your screenplay, fine. But just get your character down on paper. Let your characters discover who they are.

Do the same with the professional, personal, and private lives of your character. Write a page or two about what your character does for a living, his or her relationships and hobbies. You might even craft a "day in the life" of your character and write what her typical day looks like. What does she do from the moment she gets out of bed till she goes to sleep at night? Write it in a page or two. If you need to write more, write more. If you can do it in less, do it in less.

If you discover any areas in a character's life you feel unsure or insecure about, write it in a page or two. Free-associate. Do some research if necessary. The relationship between you and your characters is like the relationship between two best friends. You decide what you need, then define it.

If you don't know whether you should write something or not, write it! Don't self-edit at this stage. It's *your* script, *your* story, *your* characters, *your* dramatic choices. When you have completed your assignment, you'll know your characters as if they were good friends.

7

Conflict and the Circle of Being

> "The only thing that's important is the story, and the story arises from the conflict between the characters. And you can only evolve that by beginning with their needs and motives, and by bringing them together, and they will create the story for you."
> —Frank Pierson
> *Dog Day Afternoon, Cool Hand Luke*

When you're writing the screenplay, the most essential aspect to keep in mind is that all drama is conflict. Many writers seem to forget that. If the purpose of the scene in a screenplay is to either move the story forward, or reveal information about the character, the writer sometimes feels that telling the story means moving the character through the action like a chess piece without focusing on the conflict.

Why is conflict so important in writing the screenplay?

Because it creates tension, rhythm, suspense, and keeps the readers, or viewers, on the edge of their collective seats. A movie is larger than life, and if you want to write a script that brings a certain order to the world, you need to engage the reader. That means generating conflict.

The word *conflict* means "in opposition to." In literary terms, it's usually defined as "creating the force of opposition between the characters and the actions that helps shape or motivate the plot." If you have a character with a strong and defined dramatic need, then you can create obstacles to that need and the story becomes your character overcoming obstacle after obstacle to achieve his or her dramatic need. If your character has a strong and distinct point of view, and you have another character with the opposite point of view, the result is a strong and continued conflict within the scene. And that's what it's all about, sustaining conflict either in an emotional or physical context.

Cold Mountain is a good example that illustrates the multidimensional complexities of conflict. Charles Frazier's novel, adapted by director Anthony Minghella, is set during the American Civil War, a bloody and brutal time that violently divided the nation along the lines of politics and geography.

The focus of the story is on three characters: Inman (Jude Law), a carpenter, is a man of many talents and few words. Ada (Nicole Kidman), is a young woman raised to be a Southern "belle," daughter of a Baptist Minister, who can read, write, play the piano, and be the perfect "hostess." Ruby (Renée Zellweger) is a feisty drifter who teaches Ada about strength and self-reliance and reveals a kind of world that Ada has never known or dreamed of. Three lives, uprooted by war, learn to depend upon each other to endure their physical and spiritual survival together.

And then, there's Cold Mountain, a little town sheltered in the foothills of the Blue Ridge Mountains of North Carolina, which represents a time, a place, and a way of life that has been forever lost. Cold Mountain is really like a beacon of love, a place that resides in the heart.

Cold Mountain is all about conflict and that is established and set up with the dramatic situation. The story takes place during the conflict between the states that ushers in the changing way of life in America. In change there is always conflict. The story begins in flashback, as Union soldiers tunnel under a Confederate camp planting explosives. We are introduced to Inman as he rereads one of many letters sent by Ada, sharing her hopes and dreams with him in voiceover. Already, this provides a stark visual contrast to Inman and the Confederate camp. Even while we hear Ada's words, we watch the Union soldiers light the fuse. Then all hell breaks loose.

The attacking Union Army finds itself stuck in the landfill and the Confederates stand on all sides of the crater firing their guns into the mass of humanity. So it begins.

In the midst of this madness and confusion we flash back to a time two years earlier, in Cold Mountain, and we see Inman's memories of meeting Ada. Already, the opposition of forces in the story generates the conflict: North versus South, right versus wrong, the state versus the individual, and so on.

Inman, wounded in a later skirmish, listens to the words of Ada, "Come back, my love," and chooses to desert the Confederate Army and flee this madness of war. He wants to make his way home to the woman he loves, and is driven by his dramatic need to return to Cold Mountain. Like Homer's *Odyssey,* Inman's trek is a story about a man whose desire is to return home, and during the course of his journey, he confronts all kinds of obstacles placed in his path. His story becomes a supreme test of courage, of pride, of romantic love and loyalty. He must hide and flee from the enemy as well as the Confederate bounty hunters. He must endure starvation and fatigue, and confront his own issues of fear and doubt as he travels to Cold Mountain, a journey on foot of more than three hundred miles over harsh and sometimes impassable terrain. It is an amazing journey. Every step he takes back to Cold Mountain becomes a form of conflict to confront and overcome.

The mythology of the journey is a universal theme in all human expression and is expressed and imitated no matter what our language, culture, color, or location. We're all on this same path in life, from birth to death and our job is "to decide is what to do with the time that is given to us," as Gandalf says in *The Lord of the Rings: The Fellowship of the Ring.*

The universal theme of the journey is expressed in *March of the Penguins* (adapted by Jordan Roberts, from the French documentary by Luc Jacquet and Michel Fessler). In this extraordinary documentary, we follow the Emperor penguins as they journey back to their breeding grounds in Antarctica and confront the harsh and severe obstacles of their environment. It captures their intense will to survive and in their journey we see the emotional foundation of all drama: exposition, conflict, complication, narrative progression, transition, surprise, climax, and resolution.

If we want to create the context of conflict, we see there are two kinds: one is *internal conflict* and the other is *external conflict.* Inman chooses to desert and return to Ada, so fear, doubt, love, perseverance, enduring the hazards of survival, either taking or not taking action, all represent an *internal* conflict. *External* conflict is the force or forces that work outside the character—the hazards of war, weather, physical terrain, temptations, as well as the physical hardships.

In *Cold Mountain,* Ada is a well-educated, city-bred woman who has always been protected by her father (Donald Sutherland). In the wake of his unexpected death and Inman's absence, Ada finds herself totally alone on the farm, in the middle of extreme danger, without the vaguest idea of how to fend for herself. Faced with starvation, attack, and the possibility that Inman may never return, Ada must learn to adapt and live off the land and trust the self-reliant Ruby. Ruby teaches her how to plant crops, mend and fix fences, and take care of herself. Together they find a way to survive in the midst of the hostility and bloodshed that surrounds them.

Explore your character's internal life to find and dramatize conflict within the screenplay. Waldo Salt once told me that the key to a successful screenplay is in preparing the material. Dialogue, he said, as mentioned earlier, is "perishable," because an actor can always improvise lines to make it work. But, he added forcefully, the character's dramatic need is sacred; it is what holds the entire story in place. Putting words down on paper, Waldo said, was the easiest part of the screenwriting process.

Conflict is a major factor in creating character. In most cases, the forces confronting the character will be a combination of both internal and external. Conflict in your story is a source of tension that powers the narrative thrust to move through the story line.

Sometimes, the conflict confronting your character is a reaction to the specific scene or moment in the screenplay. In *Crimson Tide,* an Emergency Action Message has been received ordering the nuclear submarine to launch its nuclear missiles. Soon after, another Emergency Action Message comes in, but the transmission is severed before the entire message can be read. What does it say? Does it confirm the launch of the missiles? Or does it cancel the previous order? What to do or not do because of this message is the major conflict within the film and tension and suspense is heightened until the proper course of action can be initiated. An uneasy truce is agreed upon while they fix the radio to see what the orders say. And it is during this wait of a few minutes that conflict is initiated by *what is not said.* It heightens and adds to the suspense of the moment. The conversation between the two main characters, played by Denzel Washington and Gene Hackman, doesn't address "the problem of the message." Instead, the characters discuss whether the famous Lipizzaner horses of Vienna are black or white. This conversation not only reflects the subtext of the scene, but also any racial implications that might exist between the two men. It's a great example of illustrating conflict within the tension of the moment.

In *Collateral,* the conflict starts with the dramatic need of the taxi driver character, Max, who is hired for the night by Vincent, a hit man contracted to commit five murders. When Max discovers Vincent's intention, he literally becomes an accessory to the crime and though he tries to get away, he cannot. Once the conflict is established, it drives the action forward, becoming the fuel that feeds the narrative. In Max's case, the external conflict gives rise to the internal conflict. For twelve years, Max has had a dream of starting his own limousine service. Every night as he begins his shift, he goes through his personal routine; he cleans the cab, inserts his little picture of a desert island behind the sun visor, and dreams about his new Mercedes limousine. But by the end of Act II, as mentioned, Max realizes he's been living a "someday" life—"someday" he'll have enough money to start his own limo service, "someday" he'll leave this taxi business behind him and do what he really wants to do. And those "someday" dreams, as we all know, never happen. The collision between a character's dreams and reality generates conflict. Wes Anderson's *Rushmore* is a good example of this.

That's the nature of conflict. As you begin creating and formulating your character(s), see if you can create an internal or external conflict that will help drive the story forward.

Remember, the purpose of the scene is to either move the story forward or reveal information about the character. The dramatic core of achieving that is generating conflict—conflict within, or conflict without.

Conflict can create dimensions that infuse the character and story line in a number of significant ways. In *Magnolia,* Paul Thomas Anderson's brilliant screenplay, the themes of reconciliation and forgiveness are woven throughout the story and reveal how the past actions of parents shape and influence the behavior of their children. Earl (Jason Robards) is dying of cancer and on his deathbed he seeks forgiveness for leaving his then fourteen-year-old son Frank (Tom Cruise) alone to care for his dying mother.

This incident of Earl walking out on his dying wife has affected Frank's life profoundly, leading him to develop a lifestyle where he channels his anger into convincing men to use sex as a weapon to "destroy the opposite sex." When Frank finally does confront Earl on his deathbed, Frank is able to complete his relationship with his dying father. This scene illustrates how certain facts uncovered within the character biography might help shape and form a character's life. Through the character biography, you can *form* your characters, then *reveal* them by showing who they are in the story line. Ibsen's great play *Ghosts* deals with some of these same themes, about the sins of the father being passed on to the son.

One of the ways to accomplish this is by performing an exercise I call the *Circle of Being.* It's a process that allows you to uncover an incident in your character's life that emotionally impacts your story line; typically, it's an incident or event that occurs to your main character when he or she is between the ages of nine and eighteen. This is a very formative time, during which a traumatic event could possibly affect the entire course of a character's life. This event might be the death of a parent or loved one, some sort of physical abuse that results in a deep emotional scar or physical injury, or a move to a new city or country.

I call this event the *Circle of Being* because if you picture your character as a circle, and then slice the events of his or her life like dividing a pie, you can evoke the physical, emotional, mental, spiritual, social, mystical, political, traumatic, and intellectual incidents or events of their life that impact their behavior. By doing this exercise, you can create a well-rounded portrait of your character that evokes the emotions, thoughts, and feelings that expand and deepen your characterization.

Thelma & Louise is a good example of the *Circle of Being* event and how it's used. Callie Khouri's screenplay does not explicitly mention that Louise was raped and unable to receive justice when she was growing up in Texas. Although it is only insinuated once or twice during the screenplay, Louise's past ordeal impacts her physical, mental, and emotional behavior throughout the movie. "If you blow a guy's head off with his pants down," she says, "Texas is the last place you want to get caught!" Carrying the anger and hurt of this burden is what ultimately leads to the incident that powers the entire story line, the shooting of Thelma's would-be rapist in the parking lot. It explains *why* Louise pulls the trigger in the first place, and why she vows to never set one foot inside the state of Texas.

"I'd rather be caught dead," she states emphatically. And, of course, it becomes a prophetic remark. From Oklahoma City, the only way to get to Mexico without going through Texas is the long way around, through Utah and Arizona. It is this decision that ultimately costs both women their lives, and at this point, they wouldn't have it any other way. This Circle of Being event, I feel, is triggered in the parking lot when Louise sees Harlan attempting to rape Thelma. Louise totally loses it and pulls the trigger, killing Harlan. To me, the Louise pulling the trigger in that parking lot is not the Louise of the present time; rather, it is the young girl who was raped in Texas many years earlier.

Later, Hal, the police detective (Harvey Keitel), tells her on the phone, "I know what happened in Texas," and a little later Thelma, referring to the rape attempt, guesses that "it happened to you, didn't it?" To the very end, Louise does not respond.

Creating a Circle of Being event for your character is an invaluable tool to use in crafting and enriching your character. If you go into your character's life and ask yourself what traumatic incident might have occurred in your character's life between the ages of nine and eighteen, see what happens. You might even explore your own life and see what, if any, traumatic event might have occurred in your life during this time frame.

Why nine to eighteen? First, because it seems to be the most formative period in a person's life and results in specific behavioral patterns that remain either consciously or unconsciously in the psyche. The noted behaviorist Joseph Chilton Pierce states there are four major periods of growth, or spurts, of human intelligence. The first intelligence growth period occurs when the child is about a year old, when they learn to walk. The second intellectual spurt occurs when the child is about four years old and learns that he or she has a distinct identity and communication skills. The third stage of intellectual growth occurs when the child is about nine or ten; that's the age when he understands that he has a singular and individual voice and begins to question authority, forming his or her own opinions about what's right or wrong and starts speaking his mind. This is a vital time in the life of the young person.

The fourth stage of human intelligence, and perhaps the most important developmental spurt according to Pierce, occurs when the person is about fifteen or sixteen—the teenager. That's the age when the young person starts rebelling against authority and tries to find his or her own voice; she suddenly understands that her parents are no longer the center of the universe, and she looks outward, into the world for models of behavior. The young person is heavily influenced by his peers, and may begin to dress differently, color his hair, get body piercings or tattoos, and experiment with drugs, actions which are more acceptable to his peers than to his parents or society. But these actions express teenagers' individuality and who they are within the context of their own peer group. They have an identity. Just look at your own kids, or your nieces or nephews, or your friends' kids, and how they dress, act, and react.

It's a period of a person's development so influential that it can leave a subconscious imprint for the rest of his life, much like furniture leaves an impression in the rug. Take a moment and look back into your own life and see how influential this time was. Just close your eyes and go back to the time when you were about that age, anywhere from nine to eighteen, or thereabouts, and see if there was any specific incident or event that affected you the most. What was the incident or event that springs to mind? Take a moment to consider how that event might have affected you and possibly changed your life.

If you go back into your character's life and create an incident or event that becomes a major influence, then you can enhance the texture and depth of any character you're writing. By creating a Circle of Being event you can generate conflict or a plot complication that will expand the dimension of your character.

One of my students, a well-known and working playwright, wanted to make the switch from writing for the stage to writing for the screen. He had an interesting story that involved the reconciliation of two sisters after an absence of many years. The story opens with the main character, a dentist, undergoing a dental procedure. While under the influence of the anesthesia, she flashes back to a time when she was a young girl and witnessed her sister being raped by their uncle. Fearful of being seen, she ran away and in her flight, tripped over a rock, fell, and injured her front teeth—the same teeth which are *acting up now.* She had totally repressed the memory of this event until now and it leads her to reconcile with her sister. This Circle of Being event sparked the entire story. The themes of reconciliation and forgiveness thus became the narrative thrust of the screenplay. I suggested to the writer that we see the Circle of Being event as the story unfolds in visual bits and pieces scattered throughout the screenplay. She recovers the incident in visual fragments, and the final script turned out to be very powerful material. *The Bourne Supremacy* uses this same kind of visual technique throughout the narrative as we see fragments of Bourne's memory as he tries to recall the murder of the politician Neski and his wife, in Berlin. It adds tension and power to the film experience.

That's the influence of the Circle of Being. Once you've created an experience or incident that affects the life of your character, then you can base the character's emotional arc on that incident and have him or her confront and resolve (or not resolve) the experience. It becomes a way of embellishing character, creating a strong, defined point of view and attitude, and contains within it the spark of conflict. Some films use the Circle of Being as the basis of the story line, and it becomes the subject of the entire film.

Quentin Tarantino's *Kill Bill: Vol. 1* is another good example of this. Both *Kill Bill: Vol. 1 and Vol. 2* deal with the theme of revenge. But it is the Circle of Being event that defines the story of The Bride (Uma Thurman) and O-Ren (Lucy Liu), her opponent in Part I. In an animation sequence, we see how O-Ren becomes the leader of the Japanese underworld. As a child, she witnesses the murder of her parents by a Japanese gangster. She lies huddled under the bed during the butchery and swears eternal revenge. A few years later, she gets her revenge by seducing her parent's killer and murdering him and his henchmen. She becomes the most notorious assassin in Japan and soon rises to the top of the Japanese underworld. This ultimately leads to the showdown between O-Ren and The Bride that occupies almost the entire second half of the first film. We see in graphic detail how the Circle of Being event changed O-Ren's life.

Sometimes you'll be able to find a Circle of Being event for your character with no problem whatsoever and it will just flow naturally from the character biography. Other times it may not be so easy. You may have to work, struggle, think, ponder, reflect, and contemplate what the Circle of Being event might be in your character's life.

In *The Silence of the Lambs,* the Circle of Being plays a prominent part in the transformation of Clarice Starling (Jodie Foster), a young FBI trainee tracking a serial killer, who must come to grips with an incident that occurred in her own childhood. That incident, the death of her father, a small-town policeman killed during an attempted robbery, creates a major gap in her life and has influenced a subconscious search for a father figure.

The extraordinary screenplay by Ted Tally focuses on Clarice's relationship with three fathers: her real, biological father, who's kind of a ghost figure during the action; Jack Crawford (Scott Glenn), the Director of the Behavioral Science Division at the FBI Academy, who's loving but stern, and remains somewhat distant; and the brilliant but deadly Hannibal Lecter (Anthony Hopkins), who becomes a kind of mentor to her, guiding and teaching her what to look for when pursuing the serial killer known as Buffalo Bill. As *The Silence of the Lambs* unfolds, each one of Clarice's "fathers" has something to teach her as she walks the path from being the student to being the professional.

The search for the father is a major theme in literature. Many times, a person's character, psychologists say, is reflected in the search for the father, but in reality, it is really searching for your own true nature. Often, a person searches for their destiny as their destiny is searching for them.

The death of Clarice's father is the Circle of Being event in her life. Because of her father's death, she is sent to live with an uncle in Montana. One night, she's awakened by the screaming of lambs being slaughtered. When she is caught trying to rescue one of the baby lambs, she is sent away to an orphanage. Hannibal Lecter forces her to look at this emotional event she's been shielding and allows her to recreate it, thus becoming free of it. By the end of the film she has transformed her life. She is now on the threshold of building a new life, not only in terms of her relationship to men but professionally as a top-notch FBI agent. Only when she is able to confront this incident in her past can she truly be free.

How can the Circle of Being affect your screenplay? In many ways, obviously, but I find its importance is that it provides a source of conflict, either inner or outer, that your character must confront during the story line.

One of my favorite examples is *Seabiscuit.* We see Red Pollard (Tobey Maguire) being given away because his family cannot take care of him. Can you imagine being given away by your parents when you're about fifteen because they can't take care of you?

This is Red's Circle of Being scene, and though it is taken from a real event in his life, it is something that could be discovered while writing the character biography. In the film, Red is watching a horse race in a carnival when his father approaches, carrying a pillowcase filled with his favorite books. "I'm so sorry," his father begins. He looks at Red. There are tears in his eyes. The trainer, his father says, "has a house. A real house... There's even a phone next door so we can call you every couple of weeks and let you know where we are...." "No," Red cries. His father reaches down, hugs his son.

Red doesn't know what's happening. "You'll be great at this [racing horses]," his father whispers. "You've got a gift... we'll come back." Then he hugs his son again wanting to believe his own words. "We will.... We will." His mother weeps.

Red watches, still confused "as his father leans back. He looks around the fading light of the race track/fairground. Mr. Pollard looks at his son for a moment as the CAMERA begins to pull back, rapidly leaving them a small part of the crowd...." Then, they cut to the next scene.

It's a small scene but quite an emotional moment. The impact on Red is enormous—it is what influences and shapes his life, a life built upon negative self-worth and deep-seated anger. Emotionally, being given away by his parents has led him to believe that he's not good enough as a person and we see that in his behavior as he lashes out at everyone he is close to.

The Circle of Being event is the source of inner conflict that Red must confront and deal with for the rest of his life. He doesn't feel he deserves anything. As the story progresses, we see his internal conflicts about his own self-respect and self-worth.

I feel a Circle of Being event can also apply to animals. As mentioned, I think Seabiscuit is a real character in this movie. He was given away at six months, just like Red Pollard, because he did not fit the image of what a racehorse should be. He was taught to lose, not allowed to win a race. Is it any wonder that he "forgot what it's like to be a horse"?

Seabiscuit is affected by his real-life Circle of Being event. The narrator tells us that: "Seabiscuit was the son of Hard Tack, sired by the mighty horse Man O' War.... At six months he was shipped off to train with the legendary trainer Sunny Fitzsimmons [who] decided the horse was lazy.... Where his sire had been a fierce, almost violent competitor, Seabiscuit took to sleeping for huge chunks of the day and enjoyed lolling for hours under the boughs of the juniper trees. So, they made him a training partner to 'better' horses, forcing him to lose head to head to boost the confidence of the other animal. . . . When they finally did race him, he did just what they had trained him to do. . . . He lost. . . . And, of course, it all made sense. . . . Champions were large. They were sleek. They were without imperfection. This horse ran as they had always expected him to run. . . ."

That is the power of the Circle of Being event in your character's life. It can be the source of conflict in the narrative line of action, whether animal or human. Film is a visual medium—a story told in pictures. As the ancient text of the *Yoga Vashista* states, "The world is as you *see* it." Your story is held together by its characters and conflict and becomes the arena where your character(s) confront the tremendous challenges of the world. Conflict and the Circle of Being are the key that ignites the engine and powers your character through the story line.

THE EXERCISE

Rent or buy the DVD of *Cold Mountain, Seabiscuit, Thelma & Louise,* or *Magnolia* and study it from the point of view of conflict and the Circle of Being. If need be, write a free-association essay of what you notice in terms of conflict.

All drama is conflict. So when you're thinking of creating your main character(s), it's important to think about finding ways to generate conflict. There are either internal or external forces working on your character that can help you articulate and define some of the conflicts your character encounters during the course of the screenplay.

Once you define the dramatic situation, see if you can break the arena of conflict into an external source, or an internal one, or any combination of internal or external conflicts. Think about the external forces working on your character. What are they? Can you define and articulate them? Just write them down in a free-association essay in about a page or two.

Go into your character biography and see what kind of Circle of Being event you can create for your character. Sometimes, an event will just "pop out" on the page and at other times you may have to dig into your character's emotional life to find it. Even if you don't actually use the Circle of Being event in your screenplay, it's good to know your character has a history that you can draw upon while writing.

8

Of Time and Memory

Jason Bourne: "What's going on in Berlin?"
—Tony Gilroy
The Bourne Supremacy

The great Italian filmmaker, Michelangelo Antonioni, once stated that "film is a language that bypasses the mind and speaks directly to the heart." There's no doubt this comment permeated his exploration into the human spirit in several of his great films: *L'Avventura, La Notte, Eclipse, Red Desert, Blow-Up, Zabriskie Point, The Passenger,* and others.

In *The Passenger,* David Locke, played by Jack Nicholson, is a world-weary journalist hunting for a story in North Africa when he discovers an Englishman in his hotel dead from a heart attack. After a long, silent deliberation, David, weary of his own life, disillusioned with his job and isolated in his marriage, assumes the man's identity and so cuts the restraints of his past life and sets out to forge a new life with a new identity. Of course, he doesn't know what the future will bring, or what the destiny is of the man whose identity he has assumed. He meets up with a detached young woman (Maria Schneider), and begins keeping the dead man's shadowy appointments in London, Munich, and throughout Spain, because "he believed in something." Only later does David learn the man was selling guns.

In one scene, David is driving a rented convertible with the top down along one of those long country roads outside London that are lined with tall trees. The girl, Maria Schneider, is in the passenger seat and she looks over at him and asks, "What are you running from?" He replies by telling her to turn around. She looks behind her and we watch from her point of view as the empty and barren road disappears behind them. The moment holds as we see that he's leaving his past behind, and moving into an unencumbered present, leading to an unknown and uncertain future. It is cinema at its highest.

When I grasped the realization of that moment, I found it affected me on a deep, and profound, emotional level. No words, only pictures and the coursing recognition that we're traveling on this road of life carrying our past behind like some unwanted luggage. I've often wondered what it would be like if we could simply drop our past and step into the present moment free of time and memory.

When I see a film I like, I respond immediately, on an emotional, intuitive level. Either I like it or I don't. Either it works or it doesn't. Oh yes, I can talk endlessly about the visual brilliance of the director, the great performances of the actors, the broad sweep of the photography, the poetry of the editing, or the ingeniousness of the special effects. But when I get right down to it, there's only one thing that holds the whole thing together—and that's the story.

Ideas, concepts, jargon, and analytical comments don't really mean a thing. Whether the movie proceeds in a straight line, in a circle, or is fractured or splintered into little pieces, doesn't make a bit of difference. Movies are all about story. No matter who we are, or where we live, or what generation we belong to, the singular aspects of storytelling remain the same. It's been that way since Plato created stories out of the dancing shadows on the wall. The art of telling a story with pictures exists beyond time, culture, and language. Walk into the Elmira caves in Spain and look at the rock paintings, or into the Accademia Museum in Venice, and gaze upon those magnificent panels depicting the twelve Stations of the Cross, and you enter the grand view of visual storytelling.

There are many filmmakers today who insist that the linear story line—where the story goes from beginning to end in a straight, narrative line—is passé, out of date, not "part of the scene" anymore. They loudly proclaim that the three-act structure is dead, no longer pertinent to the "modern movie," whatever that means. One filmmaker even went on record to state that "the Hollywood narrative film is in its death throes right now and people are looking for something else. The whole school of Act I/Act II/Act III is destructive to a thriving, growing cinema."

Since *Pulp Fiction* first fractured the "modern" cinematic structure, there have been many films that illustrate this search for a new form: *Memento* (Christopher Nolan), *2046* (Kar Wai Wong), *Eternal Sunshine of the Spotless Mind* (Charlie Kaufman), and *The Usual Suspects* (Chris McQuarrie) are just a few examples that spring to mind. These films don't necessarily illustrate a particular intellectual idea, like Alain Resnais did with *Last Year at Marienbad* or *Hiroshima Mon Amour,* they simply explore new challenges within the form of the three-act structure.

Run Lola Run (Tom Tykwer) reflects this very well. The movie unfolds like a video game. Every time Lola fails to get the $100,000 to save her boyfriend, guess what? The game's over. She goes back to the beginning and plays another game until she wins.

Filmmakers are always searching for new ways of telling their stories: *Kill Bill: Vol. 1 and Vol. 2* (Quentin Tarantino), *Being John Malkovich* and *Adaptation* (Charlie Kaufman), *The Hours* (David Hare), *The Matrix* (Andy and Larry Wachowski), *Magnolia* (Paul Thomas Anderson), *The Sixth Sense* (M. Night Shyamalan), *The English Patient* (Anthony Minghella), *The Royal Tenenbaums* (Wes Anderson and Owen Wilson), *American Beauty* (Alan Ball), and *The Bourne Supremacy* (Tony Gilroy), just to name a few, all push the form of the modern screenplay both in style and content. At first glance these films may *seem* to be in rebellion against the linear, narrative film, but the truth is they're as traditional as their predecessors.

Looking back at how the screenplay has evolved during the last twenty-five years, it's easy to see that the form of the script has changed considerably. While screenplays like *Mystic River* (Brian

Helgeland), *Cinderella Man* (Chris Hollingsworth and Akiva Goldsman), all three parts of *The Lord of the Rings, The Shawshank Redemption* (Frank Darabont), and *Sideways* are all linear story lines, (that is, told from beginning to end in a "straight" story line) there has been a tendency in recent years to create a more novelistic structure. The novel's tools, such as stream of consciousness, memories, fantasy, subjective reality, flashbacks, voiceover narration and such, are being used within the framework of the screenplay to create a new form. They've been doing this from the beginning of the silent film, of course.

Often, present time merges with memories of the past like in *The English Patient, Cold Mountain,* or the beautiful *2046,* almost a meditation on time, love, and memory. In essence, it seems we're trying to communicate a more internal perspective and get closer to the *consciousness* of the characters. It is here, in the subjective reality of the character, where the past influences the present and dreams collide with reality. This fusion of time and memory is one of the indicators of what I see as an evolution in the modern screenplay.

As of this writing, I think we're in the middle of a screenwriting revolution, a time where screenwriters are pushing the form in new directions. The traditional way of "seeing things" has changed, and we're looking for ways to match our experiences and incorporate the new technology at our fingertips.

This revolution/evolution in screenwriting seems to be based upon a new visual awareness of how we see the world. Today, the popularity of screenwriting and filmmaking is an integral part of our culture and cannot be ignored. Walk into any bookstore and you'll see shelves and shelves devoted to all aspects of filmmaking. Everybody, it seems, wants to be a filmmaker. Write a script, get a digital video recorder, film the movie, upload it onto your computer, edit it with IPro Edit, or any of the other systems, add some special CGI effects, lay in a soundtrack from a database of music, and you have a film you can then email to your friends and family. Many presentations, both in business and the arts, are now given visually, either on CD or DVD. With the dramatic rise of computer technology and computer graphic imagery, along with the expanded influence of MTV, reality TV, Xbox, PlayStation, new wireless LAN and Bluetooth technology, and the enormous increase in the number of film festivals both here and abroad, I think we're in the middle of a cinematic revolution. Already, we are making short episodic TV series for our cell phones to view during the day or project on TV. Clearly, we have evolved, and are evolving, in the way we *see* things.

In terms of the screenplay, it seems we're trying to get closer to the subjective reality of our characters in the same way that the great painters went from the objective world of landscapes and religious figures to the subjective world of the impressionists and abstract expressionism. Take a look at *The Bourne Supremacy, Kill Bill: Vols. 1 and 2, Eternal Sunshine of the Spotless Mind, Memento, Courage Under Fire* (Patrick Sheane Duncan), the remake of *The Manchurian Candidate* (Daniel Pyne and Dean Georgaris), and others.

Why is this happening? I think part of it is due to the advancement of digital film technology, which has changed and influenced the way we see and interpret our experience. Most films coming out of Hollywood are as pretty as cotton candy. They may look like they're about something, but there's nothing there but sugar and water. There's no content. As Gertrude Stein once remarked about Oakland many years ago, "there ain't no there when you get there."

If you look at the way flashback was used in a film like *Casablanca* (Julius and Philip Epstein and Howard Koch), measure it against the fragmented flashbacks in *Ordinary People* (Alvin Sargent), and compare them with the fragmented strands of memory in *The Bourne Supremacy*, you'll see a visual evolution in terms of style and execution. The flashbacks in *Casablanca* show that magical time in Paris when Rick (Humphrey Bogart) and Ilsa (Ingrid Bergman) met and fell in love. The flashback scenes showing them in Paris are simply complete scenes that are *inserted* within the narrative flow of the story line. Comparing the cinematic expressions of *The Bourne Supremacy* and *Ordinary People* is an interesting exercise. In cinematic terms, the visual attributes are impressive, and the way the action and the characters are expressed makes the films more of a subjective experience.

In *Ordinary People* (Alvin Sargent), the story is built around the fragments of memory that unfold during the story line. It is *integrated* into the story; the emotional journey of young Conrad (Timothy Hutton) reacting to his brother's drowning is what Conrad has to uncover and accept to be free of the guilt that haunts him. The story, about a young man coming of age who must accept himself for who he is, is a powerful and universal one. The inciting incident occurs before the story begins, when the two young brothers are caught in a storm on the lake and their sailboat capsizes, and, due to the violence of the storm, the older brother lets go and drowns. Conrad's mother, Beth Jarrett (Mary Tyler Moore), cannot forgive Conrad for being the son who lives. And it is this relationship, between mother and son, that drives the entire story.

The drowning is seen in small fragments during the course of the film. It is seen in the opening shots, a brief sliver of the event that haunts Conrad like a bad dream. He feels so guilty about his own survival that he cannot accept the fact that he is the one who lived. Before the story begins he had so little sense of self-worth that he tried to kill himself by slashing his wrists. We learn as Conrad learns about the hidden impact that seeps through his entire being and drives his sense of unworthiness. The drowning, the key incident, is visually woven throughout the film and seems to anticipate the sheer power that time and memory plays upon the character of Jason Bourne in *The Bourne Supremacy.*

If there is any one film at this writing that seems to embody and capture this "new style" of screenwriting, it is *The Bourne Supremacy.* Not only is it fast-paced and exciting, but the characters are well-drawn, the story powerful, and the action sequences, directed by Paul Greengrass, are visually stunning. When I first saw it I was totally blown away; it touched me on both an emotional and physical level. I walked out of the movie theater dazed by the visual brilliance and wondering how and why the film made such a powerful impression upon me.

So I went back to see it a second time and marveled at the way screenwriter Tony Gilroy had integrated the portrait of a character who is basically reacting throughout the entire screenplay. People are constantly trying to kill him, yet he still manages to capture the depth and essence of his character. Not only that, but Gilroy intercuts strands of time and memory throughout the action in a stylized, "modern" approach to screenwriting.

Watch *The Bourne Supremacy* and you'll see the shards of time and memory woven throughout the action and resolved with a moving and fitting act of redemption. With Bourne's final act of redemption, I gained new insight on Henry James' question: "What is character but the determination of incident and what is incident but the illumination of character?"

Jason Bourne is a man with amnesia, driven by the universal question of "Who am I?" Imagine waking up one day and not knowing *who* you are or *where* you are. You don't know *how* you got there, or even *why* you're there or *what* it is that you do or what languages you speak or anything else about who you are. Everything in your life is literally a blank sheet of paper. In the original Robert Ludlum novels from the 1970s, Bourne is a man who is both victim and savior whose journey deals with various political and social issues of the time that are no longer relevant today. So, if you're a screenwriter who's going to be adapting the Bourne books where the situations are out of date and revolve around a character who has no past, an uncertain present, and perhaps no future, how do you go about creating character and story?

That was only one of the many questions I wanted to ask screenwriter Tony Gilroy. Before talking to him, I went online and downloaded his filmography. I saw he'd been writing for several years, with credits on *Dolores Claiborne* (adapted from the Stephen King novel), *Extreme Measures,* and *The Devil's Advocate,* and he also adapted *Armageddon* before he did *Bait* and *Proof of Life.* That's when he got the opportunity to write *The Bourne Identity.*

I tracked him down in his office in New York where he was in the process of writing the third Jason Bourne film, *The Bourne Ultimatum.* He shared that at that particular moment, he was in a state of confusion, still thinking things through before the story took hold and got sorted out. For me, that's the most fun part—confusion is the first step toward clarity.

I asked about his background. The son of writer-director Frank D. Gilroy, he grew up in upstate New York and originally started out as a musician. He played in a lot of bands, got involved in songwriting, and told me he "just got tired of playing music." He moved to New York and began writing short stories, moved on to writing a novel, and "fell in love with writing prose."

When his brother, Dan, also a screenwriter, graduated from college, "he optioned a book that he was turning into a script and it looked like there was some interest in it," Gilroy said. "I had stopped playing music, and thought, well, I'm not going to finish this novel. I'm going to write a screenplay and make some dough. Quick. Then I'll go back and finish this book. So I spent the next 5 years tending bar while I learned how to write a screenplay and fell in love with the form of it."

"I learned a lot of things from music," Gilroy continues. "I don't read music, but making music in the recording studio and the process of recording music and rehearsing with bands and making arrangements of songs, basically just how you think about songs, seems to always be the same creative process."

"How did you approach adapting *The Bourne Identity*?" I asked, because the political situations in the book were so different then and totally out of date now. He paused for a moment, then replied that "I had to start with the character. If I were in that situation, what would I do? I mean, if I had amnesia and woke up and didn't know who I was, or didn't remember where I was, and I'm in a place where no one knows me, and I don't speak the language, I could probably figure out who I was by what I know how to do.

"So," he continues, "we discover what Jason discovers about himself at the same time. When he comes to, his mind's a blank—a clean slate. He's in an environment with no frame of reference. So, you say to yourself, if this were me, what would I do? How can I figure out who I am? The only answer seemed to be, *what do I know how to do?* Do I know how to diaper a baby? Do I know how to fold laundry? Can I change a tire? What language do I speak? What happens if the things I discover I know how to do are repulsive? If that's so, then that's a movie. That was my start point."

We see this in the early part of *The Bourne Identity*. Jason is sleeping on a park bench when he's roughly asked for his papers by two policemen. He tries to explain his situation, in German, and realizes he can speak the language. But the police are indifferent and sensing where the situation is going, Bourne doesn't hesitate; he lashes out and quickly subdues the two cops. How does he know how to do that?

Action is character, right?

Bourne gradually discovers he has a tremendous capability to defend himself, along with the ability to kill people. He has knowledge of weaponry and fluency in several languages. And he learns that people are out to kill him. So he commandeers Marie (Franka Potente) and her car and they race toward safety, wherever that may be.

When Gilroy approached *The Bourne Supremacy*, he confronted a much more difficult problem: not only was the book out of date, but he had moved so far from the source material in the first film that it was impossible to bridge back to even the most basic plot elements. How did he go about building and constructing a new story line?

Tony Gilroy approached this in two ways. At the end of *The Bourne Identity*, Jason tracks Marie down in Greece and the film ends with them together. So, the first question Gilroy had to ask himself was, what happened to Bourne and Marie during the intervening years. "Where would they have gone?" he asks. "And what would be happening to them? I thought the honeymoon would probably be over because he had escaped without really paying the emotional price of that relationship. Being with Marie was easy so I felt there was a lot of unfinished psychological business with Jason Bourne. I was sure the audience would want to know how much he was going to remember. And we had left that open. So I wanted to define for myself what might've happened to them on the run.

"First, I wanted to find a location where they would go. Bourne would be looking for a place that was 'safe'—isolated, off the beaten track, but someplace where they might have a chance of blending in. So I started looking for places which were out of the way, where people hadn't shot too many movies. Finally, I found Goa, in India, and I thought that was really cool.

"Once I had the location, then I could start sketching scenes for them. Long scenes, just getting them talking to see what might happen. They'd come together so quickly, and now their time together had been on the run, with Bourne constantly looking over his shoulder, I thought they'd probably be unhappy. What would happen if the headaches had gotten worse? What happens if his paranoia has really started to wear on her? What would the reality be for a relationship like theirs?"

That's all he had to start with. Not much in terms of story except a character on the run who happens to have amnesia. "So, what's going to happen?" Gilroy asks rhetorically. "As far as the story goes, I'm back to square one: What kind of a movie is this? Intuitively, I felt I didn't want to drag Marie through this story line because I had already done that in *The Bourne Identity.* I thought the best thing to do would be to kill her off. That way there'd be no chance of repeating the first film.

"But how? And why? I knew I needed something thematic, but since that wasn't what was coming first I thought I'd follow this line and see where it led me and maybe I'd find something larger along the way. I wrote a scene where they had this huge fight—he thinks he's seen someone following them, she's had it with running away all the time and she doesn't want to move again. It's Bourne's paranoia that led to them moving like five or six times already. And now he wants to move again. He's on edge, jumpy, and feels he might be coming unhinged. So there's this huge fight. She storms out of the house, down the street, angry, not looking. I had her get hit by a bus. Which apparently in India is a fairly common occurrence. She's dead. Just like that. It was shocking and fresh and unexpected for this kind of movie. It was very energizing. His reaction to her death—his complicity in it—seemed like an interesting place to start. But that's all it was and I was still stuck on finding a big idea."

How did he resolve this story issue? I asked. He replied, "In the novel, which takes place in Communist China, there was a doppelganger [a double, or mirror image of someone] impersonating Jason Bourne. I thought maybe I could use that—maybe someone *is* impersonating him? But why? And if I have them kill Marie and then have Bourne seeking to avenge her death, will this just become another revenge picture? If it is, what happens? I started wondering why someone would be impersonating him when he's with Marie in Goa.

"Around thirty pages in, I knew I needed another character, someone who's after Bourne, so I created the Pamela Landy (Joan Allen) character. Why was she after him? That's when I began to develop the theft in Berlin. It was at that point that I got really bummed out because I realized it would have helped if the Chris Cooper character was still alive. But I had killed him off in *The Bourne Identity*. If I knew then that we were going to do the sequel to *Identity*, I would have definitely kept Chris Cooper alive.

"I'm still sketching here, all this is just me flopping around trying scenes, trying to get some traction to see what comes to life. After Marie's death I had written a whole sequence where Pamela Landy's team starts looking for Bourne. I sketched another sequence where he's in an Indian prison and when they find him there they realize he couldn't have been in Berlin stealing their money."

Gilroy paused for a moment, then continued. "But, you know, I still felt I didn't have any big theme. I couldn't define what the movie was about. Everything I had was jazzy, it was moving well, but I could see there was going to be a lot of trouble down the road. Everything was heading inevitably toward this being a very simple revenge picture. That's when I knew I hadn't really done the real work and it was going to come back and bite me in the ass. I knew we had to get on it right now.

"So, I stopped writing. Just like that. I told everyone I really didn't have it. I wrote Matt Damon saying I didn't think any of us wanted to just do a revenge movie. Because that's the way we were going. And it wasn't going to work. And I didn't want to resurrect Marie. There were some times where I thought maybe I shouldn't have killed her, maybe I'll bring her back. But the more I thought about it, the more I knew it just wasn't going to work.

"So I kept asking myself 'what am I supposed to do with Jason Bourne?' You know, he has not paid the price. He's a guy with blood on his hands who's made this sort of instant transformation. It's been too easy. Can you really just wake up one morning and say, 'Hey, I don't remember who I am, but I'd like to start fresh thinking I'm a good person?' He didn't confront the issue head-on in the beginning. Which is why he's always looking over his shoulder, constantly feeling he has to be on the run. This is why he's so screwed up. Which is why he lost Marie. He's being revisited by all these sins because he's never dealt with what's really wrong with him—and there will never be any peace for him until he works this out.

"That's when I realized that this movie could really be about an apology. About atonement. How can I find one specific thing he can atone for? Some kind of powerful incident. So I thought, well, who could he apologize to? That's when I came up with the Neski assassination in Berlin. He was assigned to kill the father but when the mother shows up unannounced he has to kill her as well, and then to cover his tracks he makes it look like the mother killed the father and then killed herself. And somewhere out there there's this kid who is now parentless because of what Bourne did."

I thought about this as I was studying the screenplay and I began to see that this thematic overview drives the entire narrative line of the screenplay. It is the foundation of the key incident (the killing of Neski in Berlin) that is now woven throughout the entire film. Once this key incident had been determined, it becomes the structural point to build and to anchor the rest of the film. In the end, Bourne travels to Moscow to apologize to Neski's daughter, thus atoning for his sins.

At this point, Gilroy said, he had to make some distinctions. First, the agents from Treadstone, the secret CIA assassination squad, were like "soldiers and their assignments were specific and precise. That was the distinction. The people that Treadstone killed were also 'soldiers' of some sort or another. But Neski's wife was collateral damage. She wasn't supposed to be there. And Bourne's improvised solution to this—the murder-suicide—added a whole other dimension to the tragedy of it." Gilroy continued. "I've known a few people who are the children of suicide and it's a shadow that follows them always. There were, no doubt, many people that Jason Bourne could find to apologize to, but this Neski construction came about because I needed the apology to have some possibility of hope to it. It needed to be more than just, 'I'm sorry.'

"I wanted him to actually *give* something, so it wasn't just some selfish grab for atonement. And Bourne knows that if he can find their daughter, he can at least make one thing better. And when I understood that, I jumped to the end and sketched that final scene, which came very, very quickly. It felt locked in—solid from the first pass. I knew I had the ultimate landmark to navigate the film toward. And that's when the whole movie opened up."

I asked Gilroy how he structured the sequence in Berlin in terms of Bourne's memory. I know that in my own life I've had similar experiences where something happened a long, long time ago and I had no recollection of the incident or, at best, only a vague, fleeting image of it. Then, one day, I would find myself in a certain, similar situation and suddenly remember a tiny piece of fragmented memory of what happened at that particular time or place. Memory stirs something buried so deep that it can be stimulated either by a situation, a line of dialogue, or even the tea leaves left at the bottom of the cup, like Marcel Proust in *Remembrance of Things Past.*

The killing of Neski and his wife is the foundation of the story line. It is this journey of discovery that literally holds the film together. It is the source, the hub of the story line from which all things flow. Once Gilroy figured this out, then he began to weave certain fragments of this key incident throughout the film to jog Bourne's memory. That's why the fragmented dream sequence that opens *The Bourne Supremacy* is so important to the film.

It opens in a dream: inside a car; rain on the windshield, the sound of windshield wipers scraping across the windows, a misty yellow light from the hotel across the street, muffled sounds, fragmented images. We watch this unfolding in a dream with splintered, abrupt visuals, just out of the reach of consciousness.

Bourne wakes with a start and tries to clear his head. Tries to remember and cannot. Marie attempts to comfort him, but can't. We're in Goa, India. Then, we cut to Berlin. Night. A break-in. We don't know exactly what's happening as we watch two men break into an office and plant plastic explosives in the basement. The lights go out. Shots are fired. And at CIA headquarters in Langley, VA., under the command of Pamela Landy, there is chaos.

We cut back to Goa. Marie takes the opportunity to leaf through Bourne's journal. It is a good way of showing us what little we know about Bourne. Along with Bourne's handwritten notations of streets, cities, various fragments, one entry stands out: "Who am I?" Which is what *The Bourne Supremacy* is all about.

Bourne finishes his run along the beach in Goa and we watch the arrival of the Russian, Kirill (Karl Urban), who is hunting Bourne. And at the CIA, the names of Bourne and Treadstone have popped up and Pamela Landy is determined to find out what's going on—after all, two of her agents have been killed. Back in Goa, Kirill spots Bourne and a wild chase ensues resulting in the death of Marie. That incident leads us to the Plot Point at the end of Act I.

Bourne is determined to find out what's going on and who is responsible. At this moment, it appears that this is going to be a revenge film. Bourne buries the mementos of Marie and travels to Naples, determined to find out the who and why of what's happening. He is stopped, questioned, escapes, learns the identity of Treadstone, and, after the incident in Munich, travels to Berlin where he literally comes "face to face" with Pamela Landy. That is the Mid-Point.

In the Second Half of Act II he discovers Abbott (Brian Cox) is responsible for planting Bourne's fingerprints at the crime scene in Berlin. After Abbott's confession and suicide at the end of Act II, there's only one thing left for Bourne to do. He takes responsibility for his actions and boards the train for Moscow seeking Neski's daughter. It is a time for redemption. After an amazing car chase through the streets of Moscow, Bourne finally finds the young woman he has sought, asks her forgiveness, and walks away.

That's the structure of the film. Lean, clean, and tight, with a thematic foundation that unifies the elements of time and memory within the context of a fast-paced action film. It's an extraordinary film, a great example of moving the screenwriting craft forward in terms of craft and evolution.

And what holds it together are two incidents: one, the inciting incident, the death of Marie. The second is the key incident, Bourne discovering what happened in Berlin and his role in it. What happened in Berlin is the underlying foundation of the script. "Once I had that scene of what happened in Berlin, then I came to work every day ready to write," Tony Gilroy says, and from there it was an issue of infusing time and memory into a story line with skill and visual acuity.

"When I knew what that incident was, I was thinking very practically. What kind of assassination is so special that Bourne would seek some kind of atonement? And what kind of assassination makes this one so special? Those were the questions I had to ask myself and I got the answers almost immediately. It was Bourne's first assassination and there was no record of it at all. No one knew anything about it except Abbott and the Chris Cooper character.

"Intuitively, I recognized that I had tapped into the two things that are really touchstones for this film. First, there are children, and they frame a strong motif through both movies; in *Identity,* the African dictator had his kids on the boat with him and later, when Bourne and Marie are on the run, they see the kids at the farmhouse. Every time children appear, it seems they have a large amount of power in these films. I think that will also figure prominently in the third film as well, *The Bourne Ultimatum.*

"The second thing was that I had killed Marie at the beginning. Isn't that like killing Mrs. Neski? Isn't she as much a victim? Isn't she collateral damage? And that's when I knew things were working, and they were all tied together and I wasn't forcing them. Every single second counts in a film. There isn't one microsecond that doesn't matter. Everything means something. All the flashbacks are there because he's trying to recover the idea of who he is."

The great screenwriter Waldo Salt used to refer to the flashback as a *"flashpresent,"* because the character is in present time, in a particular situation, and something within that environment triggers a past memory. Gilroy agreed and added that "we didn't want to do any flashbacks in *The Bourne Identity.* We tried to do the whole movie without a flashback. So, when I came up with this key incident in *Supremacy,* I thought this is going to be beyond a flashback. Instead, I wanted this to be where the past and present actually collide within the action. I'd written a movie called *Dolores Claiborne* where I'd had a chance to use just about every kind of flashback in the bag, so I wasn't hung up about it. As I was writing I wanted to find a way to isolate each flashback on the page, so I started writing them in italics." I told him I noticed that the first time I read the script and how impressed I was with this writing style. He calls it his "cut to" style. About midway through the second act, when Bourne has commandeered Nicky (Julia Stiles) to gain information on Treadstone and find out why they are after him, he holds a gun to Nicky's head, *"about to pull the trigger—SUDDENLY—FLASHBACK! a moment—a shard—A WOMAN'S FACE—backing away—begging—begging us—begging the camera—PLEADING FOR HER LIFE IN RUSSIAN—this awful blur of desperation and panic—fear—too fast—too panicked"* and then we cut back to present time where we "Jam Back To Bourne—hesitating—stepping back—totally unprepared for the rush of images crowding into his head and before anything else can happen, we cut to" the next scene, in the building where the killing took place at the opening of the film. The script of *The Bourne Supremacy* is an amazing read; it moves like lightning.

Which raises the question, when is it appropriate to use a flashback in the story line? I hear this all the time in most of my workshops and seminars around the world. When does it work best and when is it the most effective?

Flashbacks are a tool, or device, where the screenwriter provides the reader and audience with visual information that he or she cannot incorporate into the screenplay any other way. The purpose of the flashback is simple: it is a technique that *bridges time, place, and action to either reveal information about the character or move the story forward.*

Many times, a writer throws a flashback into the screenplay

because he or she doesn't know how to move the story forward any other way. Sometimes, the screenwriter decides to show something about the main character that could be better stated in dialogue, and, in that case, the flashback only draws attention to itself and becomes intrusive. That doesn't work.

Look at the flashback as a tool that can be used to reveal information about the character or story that you can't reveal any other way. It can reveal *emotional* as well as *physical* information. It can reveal thoughts, memories, or dreams, like what happened in Berlin that Jason Bourne is trying to remember, or the drowning incident in *Ordinary People,* or the memories of the Almásy character (Ralph Fiennes) in *The English Patient,* or Inman (Jude Law) in *Cold Mountain.*

Flashbacks are really a function of *character,* not story. As mentioned, Waldo Salt thought that a flashback should be thought of as a *"flashpresent,"* because the visual image we're seeing is what the character is thinking and feeling at that *present moment,* whether it's a memory, fantasy, event, or anything that illuminates a character's point of view. Study *The Bourne Supremacy* as an ideal example of that. What we see in flashback is shown through the eyes of the character, so we're seeing what he or she is seeing, thinking, or feeling in *present time.* That's what's happening in *The Bourne Supremacy*—most of the action takes place in present time with Bourne seeking to recapture and recall certain memories from his past. The *flashpresent* is anything we see the character thinking and feeling in the present moment, whether a thought, dream, memory, or fantasy, for time has no constraints or limits. In the mind of the main character there is no time and the *flashpresent* could be a particular moment in the past or present, or perhaps even the future.

Which brings us back to the question: when is it appropriate to use or not use a flashback?

There are no "rules" about this, of course. It really depends upon whether you've designed the flashback to be an integral part of the story, like *The Usual Suspects, Memento, The Long Kiss Goodnight* (Shane Black), *Courage Under Fire, The English Patient, Ordinary People,* and *The Bourne Supremacy.* Or, you can show an event that happened and how it happened. A flashback, remember, either moves the story forward or reveals information about the character.

Remember that a screenplay is a story told with pictures. Dialogue only becomes an adjunct to the visual information that moves the story forward or reveals information about the character. It has the same purpose as a flashback. Suppose you want to show an event that has affected your character, and you decide to incorporate it into the script. So you go through the scene and find a nice transition point that leads into the flashback, which naturally results in cutting away from the middle of the scene to insert the flashback.

What happens? In the case of *The Bourne Supremacy* it works beautifully, because Bourne is in a state of amnesia, trying to recall who he is and what happened in Berlin. It is a mystery, so we learn as he learns, reacting to the forces that are working on him in present time.

You can use flashbacks for any number of reasons, but its primary purpose is to bridge time and place and to reveal a past emotional event or physical conflict that affects the character. Sometimes it gives insight and understanding into a character's behavior or solves a past mystery, as in John Sayles' *Lone Star.*

There are times when a flashpresent is effective in giving a visual expression to a thought or expectation or wishful thinking—remember the scene in *True Lies* (James Cameron) where Harry Tasker (Arnold Schwarzenegger) is driving in a Corvette with the used car salesman he thinks is having an affair with his wife and he busts him in the nose? It's only wishful thinking. It's a nice little touch. You can also use the flashback to show how or why an event happened, or maybe flashforward to an event that may or may not happen in the near future. These all are ways to incorporate the *flashback* into your screenplay and *make it work.*

If you do decide to use a flashback, think in terms of the *flashpresent;* ask yourself what is your character thinking or feeling at the present moment? If you can get into your character's head and find some thought, memory, or event which reflects on the present moment, try to *show* how it affects your character. That way, you have an optimal advantage. If need be, go into your character's *Circle of Being* (see Chapter 7) and see what you can find.

Some films incorporate the flashback as a *bookend* to their main story line, meaning they open the script with a present incident or event, then flash back to the beginning of the story, and then end it in present time. This can be very effective. Take a look at: *The Bridges of Madison County* (Richard LaGravenese), *Sunset Boulevard* (Charles Brackett and Billy Wilder), *Annie Hall, Citizen Kane,* and *Pulp Fiction.*

Once you complete the preparation work on your screenplay, then you can determine how you want to write it, either in a linear or nonlinear form.

Which brings us to the actual writing of the screenplay.

TWO

WRITING THE SCREENPLAY

9

Structuring Act I

> Howard: "This is not the finish line, my friends. This is the start of the race. The *future* is the finish line. . . ."
>
> —Gary Ross
> *Seabiscuit*

The hardest thing about writing is knowing what to write. The second hardest is figuring out the best way to write it.

That's what is coming up next in the screenwriting process. As we shall see, the blank sheet of paper is not only the beginning of a new journey, but also the end of a journey. We've gone from the necessary preparation needed to write the screenplay to actually getting ready to write the screenplay.

Up until this point we've taken a three-sentence idea and expanded it into a four-page treatment focusing on dramatic structure. We've isolated the ending, the beginning, Plot Point I, and Plot Point II. We've done character biographies, defined our character's dramatic need, determined his or her point of view and attitude and whether he or she has changed or gone through some kind of emotional transformation in life. We've done any required research on the subject or the historical times in which he or she lived.

So, now what? What's the next step in the screenwriting process?

Structuring Act I.

Now that we have the form of the story line, we can begin to lay out the content. Act I is a unit, or block, of dramatic action. It begins on page one and goes to the plot point at the end of Act I. It is approximately thirty pages long, and held together with the dramatic context known as the Set-Up. We have to set up our story, introduce our characters, define their relationships, and establish the dramatic premise, what the story is about. The context, remember, is the space that holds something in place, like the space inside a glass that holds the *content* in place. The context doesn't change; only the content changes.

Act I holds the content—the characters, dialogue, locations, scenes, sequences—in place. Everything in this Act I unit of dramatic action sets up the story: the characters, the situation, the dramatic premise. That's why Act I is so important; everything relates to setting up your story and characters. It is a unit of dramatic action that takes us from the beginning to the Plot Point at the end of Act I. It is a whole as well as a part, therefore you must "design" it carefully.

Aristotle talks about the three unities of dramatic action: time, place, and action. So this first unit of action, Act I, establishes what the story is about and who it's about. *Seabiscuit* is a good example. Here, we have a true story about four characters who are influenced by the times they live in, the Great Depression of the 1930s in America. They worked together as a team to create a story that inspired an entire nation. The first thing Gary Ross, the writer-director, had to establish was the time in which the story takes place. The story begins with a shot of the Model T Ford, and the understanding that the automobile will soon revolutionize the culture and ethics of American history. Here's the opening description and narration from the screenplay:

```
FADE IN: ON A MODEL T.

Not so much as a car as a symbol. Over the frozen,
grainy, black and white image, we HEAR the voice
that has become our history...

                    NARRATOR
      They called it the car for Everyman.
      Ford himself called it a car for the
      "great multitude." It was functional
```

> and simple, like your sewing machine or your cast-iron stove....For the first time in history, a worker didn't have to go to the parts—the parts came to him. Instead of building the whole car, he only had to build the bumper... or the gearshift...or the door handle....Of course, the real invention wasn't the car—it was the assembly line that built it. Pretty soon, other businesses had borrowed the same techniques: seamstresses become button-sewers...furniture makers became knob-turners...It was the beginning and the end of imagination all at the same time.

In this one scene, using voiceover narration along with stills, old photographs, and newsreel footage, we have sketched the times, the place, and the situation, as well as setting up the future influence of the automobile. It provides the backdrop and dramatic situation to the story and establishes the forces that will change a nation and thus set the stage for the story.

That's all found in the opening few pages of the screenplay. You may think that because *Seabiscuit* is a true story, nonfiction, that it does not follow the general rules of fiction. Not so. If you look at the opening pages of Lawrence Kasdan's classic *Body Heat,* the first few words on page one describe the entire film: "Flames in a night sky." Ned Racine (William Hurt) is established as a careless, shoddy, incompetent attorney searching for a quick score. In the first ten pages, he meets Matty Walker (Kathleen Turner), then we see him searching for her, and finally he finds her. They have a drink together and she agrees to let him come back to her place (nothing's going to happen, she insists) to see "her collection of wind chimes."

The sexual energy between them is strong, almost palpable, but when it's time for him to leave, he pauses, hesitant, reluctant. He wants her. He walks to his car and stands staring at Matty, visible through the large windows that border the front door. The music swells, lust rages through him, and, unable to stop, he charges right through the glass, takes her in his arms, and in the throes of passion makes love to her on the floor.

That whole unit of Act I is set up in the actions of the characters: they meet, he tracks her down, they have a drink, go back to her house to look at her wind chimes, and the Plot Point at the end of Act I is when they have sex. Act I is approximately a twenty- to thirty-page unit of dramatic action.

Lawrence Kasdan, the screenwriter/director of *Body Heat,* sets up the story from the very first words of the screenplay. *Body Heat* is the story of lust, passion, and betrayal, and everything in Act I establishes, or sets up, the characters and the story.

When you set out to structure Act I, the first thing you have to establish is the dramatic context. You're setting up characters, premise, and situation. Who is the main character, what is your story about, and what is the situation, the circumstances surrounding the action? You're building a direction here, a line of development that goes from the opening shot to Plot Point I.

Annie Hall is a great example of this. When the script begins, Alvy Singer (Woody Allen) stands facing the camera doing a standup monologue. At the very end he mentions that "Annie and I broke up and I—I still can't get my mind around that. You know, I—I keep sifting the pieces of the relationship through my mind and examining my life and trying to figure out where did the screw-up come. You know, a year ago we were . . . in love. . . ." The entire film is based around that little statement. What were the "pieces of the relationship"? And where "did the screw-up come"? What we see during the film are the answers to those questions.

What do you need to set up your story? Is it setting off on a weeklong excursion of the Santa Barbara wine country as in *Sideways* (Alexander Payne and Jim Taylor)? Is it Jack's (Thomas Haden Church) impending marriage, or the effect of Miles' (Paul Giamatti) divorce that needs to be established? Is it about Jill Clayburgh's marriage in *An Unmarried Woman*? Is it establishing that E.T. has missed the spaceship home and is now stuck on an alien planet? Are you setting up a strong-willed individual like Charles Howard (Jeff Bridges) in *Seabiscuit,* or setting up the context of Middle-Earth, Gandalf, and the Hobbits in *The Lord of the Rings*?

It's up to you to decide what you want to show, and only then can you figure out how to show it. But for right now it's important for you to define it and describe it.

How do you go about structuring Act I?

First, we want to create the content in such a way that it can be anchored within the context of Act I, the Set-Up. There are several ways to do this: sitting at the computer describing each scene in a few words, or outlining various scenes on a legal pad, or laying out a beat sheet. What I caution against doing is simply creating a list of scenes they want to write in a numerical order. It may work for some people but I try to keep the writing process as open in idea and content as possible, so for me, that doesn't work at all. It's too limiting and there's not much flexibility.

I like to be flexible because I want to be able to change and manipulate the scenes I'm writing, especially in this part of the process. So I use cards to outline each scene, 3 × 5 cards to be specific, though any size will do. Over the years I've learned that fourteen cards work best, and if you write one scene per card (though that's a contradiction which will be explained later), you can lay out the content of Act I, from the opening scene or sequence to the plot point at the end of Act I.

People ask "why fourteen cards? Can't I have twelve or sixteen or seventeen?" My response is based on my own experience—when I look at the cards, I can tell whether there's too much material for the Act, or whether there's not enough. If a writer is laying out the structure of Act I and has only thirteen cards it's typically not enough to set up the material. And, if you have fifteen cards it's usually too much material for Act I. Fourteen cards just work; it's an effective tool for structuring Act I. If you don't believe me, try it and see what happens.

Now you're ready to lay out the structure of Act I. Remember that the first definition of structure is "to build something, or put something together." That's what we're doing now. Take a handful of 3 × 5 cards and start writing out the scenes that you know you want in your story, one card per scene. It doesn't have to be in chronological order, either. Where does your story open? With your character arriving at the employer's trailer, like Ennis in *Brokeback Mountain*? Or does it open with a flashback like *The Bourne Supremacy*? Suppose you want a continuous line of action—maybe you'll have all three of your main characters waking up in the morning, as in *The Hours*? Or, maybe you'll want to set up the character and situation like Alan Ball does in *American Beauty,* with Lester's voiceover saying: "My name is Lester Burnham, I'm forty-two years old and in a year I'll be dead. Of course, I don't know that yet. This is the street where I live . . ." Maybe you want to open your script with your character at the office at the start of the day, or maybe you want to write an inciting incident (the incident that sets the story in motion; see Chapter 8 in *Screenplay*) where you show a crime being committed, or a murder or break-in.

Write the idea of the opening scene on a 3 × 5 card; not the entire scene, just a few words about the scene. Free-associate. You should already know Card 1, the opening, and Card 14, Plot Point I. So you only need twelve more cards. Start throwing down ideas for the scenes you think should be in Act I. Don't think about it too much. *Use only a few words per card, no more.* So many times, I've had students write the entire scene on the front and back side of the card and when they start writing the screenplay they simply transpose the scene from the card to the scene on the page. It doesn't work. At this point in the process, you still want to remain open to receive any new thoughts or ideas that may spring into your awareness. Otherwise you're going to be too self-restricting and critical in the creative process.

Then write the next scene on another card, again using no more than a few words. Then the next card. And the next card. Do it until you feel a sense of completion about the scenes and sequences you have on the cards. For example, if your story is about an American journalist on assignment in Paris who falls in love with a young woman, has an intense and passionate affair, and then leaves for home, promising to return, your first card might read, "arrives in Paris." The second card, "checks into hotel; calls home"; third card, "meets assignment editor"; fourth card, "briefed on his subject and assignment"; fifth card, "sees subject at official reception"; sixth card, "arrives at the Ministry of Culture"; seventh card, "interviews subject"; eighth card: "sees a person he is attracted to"; and so on, scene by scene, card by card, leading to the plot point at the end of Act I (card 14) when he "meets the young woman" he will fall in love with. If you are in doubt about whether to write down a scene on a card, do it. When in doubt, write it down. When you've finished, you may have ten, or twelve, or fourteen, or eighteen cards. However many cards you have on this first go-around, you'll want to go through them until you end up with fourteen cards.

Next, lay out the cards one by one, from the first scene to the Plot Point at the end of Act I. Free-associate. What happens? What happens next? What happens then? These are magic words as they will spur new thoughts and ideas into the creative process. If need be, you may want to add a word or two of dialogue on some of the cards to help smooth out the flow of the action. Your main character should be in most of the scenes on the cards. Don't get *too* specific; it's better to be vague and general at this point as you lay out the action in broad strokes. You can do it all in fourteen cards.

Take a look at *Sideways.* Card 1: Miles late to pick up Jack. Card 2: Miles driving. Card 3: Miles meets Jack's fiancée's family. Card 4: On the freeway to Santa Barbara. Card 5: Miles and Jack discuss their trip. Card 6: Jack on phone with fiancée. Card 7: Miles visits mother. Card 8: Dinner with mother. Card 9: Miles takes money from mother. Card 10: Miles and Jack sneak out. Card 11: Jack's need—to get laid. Card 12: Reach Santa Rosa. Card 13: Miles teaches Jack about wine tasting. Card 14: Miles meets Maya. That's Plot Point I.

If you want an action sequence, simply write "chase sequence," or "robbery sequence," or "wedding sequence," or "fight sequence," or "race sequence." You don't need any more than that at this point in the process.

Resist the temptation to fill out both sides of a 3 × 5 card. You don't need to write extensive description in the scene or even include dialogue. As mentioned, this is not the time to start writing the screenplay. When you do the cards, do the cards. When you write the screenplay, write the screenplay. One's an apple. The other is an orange.

Screenwriting is a *process;* it changes constantly; it can't be too defined or rigid. It must be left free and open, unlimited.

Do the cards for Act I. Free-associate. Lay down your thoughts quickly. You can always change them later. When you finish (it will usually take a few hours), read the cards over and over again, smoothing out the words to read easily from one scene to the next. Change any card you want; shuffle the cards around if necessary to make the story line read better. Each card should move the story forward, step by step, scene by scene.

Many times, people jump into writing of the first scene of the screenplay but don't really know where they're going. Most of the time they don't even know where their character is coming from or going to. They'll spend ten or twelve pages rambling, not knowing what's wrong, only that it seems "boring and trite" and doesn't seem to be going anywhere. They muddle their way through those first few scenes trying to latch onto some kind of direction to hop into the story line.

The way to avoid this potential problem is by creating a back story. *The back story is what happens to your main character a day, a week, or an hour before your story begins.*

You know the first scene or sequence of your screenplay. If you look at your opening scene or sequence, what happens to your main character *just before* that scene begins? It could be an hour before, or a day before, or a week before. Did something happen to your character that might add some emotional stress and tension to that first scene? What was it? How was your character affected? See if you can define the specific incident, episode, or event that took place. Was it an accident? An argument? Some kind of emergency? What happened? When, how, and where did it take place? And most important, what is the emotional or physical impact upon your character?

One of my favorite film openings is Antonioni's classic *L'Eclisse (The Eclipse)*. The opening shot is of a large living room. The drapes are drawn, the lights are on. A man sits on a chair, resting his chin in his hand. A woman (Monica Vitti) stands idly looking at him, then turns away as if she can't bear to look anymore. Silence, broken only by a little fan moving back and forth, back and forth, in the foreground. She wanders idly, wants to say something, stops herself, and continues looking lost and forlorn.

A few words are spoken, then silence once again. For more than four and a half minutes, the silence continues. Only then do we realize that there is nothing more to be said. They've been in a relationship, it's over, they've talked all night and there's nothing left to say.

The conversation that took place before the story began is the back story. The back story can be anything, as long as there's some kind of emotional or dramatic aspect to it. A back story, for example, is not preparing for a date and the car won't start and you can't reach the person who's expecting you. It's not about your character going to the market shopping for groceries. I'm talking about the kind of incident, episode, or event that impacts your character so he or she enters that first scene or sequence with some kind of emotional or dramatic burden.

Here's an example of a back story taken from my own life. Several years ago, I had a wonderful cat named Rosie. She was then about seventeen years old and was beginning to have some serious health problems. One night, I had a very important dinner meeting. I had been looking forward to it for some time and there was a lot riding on the project for me. The producer, director, two story executives, and I were going to meet at an exclusive restaurant in Santa

Monica. As I was getting ready for the meeting, I heard a strange sound and noticed Rosie having a difficult time breathing. I knew immediately she needed emergency treatment.

I finished dressing as fast as I could, grabbed Rosie, and rushed her to the emergency hospital on the way to the restaurant. I called the restaurant and told them I would be detained for a while. When Rosie's exam was finished, the vet told me she was in serious condition and I needed to leave her there for a twenty-four-hour medical observation.

I walked out of the vet's with more than a little trepidation as I rushed to the meeting in Santa Monica. Now, what do you suppose I was thinking about through most of the meeting?

That's the power and effect of the back story. If you have a strong back story for your character, you can start your screenplay at the very beginning, page one word one. The back story allows you to jump into the story line from the very first words on the page. So, to write an effective back story, ask yourself some basic questions. What happens to your main character a day, a week, or an hour before the story begins? Can you describe it? Articulate it? How does it affect your character, either emotionally or physically, in the first scene?

An effective back story can influence the entire screenplay. Look at the opening sequence of *The Shawshank Redemption:* Andy Dufresne is sitting in a car drinking, pulls out a gun, tries to load it as he slugs down a bottle of whiskey. He gets out of the car, then staggers toward the house, gun in hand. What do you think the back story would be? Probably when he found out his wife was having an affair with a tennis pro. It's an event that impacts the main character and sets up the inciting incident that opens the film. He intends to kill his wife and her lover and it is this scene that sets the story in motion.

In a screenplay, you've got to grab the reader immediately, from page one, word one, like *The Royal Tenenbaums, The Matrix, The Lord of the Rings,* or *Body Heat.* You don't have time to find out what that first scene is about; you've got to *know* what it's about.

Because if you don't know, who does?

The back story helps you jump into your script from the Fade In. It generates a strong sense of dramatic or comedic tension immediately. So what happens to *your* character, a day, a week, or an hour before the story begins? What incident, episode, or event is working on your character when the story begins?

Suppose your script opens with your main character arriving at work on Monday morning. The back story might be that on Friday afternoon your character went to his or her boss and asked for a raise and the boss said no.

Your character goes home and suffers through a long weekend. You can imagine what your character is thinking or feeling before the story begins. Then you open your script on a Monday morning as your character arrives at work. Imagine her getting off the elevator: Is she grim and tight-lipped, or jocular and carefree? Or is she wearing a cool and personable demeanor, showing her associates at work that everything is okay, but it's only a mask because underneath that façade are the seeds of anger, resentment, and low self-worth bubbling up to the surface. And somewhere along the line they're going to erupt.

That's the force of a good back story; it allows you to enter the action from page one, word one. This way, you know the purpose of the opening scene so you don't have to go "searching" for it, trying to figure out what's going to happen. That opening scene or sequence always seems to be the most difficult to write. Knowing your back story can help you achieve the maximum dramatic value from the very first page of the screenplay.

One of my students was writing a story about a stage director preparing her first theatrical production off-Broadway. My student was having difficulty defining the emotional state of her main character and didn't know where or how to open her story. Should she open at a rehearsal or opening night? Every time she sketched the opening, it was wordy, expository, filled with unnecessary dialogue and meaningless conflict.

She didn't know what to do. I told her to write up a back story and include something in the main character's marriage that might influence the action of the play within the screenplay. When I asked her what the story of the play her character was directing was about, she didn't know. Well, I said, if she didn't know, who did?

So she went home and wrote up a character essay about the relationship of the main character to her husband—where they met, how long they'd been married, and the emotional forces that might be working on the main character when the story begins. Then she wrote up a back story, which literally opened up the entire screenplay. What she "found" in her back story was this: the marriage was in trouble and the main character's husband wanted to start a family, but she wasn't ready for that step. Her career was just getting off the ground and she was afraid she would lose this opportunity. When the chance came for her to direct the off-Broadway play, she jumped at it. Her husband became jealous and resentful, and the gap between the main character and husband grew wider.

The back story takes place about a week before the play's opening (the opening night was Plot Point I) and she knows it's just not working. Tense and frustrated, the director gets into "another argument" with her husband about starting a family just before the final week of rehearsals begin. Angry and upset, she storms out of the apartment and jumps onto the subway. As she makes her way uptown, she gets an insight into why the play isn't working and understands what she has to do to fix it. She races to the theater to meet the actors in rehearsal.

That was the back story. Now, my student opened her screenplay with the main character getting off the subway and rushing to the rehearsal with a newfound awareness.

The back story allowed her to open her screenplay with strong dramatic tension. She was able to "leap" into her story line from the opening shot and didn't have to search for her story in the first few scenes of the screenplay. She went from not knowing how the story opened to knowing exactly what she had to do to open it dramatically, effectively, and visually.

If your screenplay has a "play within a play," like a radio show, a soap opera, a play, or a movie, you must be able to describe its premise in a few sentences. That way, you can structure a progression of the story within the story to emotionally influence the main character's dramatic need. This is especially true if you're writing a nonlinear screenplay like *The English Patient* or *The Hours.* In *The English Patient,* you have two stories moving the story forward: the one in the past, the love story between Almásy (Ralph Fiennes) and Katharine (Kristin Scott Thomas), and the one in the present, when Almásy is wounded and swathed in bandages. Both stories are structured linearly, from beginning to end, with parts of each interwoven into a continuous narrative line.

That's how the back story can help you design the first scene or sequence so you begin your screenplay from page one. What happens to your main character a day, a week, or an hour before your story begins? Remember, you've only got about ten pages to grab your reader.

Sometimes you'll discover that you like the back story so much that you want to open your screenplay with it. That's fine, but if you do this you still need to write another back story to lead into your new opening scene with a sense of strong dramatic tension. And there are times when the writer writes one back story, likes it, then writes another one, likes that one, then writes another back story, and soon the original opening of the script becomes the Plot Point at the end of Act I. If that happens, just go with it. Structure is flexible, it's like a tree in the wind that bends but does not break.

So, if that happens and you decide to open your screenplay with what was once one or several back stories, just write up another back story so you'll always know where your character is coming from. Actors do this all the time; before an actor enters a scene he has to know were he's coming from, what the purpose of the scene is, and where they're going when the scene is over. That's just good preparation.

Do the same with the back story.

Sometimes the back story will become part of the screenplay, sometimes not. It depends on the individual script.

THE EXERCISE

Act I is a unit of dramatic action between twenty and thirty pages long that is held together with the dramatic context known as the Set-Up. Remember, you are setting up your story, your characters, and the relationship between the characters.

Then structure the action of Act I on fourteen 3 × 5 cards.

You already know the opening scene or sequence and the Plot Point at the end of Act I, so you know card number one and card fourteen. Start at the beginning of your story and move through the action leading to the Plot Point at the end of Act I. Free-associate. You know where you're going, so all you have to do is get there. Lay the story line out on cards, one scene or sequence per card, using no more than a few words on each card. When you've completed the cards, read them over and over again. Don't change anything until you feel the "urge" to. Then, if you like, change a word here or there, just to make the cards read smoothly and simply. Describe the story line in broad and general strokes.

After you've done the cards, write up the back story. Remember, it will influence the action of the first ten pages. Look at your opening scene. Where does it take place? Describe it. Define it.

When the script opens, where is your character coming from? What has happened to him or her a day, a week, or an hour before the story begins?

Just free-associate. Lay it out, regardless of grammar or punctuation or any plot holes you may have. You might also need to lay out the back story in terms of beginning, middle, and end, or even have to write up a character essay in order to feel comfortable about the back story. Do whatever needs to be done, because if you don't know the story, who does?

The back story can usually be written in a couple of pages, but if you need more, use them. It doesn't matter how long or how short it is. The back story is a tool in the screenwriting process, one of the many that lead to a dynamic and forceful opening.

10

The First Ten Pages

```
Mrs. Mulwray (The phony): "My husband, I be-
lieve, is seeing another woman."
                              —Robert Towne
                               Chinatown
```

During the two years or so that I headed the story department at Cinemobile Systems, I read more than two thousand screenplays and almost a hundred novels. I read so much I couldn't see straight. There was always a large pile of scripts on my desk and no matter how fast I read I was always seventy scripts behind. Every time I thought I was caught up, my boss would walk in and tell me a new batch of submissions was coming in and that I "better hurry" if I didn't want to fall too far behind. That meant I could expect about a hundred screenplays to arrive in the next few days.

I looked for any excuse to avoid reading a script. If a script came in with a one-page synopsis, I read the synopsis only. If the writer told me the story when he or she submitted the script, then I read the first few pages, a page or two in the middle, and the last three. If I liked the story line, or the situation, and the way it was written, I read the whole thing; if I didn't, I tossed it in the return file—in this case the trash can. If I had too much to eat for lunch, or if I had too much to drink, I would lean back in my chair, read the first few pages, prop it on my lap, turn off the phones, and take a ten- or fifteen-minute nap.

My job, as I was constantly reminded, was "to find material." And yet most of the scripts I read were not very good. Either they were derivative of other movies, or old TV series, or the initial idea was simply a one-liner, meaning the entire screenplay was only about one thing—similar to the later *Analyze This* (Peter Tolan, Harold Ramis, and Kenneth Lonergan), which is only about what happens in the psychiatrist's office and the character's reaction to that, or *Four Weddings and a Funeral* (Richard Curtis), which is merely a cute and clever boy-meets-girl story. More often than not, the scripts were thin, flimsy, and weak and I had seen it all before. That was the "good stuff"; the rest of the material was just poorly written.

I began to see what Jean Renoir had pointed out to me so many times before: writing for the screen is a craft that occasionally rises to the level of art. To write a good screenplay, you have to tell the story in pictures, not words. As I was learning, the art of screen-writing is in finding places where silence works better than words.

Of the more than two thousand screenplays I read, I found only forty worth submitting to our financial partners for possible production. Why so few? As a writer taking a much-needed break from screenwriting, I was curious as to what made these screenplays better than all the others I had read.

Over the next few years, I watched as studios and producers picked up many of the scripts I had found and made them into movies. Of those forty scripts I had selected, some thirty-seven films eventually were made, including classics like *The Godfather* (Francis Ford Coppola and Mario Puzo), *American Graffiti* (George Lucas), *Jeremiah Johnson* (John Milius, Edward Anhalt, and David Rayfiel), *Alice Doesn't Live Here Anymore* (Robert Getchell), *The Wind and the Lion* (John Milius), and *Taxi Driver* (Paul Schrader), along with many others.

What made these forty screenplays better than the other one thousand nine hundred sixty I had read? I began studying these scripts, and soon began to enlarge my own understanding about the nature and craft of screenwriting. After a while, I began to separate certain styles into specific genres: action-adventure, romantic comedy, science fiction, drama, mystery, and detective stories, and I began to explore how they were put together. I started understanding the dynamics of the sequence, a series of scenes connected by one single idea with a definite beginning, middle, and end.

While I was still in this observational mode, I was given the opportunity to teach a screenwriting course at the Sherwood Oaks Experimental College. I had never taught any kind of a class before and the memories I had of my own teachers were not very flattering. The only effective models I had as teachers were Jean Renoir and one of my English professors at Berkeley during the '60's—they were teachers who sparked my desire to learn. And I remembered something Renoir had once said, that a good teacher is someone who teaches the student to see the relationship between things. Could I do that? Did I want to do that? And the bigger question: What would I teach and how would I go about doing it? The only thing I could do, I realized, was to go into my own writing and reading experience and share my observations about the craft of screenwriting.

What did I look for as a reader? First, I noticed the style of writing—whether it was active, written in present tense, with terse, visual descriptions. The style had to be established from page one, word one. For example, here's a brief description of a run-down building that is a good illustration of a strong, active, visual style: "Bright sun beating through holes in a rusted tin roof. The dirt floor has been dug up. A deep hole, lined with plastic sheeting has been unearthed. There's a FOOTLOCKER open to one side." That kind of visual description grabs my attention immediately.

The next thing I learned is that as a reader, I have to know *what* the story is about in the first ten pages. What is the *dramatic premise?* It could be as simple as the phony Mrs. Mulwray's line in the first few pages of *Chinatown:* "My husband, I believe, is seeing another woman." The answer to that question, of course, results in the uncovering of a huge water scandal and several murders.

I also needed to know *who* the story is about. *Who* is the main character? Then I can determine whether the action and characters have been "set up" within the first few pages and a strong dramatic context established. In *Chinatown,* Jake Gittes is clearly the man in charge.

The third thing that has to be established is the *dramatic situation,* the circumstances surrounding the action. In *Chinatown,* the dramatic situation is shown and talked about within the first ten pages: Los Angeles is in the middle of a severe drought and water has become a scarce commodity. Jake Gittes is a private investigator hired by the wife of a prominent man suspected of having an affair, and her husband is the head of the Water and Power Department of Los Angeles. All three things: main character, dramatic premise, and dramatic situation are related and set up the story within these first ten pages.

It wasn't too long before I discovered that I could tell whether or not a script was working within the first ten pages. If I didn't know what was going on during that unit of action, I found my interest wandering and I began to look for ways to stop reading.

You've only got about ten pages to grab the attention of your reader or audience. It is the screenwriter's responsibility to set up the first ten pages of the screenplay so the essential story information is established. These first ten pages need to be designed with skill, economy, and imagination. You don't have time to wander around searching for your story. If you haven't involved your readers within the first ten pages, you've lost them. You must set up and establish three major elements in those first ten pages:

Number one: *Who* is your story about—that is, *who* is the main character? Number two: *what* is the dramatic premise—*what* is your story about? Number three: *what* is the dramatic situation—the circumstances surrounding the action? In other words, what forces are working on your main character when the story begins? Once you determine *how* you're going to incorporate these three elements, then you can design and structure the first ten pages as a unit, or block, of dramatic action.

What is your opening scene? Where does it take place? Is it a dialogue scene or an action scene, or simply a series of shots to establish a tone? Do you want to evoke a mood, like *Cold Mountain* or

Gladiator (David Franzoni, John Logan, and William Nicholson)? Or do you want to establish the texture of a character, time, or place, like *American Beauty, The Lord of the Rings: The Return of the King,* or *Gandhi*? Or do you want to set up the characters and situation like *Y Tu Mamá También* (Alfonso and Carlos Cuarón)? Or, maybe you want to open it with an exciting action sequence like *The Matrix* or *The Bourne Supremacy*? Do you want the opening to be loud and noisy or tense and suspenseful? Do you want a car driving through the deserted city streets at night, or a man strolling through a crowded park with a child on a beautiful Sunday afternoon?

What is your main character doing? Where is he or she coming from? What is the back story? Where is he or she going to? Think about it. Define it. Articulate it. Structure it.

If need be, take that first scene or sequence and structure it into individual and distinct parts: the beginning, middle, and end. How? Start with a separate sheet of paper. Then, take the general line of action, like a chase or wedding sequence or just getting out of bed in the morning, and list the activities that happen at the very beginning of the scene or sequence. Remember that scenes are made up of shots and connected by two things: place and time. If you change either, you need a new scene. (If need be, see Chapters 10 and 11 in *Screenplay*.)

Do the same with the middle of the scene, and the end—just list the number of activities that occur during the scene or sequence. For example, if the first scene takes place in an office, the beginning might show your character preparing for the meeting or putting together the presentation that occurs in the office. He or she might be working with an associate as they go through the material for the presentation. Or, you might show the character at home after an argument with a friend, lover, or spouse, going through the material before he or she leaves for work.

Maybe your character is catching a flight later in the day on a business trip and we meet him as he's packing. Maybe he has a family and we see him getting ready for his day, like the opening of *American Beauty*, or waking up on a morning that may have a significant impact on his life, like getting the lab results regarding a serious illness.

The way to approach the scene is to define your character's dramatic need. Is this a scene that is going to move the story forward or reveal aspects of the character? What is the purpose of the scene in relation to the story? Remember that we're striving for conflict, either internal, external, or some combination of the two. What is your character doing before the scene begins and what does he do or where does he go after the scene? What happens at the beginning and end of the scene? At this point you might want to sketch in some visual aspects and details you could use in the scene.

As an example, here is the inciting incident of an original screenplay titled *After Life*, a sci-fi film set three hundred years in the future in which a cosmic event sets into motion a catastrophic reaction. The main character, a recent widower, reluctantly accepts command of the mission that is forced upon him. He is the person who is best equipped to deal with the emergency. Here are the opening scenes.

```
WE OPEN IN BLACK:

A PENCIL SCRATCHES ON PAPER, and we hear:

                    LIGHTER (V.O.)
     Looking back, it's easy to see that our
     world has changed from what it once was.
     But what happened, and how it happened...
     That's the mystery.

                                        FADE INTO:

EXT. DEEP SPACE

Black, forbidding, unknown...Then, a velvety
RIPPLE reveals the COSMOS—BILLIONS OF STARS back-
dropped with brilliant hues of GASES, STARDUST
and NEBULAE. Spiralling into position, we watch
as TWO NEUTRON STARS SPIN, conjoined in their
final nanoseconds of life, and IMPLODE IN A SPEC-
TACULAR DISPLAY OF LIGHT AND MATTER.

Alpha to Omega: the beginning and the end.
```

LIGHTER (V.O.)
What quirky little twist of fate managed to tick the clock one step closer to the end? Well...

WHITE OUT:

A MASSIVE EXPLOSION erupts, thrusting a tremendous amount of destructive energy ripping through the blackest night at the speed of light.
A phenomenon known as a GAMMA RAY BURST.

LIGHTER (V.O.) (cont'd)
That was a long time ago, back at the beginning.

THE CAMERA TREMBLES as giant pulsations of deadly radiation sweep through space, burning nebulae, exploding stars—literally gobbling up everything in its path. Layers of gases, clouds, matter and planetary bodies vanish with its passing. It travels thousands of light years, leaving an unbelievable path of destruction.

EXT. PLUTO

PLUTO, glittering in the distant light of the sun, travels quietly along its orbit. The deadly gamma rays approach our solar system. SUDDENLY the tiny PLANET is OBLITERATED, blown out of existence as you or I might blow out a candle.

FADE TO BLACK:

FADE IN:

INT. NASA SPACE FACILITY, ARIZONA—DAY

SUPER TITLE:

FEBRUARY 23, 2323

A BLINKING RED LIGHT flashes silently. We PULL BACK and gaze upon a blank computer screen.

A dazzling display of computer symbols BLASTS onto the screen; the WATCHER PROGRAM boots up and we see a graphic display of our Solar System. But something's out of whack; something's missing.

```
IT'S PLUTO.

The orbital trajectory remains the same—but there
is no planet there. PLUTO IS GONE. VANISHED.

DR. TRAVIS LIGHTER sits at the computer working
the program. Mid-forties, trim and athletic, a
space scientist, he works the program impa-
tiently. There's a glitch and he doesn't handle
them very well.

He pushes a button on the intercom.

                    LIGHTER
      Sudhi!

                  SUDHI (V.O.)
      Yes, Dr. Lighter.

He stands, sighs deeply, walks to the large win-
dow at the mountains standing guard over the
brilliant desert wilderness on the edge of subur-
ban Phoenix. Stately saguaro cacti dot the sandy,
rocky landscape in the mid-morning sun.

                LIGHTER (cont'd)
      The overnight in? I think we've got an-
      other glitch in Watcher.

                  SUDHI (V.O.)
      Yes...but you're late—again. Do I tell
      them you're coming? Or do I tell them
      that you're just late—again?

Chagrined, Lighter gives her a look.

INT. LAB CORRIDOR—DAY

Lighter and SUDHI PANARJEE, Lighter's assistant,
attractive, mid-thirties, walk quickly down the
hallway. And we

                                        CUT INTO:
```

Those are the first two pages of the screenplay. Every scene is usually about one thing—one piece of information that is needed to keep the story moving forward, or to reveal something we need to know about the main character. In screenwriting parlance, it's called *the reveal.* There is a reveal in each scene—do you know what it is? Can you define it? Is it revealed through action or character? *Character,* remember, is who the person is in terms of their human and moral behavior; *characterization* is how the character expresses themselves to the world—how they dress, what kind of car they drive, where they live, their taste in art, fashion and music. It's all an expression of who they are.

There's a good screenwriting tool that may help guide you when you're writing the scene: *entering late and getting out early.* William Goldman, the brilliant screenwriter of *Butch Cassidy and the Sundance Kid, All the President's Men, The Princess Bride,* and numerous others, tells a story about where and when to enter a scene. Goldman sets up a hypothetical situation: a reporter is interviewing a subject for a newspaper or magazine article. The beginning shows the reporter preparing for the interview and arriving at the location; the middle has him greeting the subject, getting comfortable, taking out his or her tape recorder, and beginning the interview. The ending is concluding the interview, packing up, thanking the subject, putting on his or her coat, walking to the door, then suddenly remembering something, turning around and saying: "Oh, by the way—one last question." That's the beginning, middle, and end of this hypothetical scene.

Where does the screenwriter enter the scene, Goldman asks? With the reporter arriving? Greeting the subject? The interview in progress? The answer is none of the above. The best place to enter the scene, Goldman says, is at the last possible moment, just before the reveal with the reporter asking: "Oh, one last question." That would be the best place to enter the scene because you can omit all the unnecessary stuff that happens before and focus on what has to be revealed in the scene. *Enter late and get out early.*

There's a great little scene from *Magnolia* where Claudia (Melora Walters) is sitting in a bar and a guy comes up to her and says "Hey." She says "hi." And we cut to Claudia's place as they "stumble into the apartment," do a few lines of coke, and he looks at her and says "So?" and we cut to them having sex.

It's great screenwriting. The audience can fill in the blanks; we know what's happening and don't need it explained. It's a very good example of entering late and getting out early with a beginning, middle, and end.

As you explore your options for writing this first ten-page unit of dramatic action, do you think you'll be able to establish the dramatic premise in this first scene? Or are you going to do it in the fifth scene? Is the premise clear enough in your mind to dramatize it? If you decide to open your script with an action sequence like *The Matrix* or *Close Encounters of the Third Kind* (Steven Spielberg), can you structure the action into a beginning, middle, and end? Or do you want it to be a series of shots like Vincent (Tom Cruise) arriving at LAX in *Collateral*? Or do you want to create an inciting incident to open the script, like the opening of *Basic Instinct, Crimson Tide,* or *The Pianist* (Ronald Harwood)?

These are all creative decisions. You want to choose the most exciting part of the scene or sequence and use that as your starting point. You have to grab your reader's attention. Do you see the first scene done in close shots or in a master shot of the entire location, like a restaurant or living room? Your intention is to create the best visual impression to make the scene or sequence work most effectively, with maximum dramatic value.

It is essential to set up your story line immediately, from page one, word one. You have ten pages to grab the attention of your reader or audience, so you'd better design them carefully, with skill and precision.

The opening of *The Lord of the Rings: The Fellowship of the Ring* (Peter Jackson, Fran Walsh, and Philippa Boyens), is a good example; the first few pages set up the history of the Ring; we see it forged in the fires of Mount Doom, see the struggle of good and evil played out, then learn that it must be destroyed at its place of creation. Once this is established, we cut to Gandalf arriving at Middle-Earth and the story begins to unfold.

The script opens with an action sequence which is the inciting incident, and hear a voiceover narration spoken by Galadriel (Cate Blanchett) wherein we introduce the history of the Ring. "It began with the forging of the Great Rings.... Three were given to the Elves, immortal, wisest—fairest of all beings. Seven to the Dwarf-Lords, great miners and craftsmen of the mountain halls. And Nine... nine rings were gifted to the race of Men who, above all else, desire power. For within these rings was bound the strength and will to govern each race. But they were all of them deceived, for another ring was made.... In the land of Mordor, in the fires of Mount Doom, the Dark Lord Sauron forged in secret a Master Ring to control all others.... And into this Ring he poured his cruelty, his malice and his will to dominate all life. One Ring to rule them all..."

During this opening battle for the Ring, the inciting incident occurs: the Ring is lost, then found on page 5, "by the most unlikely creature imaginable... A Hobbit—Bilbo Baggins of the Shire." We meet the creature, Gollum, anguishing over the loss of his "precious" and we learn on page 6 that "the time will soon come when Hobbits will shape the fortunes of all."

In the next scene, we enter the Shire as Gandalf (Ian McKellen) arrives and is greeted by Frodo (Elijah Wood). He then visits Bilbo Baggins (Ian Holm), and on page 10, Bilbo tells Gandalf how weary he is: "I feel it in my heart," Bilbo says. "I need a holiday—a very long holiday and I don't expect I shall return—in fact, I mean not to."

Look at what we've learned in these first ten pages: we've established the history of the Ring, introduced Gollum, showed how Bilbo found the Ring, met two of the main characters (Gandalf and Frodo), and been introduced to life in the Shire as Bilbo reveals the Ring to Gandalf and tells him of his intention to disappear. We've set up everything we need to know to move the story forward. It is lean, clean, and tight, visually designed to grab the attention of the reader and audience. And it works marvelously. This entire unit of action, the first ten pages, is what sets up all three episodes of *The Lord of the Rings.*

In *American Beauty,* we meet Jane (Thora Birch) and Ricky (Wes Bentley) as Jane provocatively asks Ricky if he'll kill her father. Then we cut into a high overhead establishing shot of the street, ending at the house where Lester Burnham (Kevin Spacey) and his family live. We see the house and hear Lester speaking in voiceover: "My name is Lester Burnham, I'm forty-two years old and in a year I'll be dead. Of course, I don't know that yet." We're introduced to Lester's wife, his daughter, and his neighbors. In a few simple strokes we know who the main character is and what the story is about—Lester regaining his "life"—and we are prepared for the key incident, when he meets Angela (Mena Suvari) at Plot Point I, where the true story begins.

Another good example of an opening scene is *Crimson Tide.* We are on the deck of an aircraft carrier, and watch as military jet planes take off, then cut to newsreel footage of Russian rebels taking over the Kremlin and threatening a nuclear strike on the United States. Then we pull back from a television screen into a birthday party for Lt. Commander Ron Hunter's (Denzel Washington) four-year-old daughter. It is a scene that exploits the situation and reveals character. It's a very visual sequence, and a great example of an inciting incident.

Whether you're writing a comedy or drama or thriller or love story makes no difference at all. The form remains constant. *Annie Hall* opens up with a monologue by Alvy Singer (Woody Allen) telling us that he and Annie (Diane Keaton) have ended their relationship and how he "keeps sifting the pieces of the relationship through my mind...." That, really, is the whole film, since those "pieces of the relationship" are then told in flashback. It's all set up on the first page of the screenplay.

Larry Kasdan's *Body Heat,* also a classic *film noir,* is another good example of setting up the story within the first ten pages. The film opens with Ned Racine (William Hurt) looking out the window at a distant fire while his one-night stand gets dressed. Racine says that it was "probably one of my clients" who started the fire. On page 3, he is in court and we learn that he is a lazy, "incompetent" attorney. The judge is irritated and tells him "the next time you come into my courtroom I hope you've got either a better defense or a better class of client." On page 4, he is having lunch with his friend Lowenstein (Ted Danson) and we learn that Racine is a man who's "searching for a quick score." It tells us a lot about him.

On page 6, we see him in his law office with an elderly client; Racine had sent her to a doctor who will not testify on her behalf, so he tells her he will find a "more understanding" doctor. "We'll sue those reckless bastards dry," he adds.

Later, on page 7, it's night and he's bored. He has a drink at the bar, then wanders over to the beachfront bandstand. He listens to the music, sees Matty Walker (Kathleen Turner), "this extraordinary, beautiful woman," walking toward him. "She passes within a few inches of him.... Racine's body sways a moment as she goes by as though buffeted by some force."

He follows her, and during their conversation she tells him she is a married woman; he replies that she should have said, "I'm a *happily* married woman." She sizes him up and says, "You're not too smart, are you?" Then, as an afterthought, "I like that in a man."

He remarks that she looks "well tended," then adds, "I need tending, but only for the night." Racine's the type of person, we learn, "whose dick gets him into trouble." When Matty spills a cherry Sno-Kone on her blouse, he gets some paper towels, but when he returns she's gone, vanished into the night.

These pages are very good illustrations of a well-designed opening.

You can see how important the first ten pages of the screenplay are in terms of setting up the story. They need to be conceived, designed, and executed for maximum dramatic value. If you set these pages up correctly, the story can unfold properly, with simplicity, insight, and understanding.

THE EXERCISE

You've done the preparation. You've clarified your story line, done your character work, structured the first act on 3 × 5 cards, written the back story, and designed the first ten pages. You're ready to start writing this unit of dramatic action to introduce your main character, establish the dramatic premise, and create the dramatic situation.

Look at some films to help illustrate some effective first ten pages, such as *Collateral, American Beauty, The Lord of the Rings, Citizen Kane, All About Eve, Chinatown, The Bourne Supremacy, The Shawshank Redemption,* and *Basic Instinct.* You can obtain a copy of the some of these scripts online at Web sites like: *simplyscripts.com* or *Drew's-Script-O-Rama.com* or *dailyscript.com.* Or you can just Google "screenplays" and see what comes up.

The first ten pages are probably the most difficult you'll write. After all, you're putting your first words down on paper, you haven't found your own style yet, so you may experience some doubt, confusion, and uncertainty. Never mind. Just sit down and do it, and be willing to write some terrible pages.

Don't think about it. Do it. Jump in. Trust the process. No matter what the results, good or bad, "true art," as Jean Renoir once told me, "is in the *doing* of it."

The very worst that can happen is that you write some terrible pages. So what? If they're that bad, just throw them away! You're not obligated to show them to anyone.

If you ask yourself how good or bad your first few pages are, you don't have to guess what the answer is. Obviously, it's going to be bad. You will know that it's boring, dull, trite, and ordinary, and you've seen it all before. That may be an accurate judgment. It may well be true. But who is it that's making that judgment? You are.

Let it go. It's only a judgment; it doesn't mean anything.

"The mind," the great Master Swami Muktananda said, "is a strange and funny thing. In the summer it longs for winter, and in the winter it longs for summer."

But judgments are part of the screenwriting process. Expect it, but don't let it interfere with the experience of writing. Screenplay form should never get in the way of your screenwriting. It's so simple it's difficult.

Screenwriting software like Final Draft will do the formatting for you. A good exercise might be to type up ten pages of a screenplay. Take any screenplay, open it at random, and simply type ten pages. Just copy everything on the page and familiarize yourself with the form. If you don't have access to any screenplays, go online and download a screenplay that you like. There are many Web sites available, so just copy these 10 pages, word for word, shot by shot. You may find it an effective way to help nudge you into the screenwriting process.

When you start writing, just lay your story line out scene by scene, shot by shot. You may find it easier to write everything in master shots: INT. RESTAURANT or EXT. PARKING LOT. Be willing to make some mistakes. You're not going to write perfectly from page 1.

Just *tell your story.*

When I was working with Jean Renoir, he remarked that beginning a new creative project, whether it be a painting, symphony, or novel, is very much like going into a clothing store and trying on a new jacket. When you try it on the first time, it doesn't look right or feel right. You take it in here, let it out there, alter it so it fits. When you try it on again, it looks all right, but it still feels a little tight under the arms. You shrug your shoulders to loosen it up a bit and make it a little more comfortable, "but you have to wear it awhile before you get used to it," Renoir said.

It's the same principle when you're writing a screenplay. You've got to get used to it.

Be willing to try things that may not work, to write awkward, stilted, or boring dialogue. It doesn't matter at this stage.

Sit down and write the first ten pages of your screenplay, focusing on your main character, the dramatic premise, and the dramatic situation.

Remember "the longest journey, begins with the first step."

11

The Second and Third Ten Pages

> Warden Norton: "Put your faith in the Lord. Your ass belongs to me. Welcome to Shawshank."
>
> —Frank Darabont
> *The Shawshank Redemption*

When I first started teaching my screenwriting workshops, my students worked very hard designing and executing the first ten pages of their scripts. But when they moved into the second ten pages, it was like night and day. New characters were added, elaborate action sequences conceived, and gimmicks introduced that had absolutely nothing to do with the story line at all. It was as if they had worked so hard writing the first ten pages they didn't know what to do in the second ten. They seemed "obligated" to create complicated scenes in order to "break free" of that opening section and let loose, regardless of whether it fit the story or not.

The results were awful. It was all confusion and no story. The reader was lost. The story line wandered around and around in search of itself, going nowhere, with no direction.

Nothing worked.

Act I is a unit of dramatic action that is approximately thirty pages long and is held together with the context known as the Set-Up. It should establish the main character, the premise, and dramatic situation. It has a sense of direction and follows a specific line of narrative and character development.

I wanted to gain some insight into what had to be done to make this particular unit of dramatic action work as a cohesive whole. So I began exploring the second ten pages of good screenplays. When I started reading scripts with this in mind, I found that in this second unit of action, we learn more about the character, who he or she is, and many times follow him or her through "a day in the life." Film is behavior, so if we follow the character through a typical day, with the dramatic forces of the story line influencing their character and their actions, then we can begin to get a greater understanding of who they are.

In *Chinatown* everything is set up in the first ten pages. Then, in the second ten pages, Jake Gittes starts the job he's been hired to do: find out who Mr. Mulwray is having an affair with.

What does Gittes do?

First, on page 11, he follows Mulwray from the city's council chambers to the Los Angeles riverbed, then trails him to the beach where, after spending most of the afternoon and night, he learns water is being dumped from the city's reservoirs into the ocean during the middle of a drought. When it gets too late, he puts some cheap watches under the tires of Mulwray's car and leaves. When he picks them up the next day he learns that the head of the Department of Water and Power was there until almost 3:00 A.M. The "guy's got water on the brain," he tells his associates. Pictures taken outside the restaurant, the Pig-n-Whistle, reveal Mulwray having a violent argument with Noah Cross (John Huston). The phone rings and Gittes learns that Mulwray has been spotted at Echo Park with "the girl."

"Jesus," Gittes says, "water again." He goes to the park, gets in a rowboat, takes pictures of Mulwray and "the little twist" he's with, and as far as he's concerned, the case is closed.

The next day, he's surprised to see the pictures he took of Mulwray and "the girl" on the front page of *The Times* with the headline "Department of Water and Power Blows Fuse Over Chief's Love Nest."

He doesn't know how the pictures got there.

That's the second ten pages of *Chinatown.* Action and reaction. Gittes is hired in the first ten pages, and does his job in the second ten pages. Notice how the thread of the story weaves through the action, focusing on the events leading up to the uncovering of a major water scandal.

Once I saw how clearly defined the action was in terms of the dramatic premise, I found that to be a pretty good "rule" for the second ten pages—*follow the focus of your main character.* He or she should be in almost every scene in these second ten pages. If we use the first ten pages to set up and establish what and who the story is about, then the next ten-page unit of dramatic action needs to focus on who he or she is.

In *The Shawshank Redemption* (Frank Darabont), the first ten pages weave three threads of dramatic action into one sequence: Andy Dusfresne (Tim Robbins) is drinking in a car, then drunkenly loads a gun, and staggers toward a distant house. Then we see Andy on trial for killing his wife and her lover. The third thread shows his wife and her lover having sex. These three lines of action are interwoven into one narrative line of action.

On page 7, we cut to the Shawshank Penitentiary where Red (Morgan Freeman) is once again rejected for his parole. We find out who he is, what he's in prison for, and what his status is among the prisoner population. On page 8, Andy arrives at Shawshank to begin serving his term of two life sentences, "back to back." On page 10, Warden Norton addresses Andy and the others by laying down the rules: "Rule number one: no blaspheming. I'll not have the Lord's name taken in vain in my prison. The other rules you'll figure out as you go along." The point is illustrated when the head of the prison guards, Hadley, severely beats down one of the convicts. "Put your faith in the Lord," Norton says. "Your ass belongs to me. Welcome to Shawshank."

That's the first ten pages. The second ten-page unit of action begins with Andy and the other prisoners being hosed down for lice, issued clothes and blankets, and then led, naked, through the prison compound to their cells. We enter the prison with Andy, see what he sees, hear what he hears. We're with Andy during the long first night of prison, hearing the other convicts bet on who will be the first of the new prisoners to break down.

The next morning, on page 17, Andy meets Red and the others, and on page 19, he is assigned to the laundry room. We see a shot of him working, then cut to the showers where he is hustled by The Sisters. He tries to be polite but they are like "jackals sizing up prey." That's the end of the second ten pages.

Look how tightly designed this second ten-page unit of dramatic action is. Andy is in every scene; we enter Shawshank with him, learn what he learns, see what he sees, and get a glimpse at what the rest of his life is going to look like as a convicted felon. This second unit of dramatic action shows us a "day in the life" of Andy Dufrense.

When you approach this second ten-page unit of action, try to design the the pages with as much care and efficiency as you did the first ten pages. Lay out your cards. Do they still apply? Do you need to add any new scenes that you hadn't thought of before? If so, put them in. Is your main character in every scene? He or she should be. Is your character *active*—does he or she initiate the action and respond to the premise and situation of the first ten pages? Remember Newton's Third Law of Motion: "For every action there is an equal and opposite reaction."

This is something to really be aware of. Your main character must be active; he or she should be making the decisions about what to do or where to go. The first ten pages sets up your character, dramatic premise, and dramatic situation. The second ten pages focuses on expanding your character and his relationships and possibly seeing him in his daily routine. Your story is always moving forward with direction, a line of development that takes us to the Plot Point at the end of Act I.

If you want to make any changes, or go off the cards, do it. Make the changes, see what happens; it may work, it may not. Sometimes, when you're writing the pages, a new scene may pop into your head. If this happens, write the scene. This is part of the creative process. It will lead you to another scene, then another scene, and then you may wonder what comes next. Just look at your cards and you'll see exactly the right place to continue moving your story forward.

If you've made a mistake with these new scenes, it will become clear to you. The worst that can happen is that you'll write a few scenes or pages and you'll be able to see whether they work or not. Maybe you'll lose a couple of days of writing. So what? Better to try something new now, than later. You'll know within a few pages whether the changes are working or not. If they are, you may reach a point where you're unsure as to how to proceed. Just ask yourself, "What happens next?" These are the magic words that can guide you into the next scene or scenes. If the pages don't work, go back to where you originally started the new scenes and move forward from there.

Add whatever scenes you need; make whatever changes you want. This is only the first words-on-paper draft and you should be willing to explore and write some really terrible pages. Do whatever you need to do to make the story line clear and concise.

This brings us up to approximately page 20 of the screenplay. We're now ready to approach writing the third ten pages, and that means writing Plot Point I. What is the Plot Point at the end of Act I? It could be a dramatic scene, like Louise killing the rapist Harlan in *Thelma & Louise* (Callie Khouri), or a dialogue scene like Andy Dufresne asking Red for the rock hammer in *The Shawshank Redemption*, or a simple action like Frodo and Sam leaving the safe environs of the Shire in *The Lord of the Rings: The Fellowship of the Ring* as they begin their journey to destroy the Ring in the fires of Mount Doom. There should be no doubt as to what the Plot Point is because the first thing you did was structure the idea and story line on the *paradigm*, so you already know the ending, beginning, and Plot Points I and II.

However, it could be that your plot point has changed since you structured your idea on the *paradigm.* Structure is flexible, like a tree that bends in the wind but does not break. Often, the plot points will change, either sliding forward or backward along the story line, so don't feel obligated to keep to your original idea of what Plot Point I or II might be. Do what needs to be done to serve the needs of the story.

Once you are clear on what Plot Point I is, ask yourself what you need to do to get there. What scene or scenes do you need to write to get to Plot Point I? Usually, one or two scenes are all you need. Can you describe and articulate what story areas you need to fill so you can reach the Plot Point at the end of Act I?

In the first ten pages of *The Shawshank Redemption,* we meet Andy, who is on trial, and Red, who is rejected by the parole board. On page 10, Andy arrives at Shawshank. In the second ten pages, we see life in Shawshank. That takes us to the end of page 20. Then we see Andy working in the laundry, hear Red's voiceover talking about Andy, and in the next scene, Andy meets Red in the yard and asks him for a rock hammer. That's Plot Point I.

Why is their meeting Plot Point I? Because this screenplay is about the relationship between these two men. And it is this scene that establishes the nature of their friendship. That's why it's such an important scene, not only from perspective of their characters, but of the action as well. The purpose of the scene is to move the story forward or reveal information about the character, and this scene does both. It reveals Andy's character when Red tells us in voiceover that "He had a quite way about him, a walk and a talk that just wasn't normal around here. He strolled, like a man in a park without a care or worry. Like he had on an invisible coat that would shield him from this place. . . . Yes, I think it would be fair to say I liked Andy from the start."

Plot Point I is "any incident, episode, or event that 'hooks' into the action and spins it around into another direction." Act I is a unit of dramatic action between twenty and thirty pages long which begins at the beginning and ends at Plot Point I and is held together with the dramatic context known as the Set-Up.

Cinderella Man (Cliff Hollingsworth and Akiva Goldsman) chronicles the life of heavyweight champion James J. Braddock (Russell Crowe), who fought the German, Max Baer, for the championship. The film opens with Braddock as a promising fighter, winning his bouts convincingly (though he has a weak left hand), and providing a comfortable life for his wife and three children. Then the great Depression hits, and Braddock struggles for fights. His abilities are diminishing and in a "last chance" bout with a journeyman fighter, he breaks his hand in several places and is unable to finish the fight. As a result, his license is taken away. He cannot fight. What can he do to earn a living and provide for his family?

That's basically the action of the first act. Plot Point I is where Braddock breaks his hand, and loses his license to fight. The first ten pages set up his success as a fighter and his relationship with his wife. The second ten pages reveal his sense of character and who he is as a person. We see his commitment to his wife and family, his beliefs, and a strong sense of moral integrity, as when he learns his young son has stolen food. Instead of punishing him, he lectures his son that "no matter what happens we don't steal. Not ever... If you take something, somebody else goes without."

That takes us up to the end of the second ten pages. Plot Point I is when Braddock breaks his hand and is suspended from fighting. So, from page 20 to the point where he breaks his hand, there are three little scenes: Braddock in the locker room prior to the fight receiving instructions from his manager/trainer Joe (Paul Giamatti). We learn that his right hand is weak and painful.

This is followed by his long walk to the ring, and then the fight itself in which he breaks his hand. In the following scene, his license is suspended. Within these second and third ten pages the thematic threads of character and story have been set up and expanded.

Ordinary People (Alvin Sargent) remains a classic example in terms of setting up the dramatic premise in the first ten pages, following focus on the main character in the second ten pages, and taking us to the Plot Point at the end of Act I in the third ten pages.

The first ten pages set up the story: We meet the family, see Beth (Mary Tyler Moore) in the kitchen, observe her "neat, organized, and perfect" household. We see Conrad (Tim Hutton) in choir practice at the high school, and meet Calvin, her husband (Donald Sutherland), returning home on a commuter train. It's like a Norman Rockwell painting, the "perfect" family. Except when Calvin leaves the train a friend says, "Cal—we're sorry—about everything." Strange.

On page 5, as Beth and Calvin return home from the theater, we see Conrad (Tim Hutton) lying on his bed, and then cut to reveal fragments of images—an angry sea, a boat, a hand reaching for help—as Conrad awakes with a start. The parents return home and on page 9, Calvin asks his son: "Have you thought about calling that doctor?"

"No," Conrad replies.

"The month's up, I think we should stick to the plan," his father continues.

"The plan was *if* I needed to call him," Conrad says.

His father backs off. "Okay, don't worry about it. Go to sleep."

Those are the first ten pages of the script. The perfect picture of ordinary people, only something's wrong and we don't know what.

The second ten pages begin with Conrad waking from another nightmare, "perspiring and scared." Conrad comes down for breakfast, and the kitchen looks great, everything clean and neat, French toast sizzling in the frying pan, a newspaper sprawled out in front of Calvin. It's perfect except for one thing: Conrad's not hungry. His mother, self-righteous and indignant, throws the French toast down the garbage disposal a little too fast, and the father tries to placate the two unsuccessfully.

On page 12, Conrad is picked up by his "buddies," but when he enters school we see he is distant and insecure. His English teacher offers him understanding and support, and says she does not want him to feel "pressured about this report." In the next scene, page 18, Conrad reluctantly calls Dr. Berger (Judd Hirsch), a psychiatrist, and says, "Dr. Crawford at Hillsboro Hospital gave me your number."

After school, Conrad goes to swimming practice and we hear the coach urging him to try harder, but something is obviously bothering him. He seems preoccupied, tense. Then he has dinner with his parents. They have a polite dinner conversation, but Conrad says nothing.

That's the second ten pages, following focus on the main character. Conrad is basically in every single scene. On page 20, he suffers an anxiety attack, and leaves school. In the next shot we see him standing in front of a large building, debating about whether to go in or not. He does, and meets Dr. Berger. On the next page we learn that Conrad was in a mental hospital for four months because "I tried to off myself." He's only been out about a month. We learn along with Dr. Berger what's been going on with Conrad. Now the conversation on page 9 between father and son about seeing a doctor becomes clear. We learn that Conrad's brother Buck drowned in a sailing accident a short time ago and this has had a major impact on Conrad's mental state.

When the psychiatrist asks, "What do you want to change?" Conrad replies, "I want to be in control... so people can quit worrying about me."

The dialogue scene with Dr. Berger is the plot point at the end of Act I.

That night, at dinner, Conrad tells his parents that he went to see Dr. Berger. His father is pleased and encouraging, while his mother is concerned and withdrawn.

That's the first thirty pages of *Ordinary People.* It sets up the entire story.

In the first ten pages we *see* there's a problem, the second ten pages *defines* the problem, and in the third ten pages we understand *what* the problem is. If we wanted to diagram it, it would look like this:

ACT I *Ordinary People*		
1st ten pages	**2nd ten pages**	**3rd ten pages**
SETS UP *the main character, dramatic premise, dramatic situation*	**FOLLOWS FOCUS** *on main character*	**DEFINES THE PROBLEM**
Something seems wrong	*In school, anxious, distant*	*Dramatize Plot Point I*
	We **SEE** *symptoms of "the problem"*	*Going to psychiatrist and learning about Buck's drowning*
		Plot Point I: pp. 23–26

That's Act I, a unit, or block, of dramatic action. It goes from page 1 to the plot point at the end of Act I, and is held together with the dramatic context known as *the Set-Up.*

THE EXERCISE

Lay out the three or four cards that make up the second ten pages of your screenplay. Follow the focus of your main character. Is he or she in every scene? If you are cutting away to another character, or incident, see if you can keep the focus on your main character. Think through the action before you start writing. See where it goes.

Tell your story, showing what is necessary. If you're writing a scene and something really "good" happens, something unexpected, something you hadn't thought about before, just go with it and write it down. Don't get in the way, just let it happen. The worst that can happen is you write some pages that don't work. So what? Don't save it for a later time or another scene. Write it.

Don't worry about not having enough to say! I tell my students that if you're working full time and writing "on the side," ten pages is a good solid week's work. Think through the action for a couple of days, then sit down to write it. Think in terms of writing the script in sections, in units of dramatic action, and you'll feel more comfortable with the process.

If you find it more convenient, write on the weekends. Spend two hours on Saturday organizing the material and then writing some pages. Ten pages are preferable, but if you can only get down two or three, just write what you have time to write. You can complete, or polish, what you've written Saturday on Sunday. That's doable and most people can handle it.

Now write the second ten pages. Don't spend too much time cleaning it up and "making it perfect." The important thing is to keep moving forward, from beginning to end. Don't go back and change something in the first ten pages because you have a better idea; it's not going to work out for you. People who spend too much time making it "right" usually run out of gas about fifty to sixty pages in and have to shelve their material. In most cases, they drop it and never pick it up again.

If you make any judgments or decisions about your writing, it will usually be negative. You'll hate it. The first words-on-paper draft is usually awful anyway, so don't worry about it. Once you get something down on paper, you can always go back and change it, clean it up, and make it better. My first draft is usually about 60 percent of what I know it can be. When I go through it a second time, I'll bring it up to about 75 to 80 percent. In my polish draft I'll do the best I can; 90 to 95 percent. Some days will be better than others.

The third ten pages lead you directly into the plot point at the end of Act I. What is it? What scene or scenes do you need to take you to Plot Point I? Clearly write any transition scenes you need that will take you to Plot Point I. Have you designed your incident, episode, or event that hooks into the action and spins it around into another direction (in this case Act II)?

Can you describe it? Design Plot Point I visually. Then write it. Are you telling your story all in dialogue, or are you using visuals?

Film is behavior. A screenplay is a story told in pictures, so think in terms of opening up your story. Show the car leaving the building and driving down the street. Show your character getting a taxi, walking into a building, and stepping into the elevator. This opens up your story, and gives it visual texture. You don't want to write your script going from INT. scene to INT. scene to INT. scene. Open it up; take it outside!

Just tell your story, and don't try to tell it too quickly. Some people write their whole screenplay in the first ten pages, then have nothing left to say. Use the first words-on-paper draft as an exercise to find your voice, your visual style.

You're going to rewrite 70 to 80 percent of what you've written anyway. When you've completed Act II and Act III, you'll know exactly what you have to do when you start the rewrite. Don't worry about that now. Just write your pages.

When you complete the third ten pages you're ready to move into Act II.

Writing is a day-by-day job, shot by shot, scene by scene, sequence by sequence, act by act. Just know that when you're writing, some days are better than others.

Enjoy the process.

12

Finding the Mid-Point

> Giovanni (Marcello Mastroianni) to Valentina (Monica Vitti): "I believe now that I'm no longer capable of writing. It's not that I don't know what to write, but how to write it. That's what they call a 'crisis.' But in my case it's something inside me, something which is affecting my whole life."
>
> —Michelangelo Antonioni
> *La Notte*

When I first started teaching my screenwriting workshops, I structured each class into eight-week sessions. The first session focused on Act I; we spent four weeks preparing the material, the second four weeks actually writing it. The goal of the class was to complete Act I.

When we completed the first eight-week session, we took a short break, then continued on into the next class. The goal in this class was to structure, design, and complete Act II.

Many of the people kept writing during the break. They didn't want to lose the discipline and creative energy they had built up during the first class. But when they returned to start the second act class and showed me the pages they had written, I was astonished. They were awful. There was no direction, no line of development, no trace of an organic story line, and almost no conflict.

In my own writing experience, Act II had always been the most difficult material to get through. To face sixty blank sheets of paper can be daunting. It's easy to go into "overwhelm" or just "check out" or simply "get lost" in the maze of your own creation. The hardest thing about writing, after all, is knowing what to write.

What was happening to my students really showed me how *not to do it.* When they jumped into these blank pages of dramatic action they were overwhelmed; they didn't know where to go or what to do. They lost their overview and did not focus on telling their story. As I was fond of saying, they were like blind men in a rainstorm—they didn't know where they were going and they were all wet.

Act II is a unit of dramatic action approximately sixty pages long that is held together with the dramatic context known as *Confrontation.* Act II begins at the end of Plot Point I and ends with the Plot Point at the end of Act II. We enter Act II by defining the main character's dramatic need. If you know your character's dramatic need—what the main character wants to win, gain, get, or achieve during the course of the screenplay—*you can create obstacles to that need* and then your story becomes *your character overcoming obstacle after obstacle to achieve his or her dramatic need.*

If you understand that conflict is what drives the narrative line of Act II forward, it becomes the key to sparking the engine of the story. Plot Point I is the true beginning of your story, whether it's told in nonlinear form, like *Cold Mountain, Kill Bill: Vols. 1 and 2, The Bourne Supremacy, American Beauty,* or *Pulp Fiction,* or whether it's in a linear form like *King Kong, Brokeback Mountain, The Shawshank Redemption, Thelma & Louise,* or *Witness* (Earl Wallace and Bill Kelly). Conflict, either internal or external, as mentioned in Chapter 6, takes you directly into the heart of your character. Not only does conflict *reveal* character but it also influences the characterization in the way he or she chooses to present himself or herself to the world.

As stated several times earlier, all drama is conflict—without conflict you have no action; without action you have no character;

without character you have no story; and without story, you have no screenplay.

So where do you begin when you're approaching Act II in the screenplay? How do you get from Plot Point I to Plot Point II?

Look at the *paradigm.*

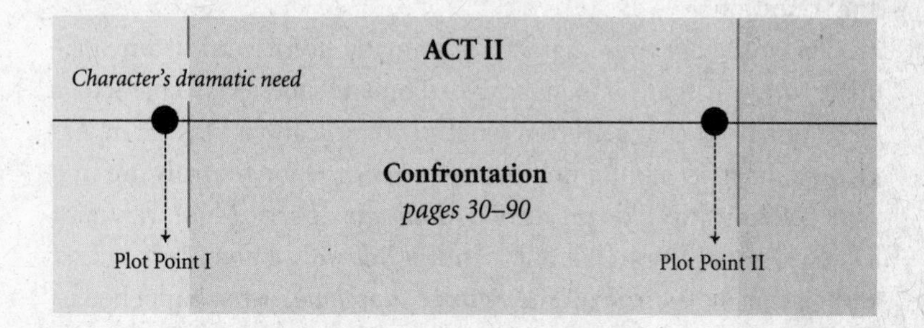

As mentioned, we enter Act II by defining your character's dramatic need—if your character's need has changed, it will change at Plot Point I. In *Thelma & Louise,* the two women set out for a weekend holiday. But, after Louise kills Harlan at Plot Point I, their need changes. No longer is it to have a good time in the mountains. It now becomes two women on the run, wanting to escape safely to Mexico. Can you define your character's dramatic need? Has it changed since the story began? In *Cold Mountain,* Inman's need was to fight in the Civil War. But at Plot Point I, he learns from Ada's letter that she is in love with him and wants him to return to Cold Mountain. Coming home to the love of his life also represents a state of mind—Cold Mountain before the war was a place of peace, warmth, and love. Inman's need is not only to return on the physical level, but also on the emotional level. That need drives him over three hundred miles on foot, enduring bad weather, starvation, being shot at, capture, escape, and more.

In *Chinatown,* Act I sets up Jake Gittes as a detective hired by Mrs. Mulwray to find out whether her husband is having an affair.

But at Plot Point I, Gittes returns to the office to find the real Mrs. Mulwray (Faye Dunaway) who states that she did not hire him. But if she didn't hire him, who did? That becomes Jake's dramatic need, and that's where Act II begins: with the search for who set him up and why. During this period of dramatic action, Gittes encounters obstacle after obstacle in the way of his finding out the answer to that question.

Do you know your character's dramatic need? What is the incident or event that happens at Plot Point I? Does your character's dramatic need change? From what to what? Can you define it? Articulate it? Is it maintaining the integrity of who you truly are in a love relationship like *Brokeback Mountain* (Larry McMurtry and Diana Ossana)? Or to kill Bill as in *Kill Bill: Vols. 1 and 2*? Or to find out, like Jason Bourne in The *Bourne Supremacy,* what happened in Berlin?

Where is your story going? What changes will your character be going through? What obstacles will be confronting your character? Are they a source of internal conflict, like *Brokeback Mountain*? Or external conflict, like *King Kong* or *Cold Mountain* or *Kill Bill*? If you look at Plot Point I as the true beginning of your story and you know your character's dramatic need, you're ready to move into the second act.

During my early screenwriting workshops, I knew that in order to map out the action in Act II, you had to structure the action before writing it, which meant that my students had to prepare their material first. This might seem obvious, but from my students' point of view, they didn't want to stop to prepare the material for Act II. So they just jumped in and started writing. No wonder they were confused! When you approach writing the second act of your screenplay, the first thing you need to do is gain some control over the material. You want to know where you are going, then figure out how to get there.

What could I do, I asked myself, to create, or organize, some kind of tool that would effectively help the writer conceive and write Act II? Something that would give the writer some kind of "control" while he or she is writing this sixty-page unit of dramatic action.

(Although "control" over the material is a misnomer; like trying to hold a bundle of water.)

As I was pondering this question, I got a phone call from an old friend of mine, Deneen Peckinpah. Deneen and I had both attended UC Berkeley and we had worked and acted together with Jean Renoir during the world premiere of his play *Carola.* Deneen had played the lead character, Carola, while I had played her lover, Campan, the stage manager. We had kept in touch periodically over the years but we hadn't seen each other for a long time. She told me she was in town staying with her uncle in Malibu. Suddenly, the name Peckinpah struck a chord. Was her uncle, I asked, Sam Peckinpah? She laughed, and said yes and invited me out to the house.

I had been a fan and admirer of Peckinpah ever since I wrote my first film review on *Ride the High Country* for a film magazine and a few days later I eagerly drove out to Malibu—a little too fast, a little too recklessly—but I was excited to see her again and possibly meet Sam. When I arrived, Sam was in a meeting so Deneen and I walked along the beach and talked about the changes in our lives over the last several years. During the conversation, I couldn't help telling her how much I liked *Ride the High Country,* and how I wanted to write screenplays like that. She smiled and said Sam would like to hear that, especially now. I didn't know what she meant, but I would soon find out.

When we went back to the house, Sam was there, and we spent the afternoon together, talking mainly about film, movies, and life in general. I'd heard a lot of stories about Sam, of course, about his drunken antics, the difficulties he had on the set with his crews, his sense of "perfectionism," and the conflicts he had with the studios and producers, so I didn't really know what to expect when I met him in person.

I found Sam to be likable and totally unpretentious, with a keen sensibility and understanding. He wasn't drinking the "hard stuff," he said, only two beers a day, and during our conversation I learned he had not made a film since *Major Dundee,* some four years earlier. Co-written with Oscar Saul, *Dundee* had been made right after *Ride the High Country,* and ended up being a traumatic experience for him, a "personal disaster." It was while working on *Dundee* that he got the reputation of being "difficult," meaning "unemployable" in the Hollywood vernacular. He couldn't get any work after that and was only now being given a chance to rewrite and direct a new screenplay called *The Wild Bunch.*

Over the next few weeks, I spent a lot of time in Malibu and late one afternoon, after Sam had finished his day's writing on *The Wild Bunch,* we were sitting on the deck watching a glorious Malibu sunset, when I asked how he structured his stories. He paused for a moment, then told me that he liked to "hang his stories" around a centerpiece. Typically, he said, he would build the action up to a certain event, about midway through the story, then let everything else be the result of that event. When I thought about *Ride the High Country* I saw that this "centerpiece" event was the wedding scene in the brothel. Once he had set up the story and characters, everything led to that wedding sequence, and then the rest of the movie was the result of that sequence. That started me thinking again about what I might be able to do to make the writer's task of writing Act II easier. Theoretically, I thought, I could build a dramatic story line, and also "hang" it around some kind of centerpiece event.

When I thought about my students writing Act II, I wondered whether I could find some kind of incident, episode, or event, to act like a "centerpiece." It would not only move the action forward but would also break Act II down into two separate units of dramatic action. I knew that everyone could work in thirty-page units of action. If such an incident occurred around page 60, it would break Act II into two separate thirty-page units of action. The First Half of Act II and the Second Half of Act II would be connected by this midpoint event.

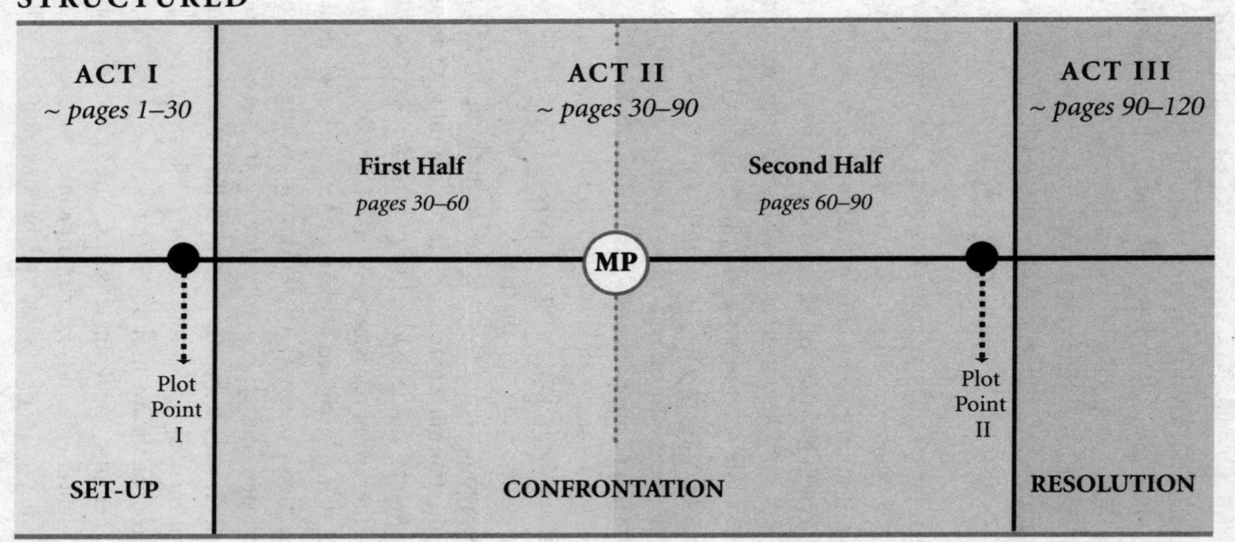

MP = A link in the chain of dramatic action; it CONNECTS the first half of Act II with the second half of Act II

Intuitively, that felt right to me, and more importantly I knew it would work—that some kind of scene or sequence in the middle of Act II would anchor the material within the context of structuring and writing the action. At this point, I began looking at films from this new perspective. I had learned, through my own screenwriting experience, that the process of writing is asking yourself the right questions and then waiting for the right answers; it will be revealed when least expected. And that's exactly what happened.

At that time, back in the late '70s, I was using Paul Mazursky's *An Unmarried Woman* as a teaching film. So I looked at the film again, studying it, seeking some kind of insight about why the second act worked so well. As mentioned in an earlier chapter, the set-up deals with Erica's (Jill Clayburgh) successful seventeen-year marriage. We meet her while she's jogging with her husband, Martin (Michael Murphy), enjoys a "quickie" with him before he leaves for work, and then we see her getting her teenage daughter off to school, working part-time in an art gallery, and "hustled" by Charlie (Cliff Gorman), a painter. We see her with her friends at lunch and from all outward appearances she is happy and content. So far, so good; Act I shows us her good life and good marriage.

Then, about twenty-five minutes in the film, she and Martin are leaving a restaurant where they've been planning their summer vacation when he suddenly breaks down and blurts out, "I'm in love with another woman. I want a divorce." Plot Point I.

From being a married woman in Act I, Erica suddenly becomes an unmarried woman in Act II. Almost overnight, she is forced to adapt to a new lifestyle, a new beginning. It's not easy. She has trouble being alone, she has trouble with her daughter, and she hates men—all men. She goes into therapy. When a blind date makes a pass at her, she throws him out of the taxi.

Her therapist, a woman, tells Erica she's got to give up her anger toward men; she should experiment a little, take some risks. "I can't tell you what to do, of course," the therapist continues, "but I know what I would do."

"What?" Erica asks.

"I would go out and get laid."

That happens on page 60. The next scene shows Erica at a singles bar, where she meets Charlie the painter. She returns to his studio apartment and spends the night with him. It's not the best of experiences. From then on, all the way through to the end of Act II, when she meets Saul (Alan Bates), she explores her sexuality in a number of one-night stands. She doesn't want a relationship. When Saul tells her he wants to see her again, she says no. "I'm experimenting... I want to know how it feels to make love with a man I'm not in love with."

The scene with the therapist on page 60 bridges the action between the First Half of Act II and the Second Half of Act II. From approximately page 30 to page 60, the main character is "anti-men"; from about page 60 to page 90, she "explores her sexuality" with a series of one-night stands.

Interesting.

When I drew it on the *paradigm* here's how it looked:

An Unmarried Woman

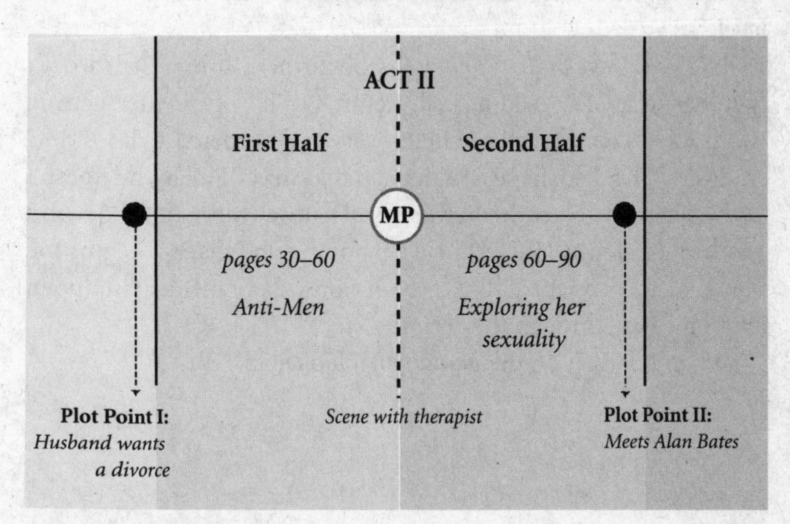

Once again I thought about what Peckinpah had told me about the "centerpiece." At this point, I wasn't sure whether I was trying to force some kind of incident or event to fit my expectation, or whether my observation was a natural, intuitive moment in the storytelling process. I didn't want to try and fit a round peg into a square hole.

But a while later I recalled Paul Schrader (*Taxi Driver, Cat People, American Gigolo*) telling me that when he writes a screenplay, "something happens" around page 60.

Page 60. Like Sam Peckinpah, it seemed he would hang a story around a *centerpiece.* Thinking about the relationship between these three things—Sam's statement, Paul Schrader's conversation, and *An Unmarried Woman,* I wondered if the same thing happened in other screenplays as well. So I started exploring several screenplays that I had been using as teaching films such as: *Annie Hall* and *Three Days of the Condor* (Lorenzo Semple, Jr. and David Rayfiel), among others. In *Annie Hall,* Alvy and Annie meet at Plot Point I. The first part of Act II deals with establishing their relationship, and then, midway through the second act, they decide to move in together. Wouldn't that be some kind of Mid-Point? I wondered. After they move in, their relationship moves to a new level.

In *Three Days of the Condor,* Joseph Turner (Robert Redford), a member of a CIA "reading cell," returns to his office after getting lunch for his colleagues and finds everyone murdered. Who did it? And why? Shocked, he seeks safety on the streets. Finally, he doesn't know where to go or who to trust. And halfway through the Second Act, he takes Kathy (Faye Dunaway) hostage and that act begins the bonds of their relationship. In both films, these incidents happen about midway through the Second Act.

When I drew it on the *paradigm,* it looked like this:

Three Days of the Condor

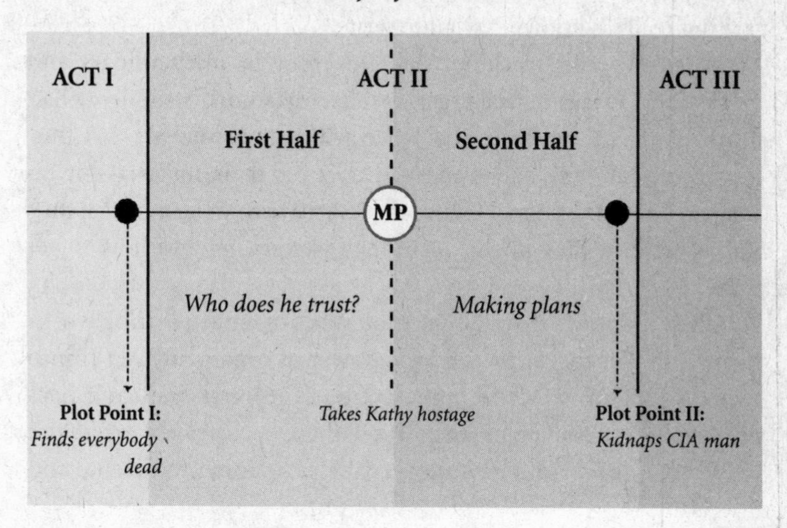

It seemed to make sense. And the more films I saw, the more scripts I read, and the more I thought about it, I began to see there was definitely some kind of incident that occurred in the middle of Act II that could be used as an anchoring point to organize and structure the action throughout the Second Act.

So, I called it the *Mid-Point;* it is some kind of incident, episode, or event that occurs around page 60, and breaks Act II into two basic units of dramatic action: the First Half of Act II, and the Second Half of Act II.

The incident I called the Mid-Point is a plot point, yes, but more important, its function in the Second Act is to be *a link in the chain of dramatic action,* and to break Act II into two distinct units of dramatic action: the First Half of Act II goes from the end of Plot Point I to the Mid-Point, and the Second Half of Act II goes from the Mid-Point to Plot Point II.

I started using the construct of the Mid-Point in my screenwriting workshops, my consultations, and in the analyzing of screenplays. I saw how beneficial it was, in terms of teaching and evaluating the screenplay. Once again, it showed me that the hardest thing about writing really is knowing what to write.

When I began teaching the Mid-Point in my seminars and workshops, I was amazed at the results. My students suddenly had a firm grasp on Act II. In their own words they told me that they now felt as if they had some control over their material—it no longer controlled them. Now, as they were writing the material they didn't get lost; they knew where they were going and how to get there.

Since that time, I've taught thousands of screenwriting workshops, all over the world, and the power of organizing Act II into two distinct units of dramatic action (the First Half and Second Half, connected by the Mid-Point), has proven over and over again, beyond any doubt, to be functional, efficient, and liberating.

Take a look at how it works in contemporary film. In Chapter 8, we saw how the key incident in *The Bourne Supremacy* structurally holds the whole film together. The Mid-Point, when Jason Bourne confronts Pamela Landy (Joan Allen), bridges the action and moves the story forward. It is the first time that Jason puts a name to a face and learns who, specifically, is after him. In *King Kong* (Peter Jackson, Philippa Boyens, and Fran Walsh), the first half of the film sets up the situation and characters, and chronicles their voyage until they reach the island at Plot Point I. That is the true beginning of the story. Midway through the Second Act, we meet the giant gorilla.

Introducing King Kong at the Mid-Point is the incident that links the action of the First Half of Act II to the Second Half of Act II. Truly, it is a link in the chain of dramatic action. It moves the story forward and amps up the emotional and physical action in the Second Half of Act II.

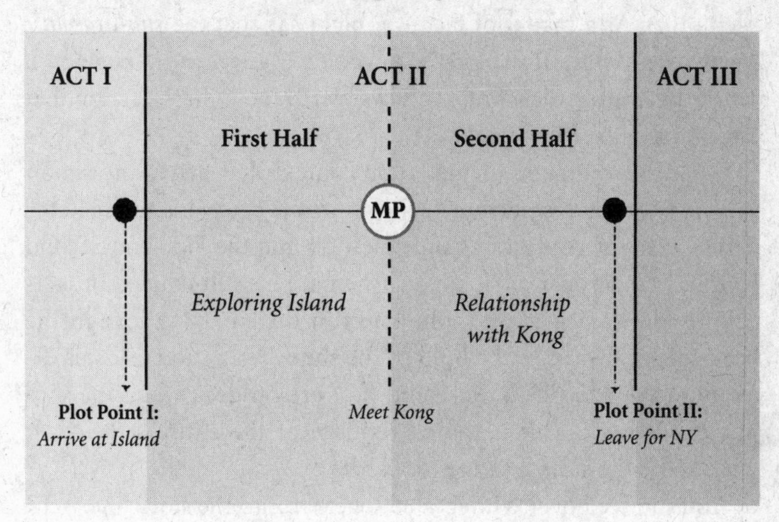

So, what's the best way to determine the *Mid-Point*? Let's do a little review. First, we started out on this journey of writing a screenplay by defining four things: the ending, beginning, Plot Point I, and Plot Point II. So at Plot Point I, what kind of incident, episode, or event would keep the action moving forward to get us to Plot Point II? It's essential to remember that the Mid-Point is *a link in the chain of dramatic action;* it connects the First Half of Act II with the Second Half of Act II. That incident is a story progression and leads us into the Second Half of Act II and keeps us on track to get to Plot Point II.

The Mid-Point is an important structural ingredient in the second act of your screenplay. A good example is *Titanic;* at Plot Point I, Jack (Leonardo DiCaprio) saves Rose (Kate Winslet) from jumping overboard. That incident is what begins their relationship, and it's this relationship that governs the action during the first half of Act II—they get to know each other, they confront the obstacles of Rose's fiancé and her mother.

As a reward for saving Rose, Jack is invited to dinner in the first-class salon. He dresses in a borrowed tux, clearly states his point of view at dinner, and little by little, they begin to share themselves with each other. As a matter of fact, we might say that the *sub-dramatic theme, the context* of the First Half of Act II, is *getting to know each other.* Illustrating that context allows you to focus on the action that takes you to the Mid-Point.

That sub-dramatic theme is the context that drives the action forward during this portion of the screenplay. Act II is still held together with the context of Confrontation, but the First and Second Half have their own sub-dramatic theme. This sub-context of "getting to know each other" culminates in their making love in the back seat of the car in the hold of the ship. This action leads us directly to the *Mid-Point:* Rose and Jack are on deck when the ship hits the iceberg. This is the centerpiece of the entire screenplay; what keeps the story moving forward.

You can see how it's integrated together into the story line. Act I sets up the individual lives of Rose and Jack. At Plot Point I, Jack saves Rose from jumping overboard. The action of the first half of Act II is their relationship, getting to know each other as they overcome obstacles like class and situation, and leads to the culmination of their relationship when they make love. The Mid-Point is when the *Titanic* hits the iceberg, which now leads us into the Second Half of Act II, which deals with their safety and survival. But the story is really about Rose and Jack, set against the sinking of the *Titanic,* and how this relationship frees Rose from the constraints of family and society to live a life of full self-expression.

Hitting the iceberg is the action that leads us into the Second Half of Act II and takes us to the Plot Point at the end of Act II: when Rose leaves the davit she's on and runs back to join Jack. If she dies, she will die in the arms of her lover. The sub-dramatic theme for the Second Half of Act II could be called *Rose and Jack staying together.*

That's the importance of the Mid-Point—it connects the first half of Act II with the Second Half of Act II. The Mid-Point is the link in the chain of dramatic action.

Titanic

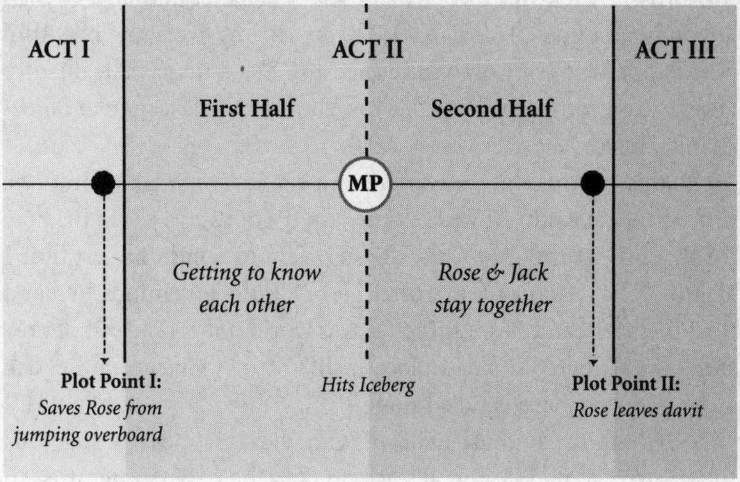

ACT I

ACT II

ACT III

First Half

Second Half

MP

Getting to know each other

Rose & Jack stay together

Plot Point I: *Saves Rose from jumping overboard*

Hits Iceberg

Plot Point II: *Rose leaves davit*

What is so interesting to me is that the Mid-Point not only conveys a new approach to the Second Act from a structural perspective, it also expands the character's depth and dimension.

In *The Shawshank Redemption,* Andy Dufresne (Tim Robbins) meets Red (Morgan Freeman) at Plot Point I. They begin their relationship and Andy settles into his routine in prison.

As he begins to gain the warden's respect, he is assigned to the library, and seeks aid from the legislature for additional funds. For six years he writes one, sometimes two, letters a week, in order to raise the funds to expand the library. Action is character, right?

Finally, when a check and a few cartons of books arrive, Andy examines the items. One of them is an album of Mozart's opera, *The Marriage of Figaro.* Anxiously, he locks the doors to the warden's office, puts the record on, and turns on the P.A. system so the strains of the aria can be heard throughout the prison. Everywhere within the prison walls the music plays, lilting and soaring with Andy's "ecstasy and rapture." As Red says in voiceover: "I have no idea to this day what them two Italian ladies were singin' about . . . I like to think they were singin' about something so beautiful it *can't* be expressed in words.... I tell you those voices *soared.* Higher and farther than anybody in a gray place dares to dream. It was like some beautiful bird flapped into our drab little cage and made these walls dissolve away... and for the briefest of moments—every last man at Shawshank felt free."

As this is going on, the warden and guards are breaking into the office to get at Andy. As Red tells us, "Andy got two weeks in the hole for that little stunt." But Andy doesn't seem to mind. "Easiest time I ever did," he tells his friends after getting out. He reminds Red and the others "that there are things in this world not carved out of gray stone. That there's a small place inside of us they can never lock away, and that place is called hope."

Red disagrees, because in his point of view, "Hope is a dangerous thing. Drive a man insane. It's got no place here. Better get used to the idea." This incident of Andy playing the music is the Mid-Point and drives the story forward in order to give us more insight into his character in the Second Half of Act II.

These three elements—*Plot Point I, Mid-Point,* and *Plot Point II* are the structural foundation that holds the entire second act in place. You cannot determine the Mid-Point until you know both Plot Points I and II. The way it works is this:

First, you decide your ending. Second, you choose your opening. Third, choose Plot Point I, and fourth, choose Plot Point II. Only then, after these four elements are placed on the paradigm, can you determine the Mid-Point. Of course, all the structural components of the screenplay are flexible, but they must be in place to guide you before you begin.

For me, the significance of the Mid-Point is an essential aspect of gaining insight and understanding in terms of organizing and structuring Act II. This story point will assist you in designing and structuring the narrative line of action that is Act II.

When you're in the paradigm, you can't see the paradigm.

THE EXERCISE

Find a couple of movies you like and get them on DVD. Watch them two or three times. The first time, simply enjoy the film and let it wash over you.

When you see it the second time, study it. Get a pad of paper and take notes. Isolate and define Plot Point I and Plot Point II. See if you can find the structure of Act II. Start at Plot Point I; it occurs anywhere between twenty and thirty minutes into the film. Check your watch if need be.

After you determine Plot Point I, follow the action of the main character. Then, about fifty to sixty minutes into the film, see if you can locate the Mid-Point. Check your watch. When the film is over, see if your definition of the Mid-Point is accurate.

Why is it the Mid-Point? Does it link the chain of dramatic action connecting the First Half of Act II with the Second Half of Act II? Then watch the movie again from start to finish. Check it out. You might even draw it on the *paradigm*. At that point, we can move to the next step.

13

First Half, Second Half

Noah Cross: "You may think you know what's going on. But, believe me, you don't."
—Robert Towne
Chinatown

I've always known that Act II is the most difficult material to write. Not only is it twice as long as Acts I and III, but the material is demanding, more complex, and requires more ingenuity and skill to execute. Just finding your story line and keeping it moving forward is a challenge. Act II is approximately a sixty-page unit of dramatic action and you always have to keep your end point in mind when you're writing; if you know where you're going, then you can figure out how to get there. For that to happen effectively, you must plan and craft your character's course of action. What happens to your main character from Plot Point I to Plot Point II, either physically, mentally, or emotionally? What obstacles does he or she confront? Does your character arc change during this action and, if so, what is the change? Are the stakes high enough to keep your story interesting, suspenseful, tense, and well-paced?

We started writing Act I as a specific unit of dramatic action. When you approach writing Act II it's important to keep your direction moving forward. What happens in the First Half of Act II? What is your character's dramatic need? What are the obstacles to that dramatic need? What happens, physically and emotionally, to your main character? What happens from Plot Point I to the Mid-Point? What *holds* it all together? That's the first thing you have to know. Once we determine the *sub-dramatic context* of the First Half, then we can provide *the content*, the individual scenes or sequences needed to make it work.

Context, remember, is the space *inside* the empty glass that *holds* the dramatic or comedic content in place.

Do you know what the *sub-dramatic context* is in the First Half of Act II? What idea or principle holds the action in place? Can you describe it in a few words? Is it a relationship? A journey? The start of a vacation? Is it suddenly losing a job, or getting one? Or maybe it's the beginning of a marriage or the beginning of a divorce?

Can you define it? Articulate it. Draw it on the *paradigm.*

Once you determine the sub-dramatic context for each half of Act II, you can design a line of action that executes your story line in the most dramatic fashion. That's what dramatic context does for us: it "holds" the action, the content, in place.

When I first started teaching the concept of the Mid-Point to my screenwriting students, I knew it was a very effective tool, but at that point I didn't have too many explanations, or reasons, or examples of the sub-dramatic context of the First Half and Second Half.

It was about this time that I was approached by two Belgian filmmakers, representatives of the Ministry of Dutch Culture, who asked me to teach a special screenwriting workshop in Brussels that summer. During our discussion, one of them asked if I had discovered anything new, in terms of structure, since the publication of *Screenplay* a few years earlier. I told him about the Mid-Point and how I was beginning to incorporate the material in my screenplays and workshops.

Since I was taking the film and script of *Chinatown* with me to Brussels, he asked me what the Mid-Point of *Chinatown* was and how it affected the action. I told him the truth, that at this point I really didn't know. I tried to cover my ignorance by declaring that all I had to do was open the script to page 60 and see what was there. So, we opened the script to page 60, which turned out to be the scene in which Jake Gittes talks with Evelyn Mulwray in a bar soon after her husband's death. He takes an envelope out of his pocket, thanks her for the check she sent him, but adds that she has "short-changed" him on the story. "I think you're hiding something, Mrs. Mulwray," Gittes tells her. He points to the monogram on the envelope that reads ECM. He casually asks what the C stands for.

She stammers slightly before she answers. "C-Cross," she says.

"That's your maiden name?" he asks.

Yes.

He thinks about it for a moment, shrugs his shoulders, and changes the subject.

I put down the script, and he saw the confusion in my face. "Is that the Mid-Point?" the filmmaker asked. And if it is, why? I looked at him and tried to justify the scene as the Mid-Point, then gave it up because it was obvious I didn't know what the hell I was talking about. The truth was that I didn't know if that was the Mid-Point or not, and if it was, why. I tried to laugh it off, and quickly changed the subject.

They left and I started preparing the workshop. I reread *Chinatown* and viewed the film several more times. I finally decided the Mid-Point was not the scene in the bar on page 60, but the scene right afterward, in the parking lot outside, on page 63, where Gittes tell Mrs. Mulwray that her husband "was murdered, in case you're interested... and somebody's dumping thousands of gallons of water out of the city reservoirs when we're supposedly in the middle of a drought... and I goddamn near lost my nose! And I like it. I like breathing through it. And I still think you're hiding something."

As far as I was concerned, that was "it." I took the film and script to Brussels with me, showed the film, talked about it, referred to it in the lectures and workshops. It became a teaching film.

Learning is being able to see the relationship between things, and the more I talked about the film the more I learned from it. (I still think it's one of the best American screenplays written in the last thirty years.)

One overcast Saturday morning, at the Palais des Beaux Arts, I showed the film to several European filmmakers, and after the screening we sat around and discussed it in front of a large audience. I started talking about the Mid-Point, and how it starts the connection between Hollis Mulwray, Jake Gittes, and Mrs. Mulwray. In the scene, Gittes wants some information from Yelburton, the new head of the Department of Water and Power. The secretary tells him that Yelburton is in a meeting and will be tied up indefinitely. "I'll wait," Gittes says. He lights up a cigarette, plops down in the chair, and makes himself at home. "I take a long lunch," he mentions to the secretary. "All day, sometimes."

He starts humming to himself, and the secretary gets nervous and edgy. Then, he gets up and prowls along the wall, looking at the photographs that detail the history of the department. There are several photographs of Hollis Mulwray and a man named Noah Cross (John Huston) standing together at various construction sites.

Cross. The name rings a bell to Gittes. He takes out Evelyn Mulwray's envelope and looks at the monogram: ECM. He asks the secretary if Noah Cross worked for the water department. Flustered, the secretary says yes, then no. "Noah Cross *owned* the water department," she tells him, "along with Mulwray." They were partners, she explains. Mulwray felt the public should own the water but Cross didn't agree, and they had a falling out.

Something clicks for Gittes. Evelyn Mulwray is Noah Cross' daughter; that means she married her father's business partner. Whose side is Evelyn on—her father's or her dead husband's? Suddenly Gittes realizes that Noah Cross could have a very strong motive for killing Hollis Mulwray.

Now things start to make sense; the information is a vital link in the dramatic action of Act II, and the first clue that points to the solution of the puzzle. Ultimately it leads to Gittes proving that Cross is the man responsible for the murders and the water scandal. It is a link in the chain of dramatic action, an essential clue to Gittes understanding of what's going on.

"You may think you know what's going on," Cross tells Gittes early on, "but you don't." Jake still doesn't know who set him up or why, but he's on the trail. That's what makes the Mid-Point such an important story progression. It sets up the First Half of Act II by focusing on Gittes searching for information, for pieces that will help in solving the puzzle. The connection between Evelyn Mulwray, Noah Cross, and Hollis Mulwray is made at the Mid-Point and it provides the link in the chain of dramatic action between the First Half of Act II and the Second Half of Act II. In the First Half, Gittes finds out *what's going on;* in the Second Half, he finds out *who's behind it.*

When I drew it on the *paradigm* it looked like this:

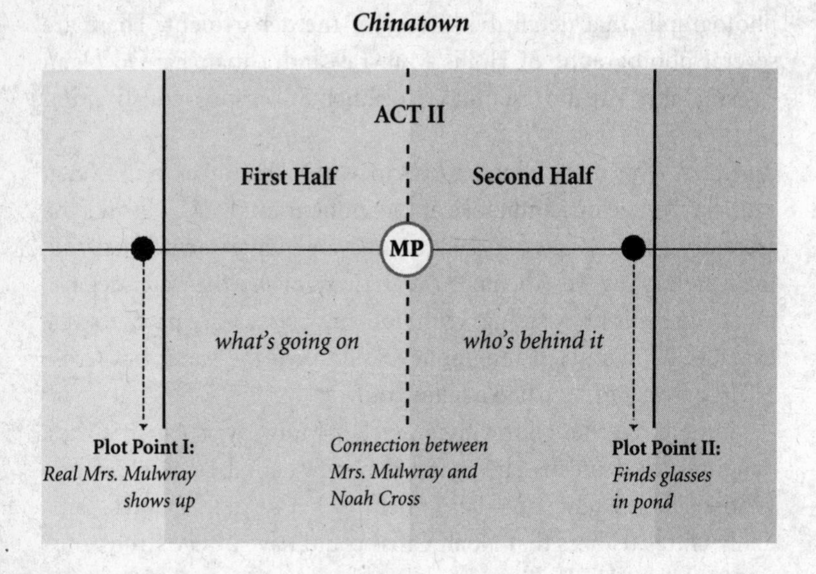

Once I saw that connection, the entire second act fell into place. When I looked at it, everything tied together, like the intricate weave of a sixteenth-century Belgian tapestry. That information, that connection, is the story progression that moves the story forward, step by step, incident by incident, scene by scene, leading us to the Plot Point at the end of Act II.

Knowing the Mid-Point is an essential tool that allows you to focus your story line into a specific line of action. With it, you now have a direction, a line of development. Once you know your Mid-Point, you can structure and organize your material by establishing the sub-dramatic context for the First Half of Act II, and the Second Half of Act II. It is an anchoring point so you can "build" your story line, confident and secure that you know where you're going. It becomes the story progression to move your story forward into the Second Half of Act II.

Sometimes, when you're organizing your material for the First and Second Halves of Act II, you'll find new scenes, new ideas, new relationships, even new characters emerging that you had never thought about. When you're writing, you want to go with what's working "right now." Trust the screenwriting process. It's larger than you are. Do what feels right. Don't worry about what you decided a long time back.

Stuff happens. People change. Things change.

The only relevant question is: does it work? If it does, use it; if it doesn't, don't. When you're writing and suddenly you get a new thought, or a new direction, something you hadn't planned on or thought about, just write it down, try it out, see if it works.

As I tell my students over and over again: when in doubt, write. If you're not sure whether to write a scene or not, write it. The worst that can happen is that you find out it doesn't work. You'll learn it's easier to cut a scene than it is to add a new one. Go ahead and write a one-hundred-seventy-five-page first words-on-paper draft. You'll have to go back and rewrite some pages. So what? In my workshops, we make an agreement that the workshop is going to be an educational opportunity; that means the willingness to make mistakes. Try things that may not work. It's the only way to grow and evolve, to sharpen your skills.

To repeat, the *First Half of Act II* and the *Second Half of Act II* are each approximately thirty pages in length. Both units of dramatic action are held together with a *sub-dramatic subtext.* The overall context for Act II, Confrontation, doesn't change; that will always remain the same. No matter how long or short your script is, you will be able to vary the pages accordingly.

What's the best way to structure Act II? We know the three basic structural points: Plot Point I, Plot Point II, and the Mid-Point. The next thing we have to do is determine the *sub-dramatic context* for the First Half of Act II—what is the main action, or story line, or concept, that holds the material together.

In *Brokeback Mountain,* Act I sets up the relationship between Ennis Del Mar (Heath Ledger) and Jack Twist (Jake Gyllenhaal) as they meet and tend a herd of sheep on Brokeback Mountain. There, unable to restrain their physical feelings, they have sex, but deny, or mask, the emotional feelings between them. At Plot Point I, they descend the mountain and go their separate ways. Act II begins with Ennis getting married to Alma (Michelle Williams) and quickly having two children. He drifts from one job to another and his life seems to have no purpose. Jack follows the rodeo circuit and meets Lureen (Anne Hathaway), the daughter of the owner of a prosperous tractor company. They get married and have a child a short time later.

But both men's marriages leave much to be desired. That's what the action of the First Half of Act II focuses on: their inability to have loving, sustaining relationships with their families. This is the sub-dramatic context. It is the line of action that holds the action together during the First and Second Halves of Act II. In the First Half of Act II of *Brokeback Mountain,* the sub-dramatic context is *revealing their relationships.* This context sets up the Mid-Point, when the two cowboys, after a long absence, get together once again, and their passion is seen by Ennis' wife, Alma. Love becomes the force that draws them together and they return to Brokeback Mountain where they had their first times together. That's the Mid-Point.

What happens now? The Second Half of Act II covers several years and expands upon their unhappy marriages while the two cowboys get together a few times a year. But this is totally unsatisfying to both of them, especially Jack. We see their unhappiness; Jack strolls the Red Light district in Mexico seeking a substitute for Ennis; and Ennis, unable to enjoy his relationships with his family, runs away from intimacy. Finally, his wife gets a divorce. Ennis becomes a lonely, ornery cowboy, drifting from one job to another. He begins a relationship with a waitress who is totally taken with him but Ennis offers her nothing emotionally, and she leaves him in tears and heartbreak.

This takes us to Plot Point II where, after twenty years, Jack is no longer able to deal with Ennis' resistance to taking the emotional plunge to stay together. Ennis is driven by his childhood memory of being taken to see the dead, mutilated body of an older "queer" cowboy, found in a gulch. That memory is what drives him to refuse to commit to his lover, Jack.

The context of Act III resolves this dilemma and illuminates the unhappiness of both men. This is what gives the story its power, its emotion, its universality.

In *The Shawshank Redemption*, the First Half of Act II focuses on Andy's survival (the sub-dramatic context) in prison, and his developing relationship with Red. The Second Half of Act II deals with Andy established in his prison life, and how he wants to contribute and pass on his education (the sub-dramatic context) to others.

In *Titanic*, the sub-dramatic context of the First Half is Rose and Jack getting to know each other. We see that illustrated when Jack is invited to dinner in appreciation for his rescuing Rose at Plot Point I. It's an important sequence because we see that he not only holds his own with the "upper class," but that Rose and the others are impressed with his values and point of view. This leads directly to the Mid-Point where they make love, just before hitting the iceberg. The Second Half of Act II deals with their survival and staying together.

The sub-dramatic context is an important cog in determining the content of these two units of dramatic action.

Since Plot Point I is the "true beginning" of your story line, you might find that when you're writing the First Half of Act II, there might be occasions when you *lose your way* in the story. If and when that does happen, just continue writing and you'll find yourself getting back on track around the middle of the First Half of Act II.

Defining the dramatic context puts you in a position of choice—

it gives you a basis for designing the action that is needed to tell your story. That's the function and the importance of the dramatic context. It holds everything together; it *is* structure.

Think about your story line. What happens in the First Half of Act II? The Second Half? Think about it. Define it. If you choose, write a short essay on what happens just to clarify things in your own mind. Once you define the context of the First and Second Half, then you can determine the time frame of the narrative action.

Aristotle considered time, place, and action to be the three unities that hold dramatic tragedy in place. In his *Poetics* he expressed the view that the time of action must correspond to the length of the play. A play of two hours could cover only two hours in the hero's life; the time of the play became the time of the action. Unlike the writer of an epic, who could represent years of action on a many-sided canvas of mythological proportions, a playwright was limited to a single time, place, and action. We don't see Oedipus killing his father, we hear somebody telling us about it.

That was the way it was until the sixteenth century, when Shakespeare and his contemporaries bridged the unity of time by portraying years in a character's life, while "[this] poor player . . . struts and frets his hour upon the stage and then is heard no more." By dramatizing a scene here and a scene there, time was bridged, condensed, and held together by the vast spectacle of action.

Shakespeare's method was cinematic but placed and written for the stage. What Homer did in his epics, and Shakespeare did in his plays, is basically what George Lucas and Steven Spielberg and Peter Jackson are doing today in their stories of myth and ritual and imagination. Epic films like *Star Wars, The Lord of the Rings,* and *The Matrix* (Larry and Andy Wachowski) cut through space and time in whatever age you're living.

If you're writing a screenplay that covers a period of time of many years, like *Brokeback Mountain* or *The Shawshank Redemption,* or a shorter time period like *The Best Years of Our Lives* (Robert E. Sherwood) or *48 Hours* (Roger Spottiswood, Walter Hill, Larry Gross, and Steven E. de Souza) or *American Beauty,* what incidents can you show that will reveal the passage of time? Do you want to use subtitles? Or do you want to illustrate the passage of time by showing a scene in sunshine, and the next in snow with Christmas trees? Or maybe you have the character wearing a tank top in one scene and a fur coat in the next? Ask yourself what you *don't* show. What makes "this" incident more important than "that" incident? Stories covering many years are difficult to write, and beginning screenwriters usually "scatter" the incidents like buckshot, hoping that luck, good fortune, and the muses will be with them. They usually are not.

Planning, preparation, and persistence are the keys to writing a successful screenplay. Figure out the time frame of your story. How long a period of time does it cover? *The Shawshank Redemption* covers more than nineteen years; *The Hours* (David Hare) covers a little more than a day but in three different time periods—1923, 1951, and 2001.

Think about it.

If your action takes place over three hours, three days, three weeks, three months, or a three-year period, you can choose to visualize the passage of time by certain transitions to focus the narrative line into a sharp visual presentation (see more about this in *The Screenwriter's Problem Solver*). If you're adapting something—a novel, play, biography, article, or news story—you can bridge and accent time. The novel *Six Days of the Condor* by James Grady was changed to *Three Days of the Condor* in order to make it a tighter, leaner visual presentation that generates greater tension and drama.

You may decide that Act II takes place within a two-month period. The First Half may be two weeks, the Second Half six weeks. The passage of time can be marked in several ways as mentioned: by seasonal changes, or by specific dialogue references to events like Memorial Day, Labor Day, Christmas, or Halloween, or using an event like an election, a birth, a wedding, or a funeral.

What is the time frame that occurs during Act II? Think about the First Half of Act II: What is the time frame for your action? Decide how long or short it is. Find a workable time frame within which to operate. Trust that the story will tell you what the time period is. Don't get too hung up with it. Don't make it too significant or important.

The time frame is what keeps your story in motion, moving forward from scene to scene, sequence to sequence, act to act. It supports the action, and is held together by the context.

When you begin to outline the action for the First Half of Act II, you have the sub-dramatic context and the time frame which will hold it all together. You have a direction, a line of development that determines what happens in the action leading to the Mid-Point and from there to Plot Point II.

The importance of sub-dramatic context and the time frame gives you greater structural support and enhances the dramatic tension by highlighting the obstacles your main character needs to overcome in order to achieve his or her dramatic need.

When you've completed this for the First Half of Act II, do it for the Second Half. The two units of action are separate and independent even though they are part of the larger whole of Act II and connected by the Mid-Point.

One of the things I discovered in my many workshops here and abroad is that to build this First and Second Half of Act II, there needs to be one major sequence that holds the material together.

During the screenwriting workshop in Brussels, I worked with three European screenwriters, one on one, in front of a large audience of about a hundred people: filmmakers, writers, directors, actors, and many producers. The writers worked on their scripts during this particular two-week workshop. They would discuss their stories and the pages coming up, the audience would raise questions, and when the session was completed, they would go home and write pages for the next session. Then they would come in with their work, anywhere from five to ten pages, and everyone in the course would read them silently together. They were translated for me as I don't read French or Flemish. Next, I would comment on the pages. Questions were raised and dramatic choices explained: Why is this scene better "here" than "there?" Why use the main character here and not another character? Can we change this scene to another locale, or to another act? Do we have to know what happens to the characters between the scenes? What's the purpose of that scene?

We began working on the material for Act II. As we started outlining and building the material from Plot Point I to the Mid-Point, I realized that all we needed was one key sequence to hold the entire First Half of Act II in place. Why? Because the dramatic context holds the story in place, but at the same time, moves it forward.

Look at the* paradigm*:

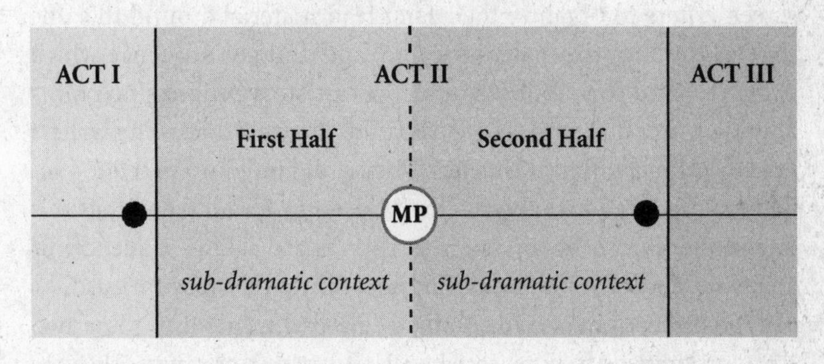

All you need is one important sequence occurring around page 45 in the First Half, and one sequence occurring around page 75 in the Second Half to anchor the thirty-page units of action in place. That's all you need to "hold" these pages together. In the First Half of Act II, that means you need about fifteen pages to get you to that particular sequence and after it's written you only need about fifteen pages to get you to the Mid-Point. Same with the Second Half of Act II. From the Mid-Point to this particular sequence you need about fifteen pages and once you've written it, another ten to fifteen pages to take you to the Plot Point at the end of Act II. Two incidents, each one a story progression, one on approximately page 45 and one on approximately page 75, and you now have two stabilizing sequences that hold these two units of action in place.

In *Chinatown,* which I was using as my teaching film, Hollis Mulwray's murder is discovered on page 45 and is enough to move the story forward to the Mid-Point. The event which is the Mid-Point (the connection between Evelyn, Cross, and Mulwray) is enough of a story progression to move the story forward to the point where Gittes discovers that all the land in the Northeast Valley has been sold to people who are dead or people who are in retirement homes. That story progression moves the story forward as Gittes discovers that Noah Cross is responsible for the murders as well as the water scandal.

During the remainder of the Brussels workshop I advised my screenwriters to organize their First Half material around this one sequence, at approximately page 45, and another sequence which occurs around page 75. Both sequences are story progression points and their function is to simply keep the story on track. The writers loved working with these scenes. They could build up to them, execute them, then move toward the Mid-Point. I've learned that this one sequence can be an action sequence, a dialogue sequence, or anything you want it to be as long as it moves the story forward.

The screenwriters told me that I needed to identify these two story progression points, so when I returned from my workshops abroad I started using these two sequences and my students immediately confirmed their importance. They told me it was the most important element in writing Act II.

I decided to call these two sequences Pinch I, in the First Half of Act II, and Pinch II for the Second Half of Act II. I thought labeling them as *Pinch I* and *Pinch II* was appropriate because these sequences simply "pinch" the story line together to *keep your story on track.* That is their function.

The definition of a Pinch is simple: it is a sequence that keeps the action moving forward to the Mid-Point, or to Plot Point II. It is just a *little pinch* in the story line that keeps the action on track, moving the story forward either to the Mid-Point or Plot Point II. Yes, it is a Plot Point, but more important, it is a sequence the keeps the story on track and moving forward.

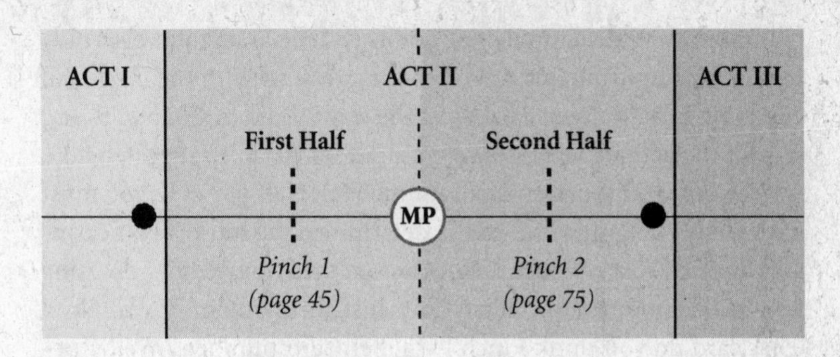

Sometimes there's a relationship between Pinch I and Pinch II, some kind of story connection. In *Thelma & Louise*, at Pinch I the two girls pick up J.D. (Brad Pitt), only to have him steal their money at the Mid-Point. Pinch II occurs when J.D. is picked up by the police and tells them that Thelma and Louise are heading to Mexico. This kind of symmetry doesn't happen all the time; it really depends upon your story line and situation.

The more I use Pinch I and Pinch II as an anchoring sequence in the structuring of Act II, the more valuable I find them. When you approach structuring Act II, you build the story line in units of dramatic action; we build the First Half of Act II, then the Second Half of Act II. As mentioned, first we determine the Mid-Point, then establish the sub-dramatic context of the First Half, then the sub-dramatic context of the Second Half. Only when you have the context of this unit of action can you determine Pinch I. What is the incident, episode, or event that keeps the story on track?

Once you establish that, you can move forward into the Second Half of Act II. You know the Mid-Point and you know Plot Point II. What is the theme of action that keeps the story moving forward to Plot Point II? That's your sub-dramatic context. Write it down on the paradigm. Next, determine Pinch II, that sequence that keeps the story on track heading toward Plot Point II.

Now, the nice thing about structure is that it's flexible. We can always move these structural points up and down, or forward and backward, on the paradigm. We always have to keep in mind that this is just the starting point, not the end point.

Once you've structured these points on the paradigm, we're ready to begin structuring Act II. We're going to start with the First Half of Act II. Take fourteen cards, just the way we did in Chapter 9, and lay out the action the same way you did for Act I. To repeat, before you lay out your fourteen cards for the First Half of Act II, you must have established your Mid-Point, determined the sub-dramatic context, and established Pinch I. Now, lay out these fourteen cards, using free-association, for the First Half. Just throw them down. Now, what card do you think Pinch I will be? Card number 7. Why? Because it occurs about halfway through the First Half of Act II, approximately page 45.

Go over and over the cards until they feel comfortable. Remember that the essence of Act II is conflict, so seek out those conflicts, either internal or external, whenever and wherever you can. And remember, the purpose of each scene is to either move the story forward or reveal information about the character.

If you get lost somewhere in the creative maze that is Act II, you could spend days, perhaps weeks, in frustration and despair trying to find your way out of the pit. But as you're writing Act II, you have to understand that you have no objectivity at all. If you doubt yourself in terms or the material, you'll start censoring everything, and you won't be able to write anything! If you don't watch out, that's when you'll become your own victim and start to experience writer's block. Don't let that happen.

Keep writing no matter how you feel about it, whether you think it's good, bad, or indifferent. Just write your story, page by page, scene by scene, shot by shot, and leave all your judgments and evaluations in the nightstand drawer next to your bed.

Breaking Act II into the First and Second Half, then establishing the sub-dramatic context and time frame, then Pinch I and Pinch II, allows you to gain a structural overview that keeps your story on track. It will guide you through the obstacle course that leads to the next step in the screenwriting process—the actual writing of Act II.

THE STORY: *A young woman, a painter in an unhappy marriage, enrolls in an art class and has an affair with her teacher. Against her will, she falls in love with him, then learns she is pregnant. Torn between her husband and lover, she decides to leave both and raise her child by herself.*

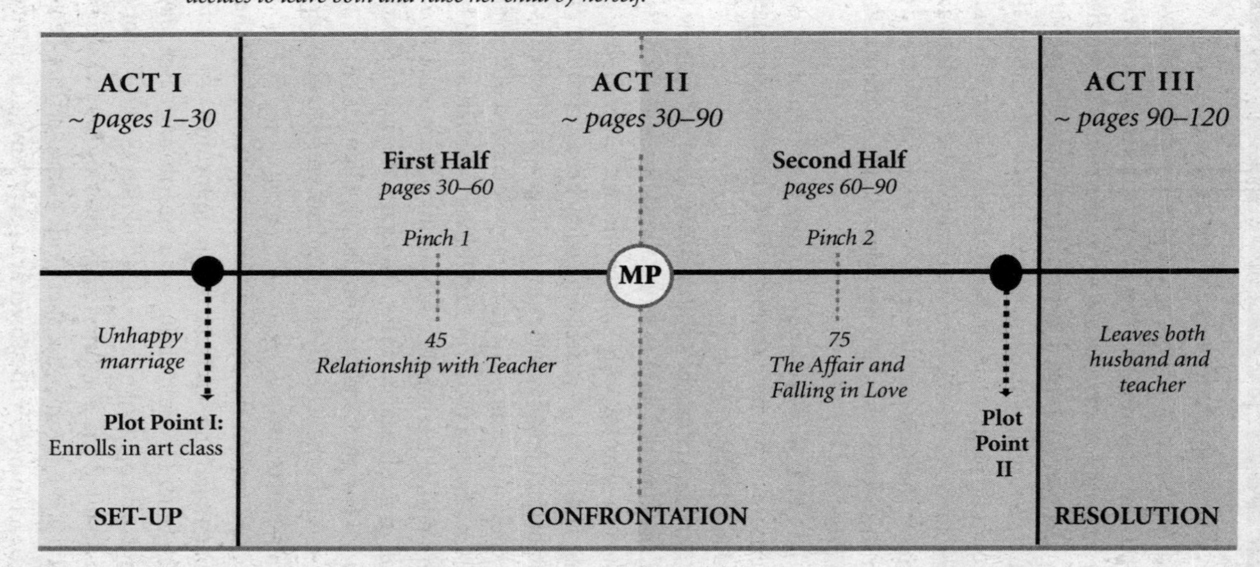

MP = A link in the chain of dramatic action; it CONNECTS the first half of Act II with the second half of Act II

THE EXERCISE

Let's do the following exercise as a "tune-up."

Look at the *paradigm* (on the previous page): we have a story about a young woman in an unhappy marriage who enrolls in an art class and ends up having an affair with her teacher.

The way it's broken down and structured is the same way we structure all our exercises: we choose the ending first, the beginning next, then Plot Points I and II, then the Mid-Point, then the time frame, then we establish the sub-dramatic context for the First Half of Act II, than the sub-dramatic context for the Second Half, and only then do we determine Pinches I and II.

In Act I, we set up our story by establishing the unhappy marriage of our main character. Plot Point I is when she enrolls in the art class.

Since we know she's going to have an affair with the teacher, and become pregnant at Plot Point II, the Mid-Point would be when she has sex with him for the first time. In that way, the First Half is where we see her juggling her art class, her painting, and her marriage, as well as her feelings about herself as she gets to know the teacher. The sub-dramatic context of this First Half of Act II would focus on establishing the relationship between her and her teacher. The sub-dramatic context of the Second Half of Act II deals with her falling in love with her teacher.

Take another look at it on the paradigm.

Go over the action. What incident, episode, or event do you think Pinch I is?

Let's look at the possibilities: It might be where the young woman and the teacher have an opportunity to get to know each other for the first time on a one-to-one basis. Maybe she wants an appraisal of her work and they go out for coffee after class; or her car won't start in the parking lot and she borrows his cell phone; or he gives her a ride home and they decide they like each other; or they meet at a party. Any such situation will work as Pinch I.

Our character is not about to jump right into bed with her teacher, no matter how unhappy she might be with her husband. She is cautious, and her actions will be appropriate to the circumstances. Otherwise, we don't have any sympathy for her, and your main character must always be sympathetic. And what about the teacher? Who is he? What kind of person is he? You would do a character biography on him just to see what kind of a person he is. Student and teacher would spend time together getting to know each other, which we could show, and then, at Mid-Point, they have sex for the first time. That gives you about fifteen pages of script to visually reveal their relationship.

During the Second Half of Act II the student falls in love with the teacher, leading us to Plot Point II, where she discovers she's pregnant. It could be a scene in a doctor's office, or the results of a pregnancy test. If they have an intense and passionate scene making love, this might be the scene where she conceives.

In this scenario, what scene do you think Pinch II is? Think about it. Study the *paradigm.* Write down a few ideas.

Going to the doctor's office
Having a fight with her husband
Getting into an argument with the teacher
Leaving her husband
Telling the teacher she loves him
Learning the teacher has a wife
A weekend trip where they make love and she conceives

Any one of these sequences will work effectively. What do you think?

I know what I would do: Pinch II would be where she first misses her period. That incident sets up choices: is she pregnant? Finding out leads her to her choices: have an abortion; tell her husband about it; leave her husband; leave both husband and lover and have the baby on her own and start life over again as a single person, mother, and painter. Or, does she want to start a new life with the teacher? In other words, how does she resolve her dilemma in Act III?

You don't have to use *my* ending. You may have a different one. All the dramatic choices listed above can work. The right one is the one that works for you.

If it works, use it; if it doesn't, don't. That's the rule. Try it. If it doesn't work, see what does work. Don't be afraid to make some mistakes. When you are writing a screenplay you've got to be open and receptive to all those little "accidents" that mysteriously happen on the blank sheet of paper.

Don't get too hung up on what you want to happen; let it happen. Screenwriting is a process, it continually changes and endures.

That's the real joy of writing.

14

Writing Act II

> "The idea emerges and once it gets to the writing stage, all the work's been done. It's really all the pre-work that's the real heavy work. Once you get to the point where you sit at the typewriter [computer] all the hard work is over and it's really just getting it down, which is no problem at all."
>
> —Woody Allen

As mentioned earlier, the best and most effective way to enter Act II is from your character's dramatic need. It's important to redefine what your main character wants to win, gain, get, or achieve during the course of your screenplay. What is it that drives him or her through the action to bring a resolution to whatever crisis or situation, either emotional or physical, your character finds himself in? Can you define it? Articulate it?

Has your character's dramatic need changed at Plot Point I? Remember, if your character's dramatic need changes, it will change at Plot Point I. That is the true beginning of your story.

During the preparation of Act II, did you think about what obstacles your character might confront during this course of narrative action? Preparing to write Act II means that you need to know approximately four major obstacles that your character confronts to get through the story line. As with all obstacles, they can either be internal or external, physical or emotional, mental or spiritual.

The foundation of all good writing is *conflict.* Stating it once again, all drama is conflict; without conflict you have no action; without action you have no character; without character you have no story. And without story you have no screenplay. Films like: *The Hours, Chinatown, The Manchurian Candidate, A Place in the Sun* (Michael Wilson and Harry Brown), *Cold Mountain,* and *American Beauty* have both internal and external conflict.

External conflict is where the conflict is outside the character, and the characters face physical (and in some part, emotional, of course) obstacles, such as in *Cold Mountain, Collateral, Apollo 13,* and *Jurassic Park* (Michael Crichton and David Koepp). Creating conflict within the story through characters and events is one of those simple, basic "truths" of all writing whether it be novel, play, or screenplay.

So what is *conflict*? If you look at the word it means to be "in opposition to," and the hub of any dramatic scene is having the character(s) be in opposition to some*one* or some*thing.* Conflict can be anything, a struggle, a quarrel, a battle, or a chase scene, fear of life, fear of failure or success, internal or external, any kind of confrontation or obstacle, and it really doesn't matter whether it's emotional, physical, or mental. If you do not have enough conflict, you'll find yourself more often than not caught in a quagmire of dull writing.

Conflict can be expressed either physically or emotionally. You can talk about it through dialogue, or you can express it through physical acts, or you can have your character respond to it. Conflict, no matter what form it takes, becomes the engine that drives the story line through the second act.

Remember too that dialogue is a function of character. Let's review its purpose. Dialogue:

- moves the story forward
- reveals information about the character (after all, they do have a history)
- communicates necessary facts and information to the reader

- establishes character relationships; makes them real, natural, and spontaneous
- gives your characters depth, insight, and purpose
- reveals the conflicts of the story and characters
- reveals the emotional states of your characters
- comments on the action

Your first attempts at writing dialogue in Act II will probably be unnatural, clichéd, fragmented, and strained. Writing dialogue is like learning to swim; you're going to flounder around a bit, but the more you do the easier it gets. When you enter the First Half of Act II it may take you several pages to get into a rhythm of both story and dialogue.

Don't worry about it. It takes anywhere from forty to fifty pages before your characters start talking to you. And they *do* start talking to you. Just let it be okay to write shitty pages, with stilted, direct, dumb, and obvious dialogue. Keep writing. Dialogue can always be cleaned up during the rewrite. "Writing is rewriting" is the ancient adage.

A word to those of you who are looking for "inspiration" to guide you during this process; sorry to say it but you're probably not going to find it. Inspiration is measured in moments, a few minutes, or hours. A screenplay depends on diligence and discipline and is measured in weeks and months. If it takes you a hundred days to write a screenplay and you're "on" for ten of those days, consider yourself lucky. Being "on" for one hundred days, or twenty-five days, just doesn't happen. Especially writing Act II. You may "hear" that it does, but in truth it's the pot at the end of the rainbow—you're chasing a dream.

"But..." you say.

But what? You mean, those stories, rumors, or hearsay that tells you that so and so wrote his or her screenplay that sold for millions in a week or two? Or, the second cousin of a friend of a friend's friend knows someone who wrote the entire screenplay in two days? Is that what that "but" refers to?

Forget it. Writing, as I tell everyone who's even thinking about writing a screenplay, is a day-by-day job, two to three hours a day, five or six days a week, either during the day or on weekends, three or more pages a day, ten pages or more a week. Shot by shot, scene by scene, sequence by sequence, page by page, act by act. And some days are better than others.

Just remember that when you're *in* the *paradigm,* you can't *see* the *paradigm.*

Even though the card system is your map and your guide, the Plot Points, Mid-Point, sub-dramatic context, and Pinches I and II are your checkpoints along the way, the "last-chance" gas station before you hit the high desert which is the ending—your destination.

What's nice about the card system is that once it's done you can forget it. But at this stage, where we're writing Act II, we're going to use the cards to build the First and Second Halves of Act II.

In review, one card equals one scene, but when you're writing the screenplay, that is a contradiction. As you're writing Act II, you'll suddenly "discover" a new scene that you hadn't even thought about, or a scene that simply works better than what you put down on the cards. If you're in doubt about whether to use it or not use it, use it. That scene will lead you to veer off the path of the cards into a few new scenes or sequences that you hadn't even considered. I think that's great. Do it. Write it. Pinches I and II and the Mid-Point will be your structural guidelines, keeping you on the path of your story. If that happens, just go with it because it's important to write those scenes or sequences. You can tell within a few pages whether they are working or not. You'll finish these new pages, feeling satisfied with your efforts, but then a sudden question might hit you: what happens next? And, you don't have a clue, you don't know what to do, or where to go. Take a breath and just look at the next card. You'll find you have a perfect lead-in to the next scene you have organized on the cards. And if those new scenes don't work, just know that all you've lost is a couple of days, but you've maintained your creative energy. In reality, you haven't lost anything.

Your creative mind has assimilated those new scenes so you can throw out what you thought might work and still be following the *direction* of your story.

Remember, when you're doing the cards, you're doing the cards. When you're writing the screenplay, you're writing the screenplay. Forget rigid adherence to the cards. Let them guide you; don't be a slave to them. What's the point? If you ever feel a spontaneous moment that gives you a better, more fluid story, write it.

As you're laying out the scenes, you'll find once again that the actual writing experience differs from the way you laid out the cards. Don't worry about changing the cards to fit the story, or adding new things in the development of the story and characters. At this point, you should be starting to feel comfortable with the form.

Begin Act II by designing the opening scene or sequence. You have your character's dramatic need clearly in focus. Now you can think about where to enter the scene. Think about entering late and getting out early. That is, try to enter the scene at the last possible moment just before the major "reveal" is established. "Reveal" is what the scene is all about; either it moves the story forward or reveals information about the character. Each scene should be about one thing, should have one "beat" to it. Do you know what the purpose of the scene is? Where did your character come from? Where is he or she going to? Did you have to change his or her dramatic need? What about the conflict within the scene? Is it internal, or external? What is the obstacle that keeps your character from achieving his or her dramatic need? If you don't know, who does?

How are you going to enter the scene? At the beginning? In the middle? Or, right at the end. Most of the time you'll enter the scene right before the purpose of the scene is revealed. As you're sketching in the context, it may help you to find the elements, or components, of the action. Does the scene you're writing fall into the space of the sub-dramatic context for the First Half of Act II? For example, if your context is a young woman—an artist—in an unhappy marriage, fill in and dramatize the context of her relationship with her husband. Do the same with her painting, with her friend(s), and with herself. These four elements can fill an entire thirty-page unit of action.

Make the story line clean and simple; don't clutter it up with too many details or too many twists and turns of plot. Once again, screenwriting is telling a story with pictures, of finding places where silence works better than words. And, to repeat once again, the purpose of each scene is to either move the story forward or reveal information about the character.

Write the first ten pages of the Second Half. Just tell your story, don't worry about frills or gimmicks. Make sure you are clear on your dramatic context and time frame. Again, work in ten-page units, moving the action forward through Pinch II to the plot point at the end of Act II. If you want to clean up your ten-page sections, do it. Then move on. Always move forward from beginning to end, beginning to end. Don't spend time rewriting now. You'll do that later.

If need be, reread Chapter 10 of *Screenplay*, "The Scene." If a new scene springs out of the page, write it down. If you find that you're leaving the action you wrote on the cards and you feel you want to follow this new direction, do it. The worst that can happen is you write a few scenes and realize they don't work. No problem. Just go back and pick up the story where you left off. What you try that doesn't work will always show you what *does* work; mistakes and changes are part of the writing experience. I don't know why it happens or how it happens—all I know is that it does happen. It's the writing process; it's larger than we are.

Be clean and tight; don't clog up the action with a lot of description or dialogue, or new plot twists and surprises. The context is *confrontation;* your character is confronting obstacles that keep him or her from achieving his or her dramatic need.

After you complete the first ten pages of the First Half of Act II, move into the second ten pages. You're heading toward Pinch I, so design these second ten pages carefully. Your cards may be a great help to you here, or not. In my own screenplays, when I'm writing this unit of action I always let my creative impulse guide my direction. Since I have my structure in place, I don't worry about whether I'm doing something that may not work, or may not be able to change.

Do you know what scenes you have to write before you get to Pinch I? Describe them. Define them. Then write them. Follow your story line. Or, follow the new story line that seems to be emerging on the pages. I've found that when I'm writing the First Half of Act II, they always seem to be the most difficult pages. I think this happens because you have to *rediscover* your story. If Plot Point I is the true beginning of your story, how do we begin to keep the story on track with tension, pacing, and suspense? It's like starting over again, from the beginning, only this time it's the second act. So, don't be surprised if you find your story line or the direction of the story starting to wander a little bit. Around page 50 or 60 you'll begin to get back on the narrative path—the Mid-Point is that great anchor that keeps your story line rooted in your structure.

Pinch I helps you get to the Mid-Point. If you feel your story's too long, and there are too many scenes or pages, don't worry about it. The questions that always seem to come up when you're writing are: "Is this scene necessary? Should I write it, or not?" And the answer is this: *when in doubt, write.* If you start censoring yourself as you are writing the first words-on-paper draft, you'll find that you are starting a process within your own head that will not serve you or your writing experience. If you start criticizing yourself too much you'll keep telling yourself that you don't need this scene, or that scene, and if that happens, more often than not, you'll find that the impulse to second-guess or criticize your own work will impede your writing process. If you are in doubt about whether to write a scene or not, just write it. The worst that can happen is that your first words-on-paper draft is one hundred seventy to two hundred pages long. So what? It's easier to cut out scenes than it is to write new ones. Trust me on this.

Just keep writing, moving forward, page by page, scene by scene, from Mid-Point to Pinch II to Plot Point II. Writing, as I have to constantly remind myself, is a day-by-day process, three pages a day, five or six days a week. If you have a full-time job, think about the ten pages you're going to write during the week, then on the weekend sit down and write them. In this way, you can do ten pages a week easily.

Writing Act II will be about the same as writing Act I, except now, working with screenplay form is easier, and by now you've built up enough discipline so that you can sit down for a few hours each day and work on your script. But you're making more changes now than in Act I. And that sometimes creates a problem. It's easy to get lost or confused in the maze of your own creation.

You may become aware of judgments and decisions and evaluations that pop up with regular persistence. Suddenly you'll know a line of dialogue doesn't ring true, that you're forcing it; you'll know deep down inside yourself that what you're writing is not working and you'll know that it's not very good.

You might think to yourself, if these pages are so bad, what about the other pages I've written? You might go back and read some of the pages you've written. And you know what? They're terrible. Awful.

Fear and panic and insecurity grip your heart; your mind begins racing. What am I doing? This story doesn't work at all. You try to calm yourself, but it's impossible. What to do? Drink? Drugs? Depression? Sex? A buying spree? Vacation? Isolation? Lose your identity? Feel worthless?

You need some help, you might reason, an "assessment." You'll call a friend to read your pages. You might expect the worst, but deep down *you know what you want to hear.*

Your friend reads what you've written and confirms your doubts and fears, saying, "I think your pages are fine, there's nothing wrong with them." Of course, they're not telling you the truth, they're just trying to be nice and spare your feelings.

Or your friend will tell you your pages are not strong enough; they're "too wordy," or the focus should be on another character, and what you should do is this, and they give you an elaborate example of what they *think* your story is about. Of course, they don't know because you don't know either. What to do, what to do?

At this point, you're over the edge in paranoia and, like Bob Dylan sings, you're "stuck inside of Mobile, with the Memphis blues again."

Many people just stop right there. They believe their own judgments, their own evaluations, their own opinions. They become their own victims. The truth is you can't see anything right now because you have no objectivity and no overview at all. What you wrote may not be very good. So what? Most of the First Half of Act II is not going to be very good. It seems contrived, dull, stilted, or overwritten.

This insecurity acts as a trigger, springing judgments and opinions into play. There's only one thing you must remember about your judgments and evaluations: *who* is making these comments and decisions?

You answer that one.

You can either let your judgments and evaluations get in the way of your writing experience or not. It's up to you. You do have a choice; you do have a voice, a say in the matter. Use it.

If you find your mind racing, criticizing what you're writing, there is a simple exercise you can do to quiet your mind. Simply *give the critic a voice.*

When you're writing your pages, the "critic" part of you that's at the back of your head will be relentless and unmerciful. It will hound you, harass you, and hassle you. You're going to have to deal with it sometime—it might as well be now.

How do you deal with this? Take a blank sheet of paper. Title it the Critic's Page. Put it near your work pages, whether you write by computer or longhand or typewriter. Now there is your work sheet and a blank sheet of paper in front of you—one for the script, the other for "the critic."

Now, start writing. As you're writing you'll notice some familiar thoughts or judgments or self-evaluations coming up. Write these negative thoughts and judgments down (they're never positive, unfortunately) on the Critic's Page.

Continue writing your script. If and when another negative thought or judgment or doubt crops up in your mind, simply write it down on the Critic's Page. You might want to number each comment the critic makes.

Give the critic a voice. You'll be writing and the critic's voice will emerge. Stop working on the screenplay and write down what the critic says. See how it makes you feel. When you complete one page, use another. If you're like me, you'll probably be writing more on the Critic's Pages than you will on your script pages.

The first day you do this exercise you may end up with about two or three pages of screenplay and one or two pages of criticism. The next day, do it again. But this time you're going to be more watchful and you may end up with two pages of screenplay and three or four Critic's Pages. The next day, do the same thing and you may have three pages of script and three pages of the Critic.

When you've done this exercise for three days, put all the Critic's Pages in a drawer and forget about them.

Go back to writing your screenplay for a couple of days. After you've taken a short break from the Critic, open up the drawer and read the Critic's Pages. Just read them. You'll notice an amazing thing. All the comments the Critic made *say the same thing*! They're all negative, they're all judgmental, and they all say that what you're writing is not very good, the dialogue is poor, the story and characters are weak, and you're probably just wasting your time writing the screenplay. Or, maybe you should get a partner, or go work out or go shopping or something.

Every day that you were working and jotting down the Critic's thoughts and comments, they're basically saying the same thing. The pages are no damn good.

So what? Maybe the Critic is right; maybe the pages aren't very good *at this point*! But this is only the first words-on-paper draft. It doesn't mean you can't change them to make them better. What's so important about this exercise is that you become aware of the voice inside your head making these judgments and evaluations. No matter what you write or say, the Critic inside your head is going to say the same thing. Worthless, not good enough, or it's been done before so give it up.

You can't give it up. After all, your negative thoughts are only your own self-judgments, they don't mean too much in the broad scheme of things. Everybody has them. We either let them get in the way of what we want to do, or we sidestep them. If we react too intensely, or too seriously, we can easily become our own victims.

And I speak from experience.

"Perfection," as Jean Renoir constantly reminded me, "exists only in the mind, not in reality." Something to think about.

As you continue to write the scenes and sequences of Act II, remember your visual dynamics. Continually keep in mind that you want to keep your story visual, cinematic. Even if you are using a screenwriting formatting software like Final Draft, notice whether your scenes go from INT. to INT. to INT. to INT. with only a few EXT. scenes. Think about transitions, those lines of description or dialogue that take you from one scene to the next. Do you show your character walking out of the building? Standing on the street waiting for a taxi? Riding on the metro? Driving in a car through the crowded streets? Walking into a building? Taking an elevator? Arriving at the airport? Do you show the plane in flight? Landing at the airport? In the baggage area? Think visually. Open up your story. As an example, go from INT. to EXT. to INT. to INT. to EXT. And be aware of visual transitions.

Transitions are those scenes, or sequences, or montages that show the passage of time. Links between the scenes and sequences have to be conceived visually, for moving the action from one scene to the next requires a visual transition. *Transitions* bridge time and move the action forward quickly, visually. Whether you're writing an original screenplay, or adapting a novel, play, magazine, or news article into a screenplay, each scene or sequence can bridge a particular *time* to a particular *place* in order to move the story forward. To go from Point A to Point B in a screenplay requires making transitions which connect the two.

There are four major ways to make *transitions:* cutting from *picture to picture, sound to sound, music to music, or special effect to special effect.* There can be *dissolves, fade outs,* and *smash cuts.*

It wasn't too long ago that the screenwriter depended on the director or film editor to create these visual transitions, but it is really the writer's responsibility to write the required transitions. One of the recognizable traits of a professional screenwriter is his or her ability to write good visual transitions. At the present time, there is an evolutionary trend in the style and sophistication of the art of transition. Even a script like *Pulp Fiction,* which is sequential and episodic, uses effective transitions so the five episodes that make up the screenplay seem to be connected into a single story line. The title page even proclaims the script is really "three stories about one story." If Tarantino and Avery had not created those transitions, the script would have been disjointed and episodic and not worked as well as it does.

As far as I'm concerned, it is the screenwriter's responsibility to write these transitional scenes that move the story forward and bridge time, place, and action. Writing good transitions is also a very good way to solve a number of problems.

In *The Shawshank Redemption,* for example, the passage of time is handled incredibly well. Only one shot is needed to show us the passage of time: the large posters of Rita Hayworth, Marilyn Monroe, and Raquel Welch pinned up on the jail cell's walls visually indicate the passage of several decades. In *How to Make an American Quilt* (Jane Anderson), Finn (Winona Ryder), a young woman of twenty-six, is kneeling down looking at a book and we hear her voiceover narration: "How do two separate people fuse into this thing called a couple? And if your love is that strong, then how do you still keep a little room for yourself..." That's what the whole film is about, and when Finn stands up, we match cut to her as a little girl of five or six, looking at the women in the quilting bee as her narration leads us directly into the story line.

Why are transitions so important? Because when you're reading a script, or seeing a movie, it has to flow smoothly across a time period that is usually not more than two hours. The story line has to be a seamless parade of images across the page or screen, and time, then, becomes a relative phenomenon. Days and years and decades can be condensed into seconds, a few seconds stretched into minutes as a leap is made from one image to another. That's one of the things that makes *The Shawshank Redemption* such a remarkable movie; the passage of time does not draw attention to itself. It becomes an integral part of the fabric of the screenplay.

Transitions can be as varied and as multiple as the colors in a kaleidoscope. In *The Silence of the Lambs,* for example, the screenwriter, Ted Tally, generally plays the last line of one scene over the first line of the next. The dialogue is used to bridge time and action and shows one way that *sound* can be used as the link connecting two different scenes. Tally ends one scene with a question, then opens the next scene by answering that question.

This kind of overlapping transition scene has been done many times before, of course, most notably in *Julia,* Alvin Sargent's Academy Award–winning screenplay adapted from Lillian Hellman's *Pentimento.* But the way Tally approached his transitions pushes the boundaries of the medium in such a way that we're not even aware of them. If you're watching a movie and become aware of the visual transitions, or feel the "arty" influence of the director in each scene, chances are it's not a very good film.

The style and sophistication of the transition is evolving all the time. In *Lone Star,* John Sayles makes his transitions bridging time and action in a very unique way: he has the characters remain in present time, then pans the camera over to a character or a place and suddenly we have moved either forward or backward in time. It's very effective, extremely visual, and I think shows the remarkable versatility of Sayles as a writer and director.

Apollo 13 (William Broyles and Al Reinert) is a film based on an actual historic event, and the screenwriters bridge time and action by simply cutting back and forth, a technique called *cross-cutting,* between the three astronauts in the spacecraft and the Mission Control team in Houston. The story moves forward by action/

reaction, and is held together by the events and circumstances. *Thelma & Louise* also moves forward by cross-cutting, between the two women on the run and the policeman searching for them.

Every screenplay has its own particular style and form in terms of transitions. An action film usually has short, quick transitions, because the film moves forward at a very rapid pace and we have to be swept up into the action. But in a character-driven piece like *Brokeback Mountain* the transitions come from silence, or looks between the characters, or a few lines of dialogue. There is never any *one right way* to make transitions. The only criterion is whether *it works or not.*

There may be times when you're so engrossed in putting the story down on paper that you don't even think about the transitional flow of the script. But when you finish the first draft you might discover that you've written a screenplay that may be a hundred and sixty pages or longer. During the actual screenwriting process that's okay, but ultimately it's too long, so you're going to have to do a lot of work to cut it to length. A one-hundred-forty-plus-page screenplay is only accepted if it's by William Goldman, Quentin Tarantino, David Koepp, or Eric Roth.

If your screenplay is too long, and you feel there's too much going on, or too many things happening or too many characters, look for ways to bridge the time and action through transitions. Transitions solve many problems in screenwriting and sometimes the bridge to another time or another place can be as simple as changing the character's clothes, or using match cuts, or changing the weather, or using holidays to condense the time and action.

Don't describe too much or explain too much, and don't end up with "thick" paragraphs. Leave wide margins, left and right, at top and bottom. You want a lot of space on the page. Be sparse and simple in your descriptions, using no more than five or six sentences for each one. Read a screenplay, any good screenplay, and look for how transitions are executed.

Sometimes you may have to write a full scene—beginning,

middle, and end—before you discover you can cut it down to a portion of the beginning and a few lines of the end.

Forget about camera angles and technical information. Don't show the reader how much you know. Simply write in master scenes. INT. OFFICE—DAY, and go from there.

Your writing will feel comfortable now, and your characters will be talking to you, telling you what they want to do, where they want to go. Go with the process. Don't be too dogmatic about staying in control.

Follow the focus of your main character; be aware that you want the main character to be active, to initiate things, to cause things to happen. Your main character must always be active, like Inman in *Cold Mountain,* not passive. Action is character; what a person does is who he or she is, not what he says. Film is behavior.

If you need to restructure your story, do it. Structure is flexible, like a tree that bends in the wind but does not break. In the same way, scenes and sequences and passages of dialogue can be moved or repositioned anywhere you want them to go—as long as it works!

Until a few years ago, buildings in Los Angeles and San Francisco could legally not be more than twelve stories high because of the continuous earthquake hazard. Now high-rise buildings are going up everywhere. In their construction they are designed to roll and sway back and forth during a quake, giving in to the shock of the earth moving. Nature is too strong to resist, so we need to bend with it.

The same thing can be said for structure. Remember the definition: "to build something or put together something." It is not a rigid, unbreakable foundation, but fluid and organic to the changing needs of your story line. If you let it, structure can bend to the needs of your story. That's why the paradigm is not a formula like many people say; it is *a form* that bends and fits the needs of your story.

One of my students was writing a coming-of-age comedy about a young girl in the sixties who loses her virginity in a tacky, awful, first sexual encounter and becomes pregnant. In the end, she journeys to Mexico for an abortion and returns to the U.S. just as John Kennedy is assassinated. It is more than just a "losing virginity" story; it is the story about a young girl coming of age in a time when the entire nation is shifting its consciousness and awareness.

Originally, the story was structured like this: at Plot Point I she sees the boy she is attracted to; at Pinch I she knows this is the person she wants to make love with; at Mid-Point she has sex with the boy. At Pinch II she discovers she's pregnant, and at Plot Point II she leaves for Mexico to have the abortion. Act III deals with the abortion and her return home, a lot older and wiser.

When my student started writing and began to build and define the relationship between her main character and her two best friends, she realized she needed more time and pages to reveal their friendship. By the time she reached her supposed Mid-Point, having sex with her first love, her main character hadn't even considered birth control. (This was the sixties, remember, before the Pill.)

The writer became anxious and concerned, and I told her to simply change the structure and expand her story line. At first, she resisted, but I told her we had to bend with the needs of the story. Reluctantly, she changed it. Plot Point I now became a scene in which the girl makes the decision to lose her virginity. Pinch I became the party where she meets the boy but he doesn't want anything to do with her. The new Mid-Point is where she is determined to have sex with him. Pinch II now becomes the moment she has sex with the boy and loses her virginity, and at Plot Point II she becomes pregnant. Mexico would be a very small sequence in Act III.

All she had to do was shift the structure to accommodate the needs of the story. Structure is what "holds" the story together, but it can bend and shift to include whatever new elements you need to put in.

When you're writing Act II, your story will most likely be shifting and changing. You'll write one scene, then find you need to add another scene that will dramatize an aspect of your story you hadn't thought about when you were doing the cards. Go with it. Let it change. Right now, you're finding the focus of your story and it's changing because you can't really "see" what you've written. You have no objectivity, no overview; you're just climbing the mountain and can only see the pages you're writing and the pages you've written.

Writing should always be an adventure. The paradigm is a roadmap of your screenplay. You can get off the main highway and go exploring and if you get lost or confused and don't know where you are or where you're going, go back to the paradigm; if need be, choose a new Plot Point, Pinch, or Mid-Point and start over from there. It's only temporary. Just tell your story.

You'll learn to adapt to the needs of your story. As Renoir used to say, "learning is the ability to see the relationship between things." It took me many years to understand what he meant.

I take a lot of baths when I'm working and do a lot of work in the tub, preparing new material, planning the next scene or chapter, and so on. Dalton Trumbo (*Spartacus, Lonely Are the Brave,* to name only two) worked in his bathtub a lot, as does Nick Meyer (*The Seven-Per-Cent Solution, Time After Time,* and several *Star Trek* films).

My bathtub sits next to a large three-sided bay window; it has a big stationary pane in the middle and two smaller windows on either side.

One day while I was taking a bath, a large black bumblebee found its way into the bathroom and couldn't find a way out. He circled the room, then gathered speed and flew directly into the large middle pane of glass. He tried again and again, and the same thing happened over and over again. I tried to stifle my concern as the rage and panic of the bee became louder and louder.

I watched the bee slamming into the window for what seemed an eternity, knowing that all he had to do to get free was stop, rest a moment, get his bearings, and look around to see if there was another way out. The open side window, fresh air, and escape were only three inches away.

Couldn't he see, I wondered, that what he was doing wasn't working? As this drama unfolded, I wondered whether I had ever done the same thing, pursued something—a job, a screenplay, a scene, a relationship—trying to make something work that wasn't working. I thought about it and recalled many episodes in my life when I had pursued something that wasn't working, that I knew would never work, but I continually struggled to make it work with the same intensity as that bee slamming into the solid pane of glass.

Emotion welled up inside me. Yes, I *had* done that, I knew, and more than once. I still do it, in some ways and probably will do it again. It's a universal experience, one we all share, human as well as bee.

I watched that bee lunge into that glass again and again. I started getting angry. I wanted him out of my bathroom. I wasn't going to chase or kill him, I just wanted him out. I closed my eyes and turned inward and steadied myself with my breathing. Then I thought to myself, Bee, just stop what you're doing. It's not working. Admit it, face it, confront it, deal with it. The open window, your escape to freedom, is only inches away.

I focused on the bee, visualizing him leaving by the window that was only a few inches away. For a moment, nothing happened. Then suddenly, like magic, the bee stopped, resting on the glass. The silence was broken only by the slight dripping of water in the bath. I held my breath, afraid to move. Then the bee arched back, felt the stream of fresh air coming through the open window, and was gone.

I breathed a long sigh of relief as a wave of emotion surged through me. I had shared a common experience with that bee, learned from him, and all the sadness and unhappiness and despair and pain of remembered moments filled me. Tears welled up in my eyes. It was a somber, profound moment.

"Trying to make something work that wasn't working" has often happened when I was writing a screenplay. I'd get lost or confused about my story and then wander around searching to get back on track, not knowing where I was or where I was going. What I was doing wasn't working, but I continued to think that if I was persistent enough, and kept working and working and working, "hitting my head against the typewriter," as I described it, I would eventually find a way out of my confusion.

It never worked.

One of my students was writing a contemporary romantic comedy about a single mother, a successful career woman, who has been in a relationship with a psychiatrist for four years. When the story opens, the therapist, a successful author and also a single parent, will not commit himself to marriage.

In the back story, the relationship has been through several upheavals. At Plot Point I, the main character severs the relationship "for good" and joins a support group for people who have been in dead-end relationships. The First Half of Act II deals with the sudden appearance of the ex-husband after an absence of five years. He won't leave her alone. She resists as much as she can, then finally gives in.

She reestablishes the relationship with her ex-husband. What didn't work the first time around also doesn't work the second time around, and she ends her involvement with him. The Mid-Point occurs when she resolves to "make it or break it" with the psychiatrist.

Everything in the script was working except for the First Half of Act II. The appearance of the ex-husband never worked within the context of the story line, as funny or as cute as it might have been. The screenplay was based on a true story, and the writer was determined to make it work, come hell or high water. She wrote four totally different versions of the First Half of Act II, and none of them worked. The context, the relationship with the ex-husband, never worked to begin with; either the main character was unsympathetic or the ex-husband was unlikable.

Finally, my student threw her pages down in despair and disgust, lost, confused, angry, panicked. So I told her the story of the bumblebee. The First Half of Act II wasn't working, and she just better stop slamming against the windowpane.

Reluctantly, she agreed.

So she went back to the drawing board, and in the revised version, when the ex-husband does show up, she tells him to get lost. With her newfound independence she becomes even more attractive, and the humor comes out of her interaction with men. The Mid-Point stayed the same.

If you find your material is not working, just stop and rethink it. If it works, it works; if it doesn't, it doesn't. The things you try that don't work will always show you what does work. You have to make these creative mistakes in order to keep the focus on your story line.

The moral of the story is simple: if you do get lost, or confused, or if you're trying to make something work that doesn't work, just stop and take a look around. See if you're slamming against a windowpane.

Rethink it. You're working in ten-page segments of a thirty-page unit of dramatic action. If you do get lost, you can always find out where you are; just go back and look at your story line on the paradigm and see if you have to shift your structural components, or change the dramatic context. Ask your characters what you should do; they'll tell you what you need to know.

The hardest thing about writing is knowing what to write. By the same token, give yourself a pat on the back if something works the way you thought it would.

Confusion is the first step toward clarity.

THE EXERCISE

It's time now to sit down and "do it."

You've prepared your material well.

Start from Plot Point I and put the cards out as a reference point to the Mid-Point. Work in ten-page units, keeping Pinch I clearly in mind. Focus on conflict. Remember, if you know your character's dramatic need, you'll be able to create obstacles to that need and then your story becomes your character overcoming all obstacles to achieve his or her dramatic need. Sometimes, if you're stuck on a scene, it's beneficial to create the opposite point of view; you can write the scene from the other character's point of view, then go back and change it, writing it from your character's point of view. If your character is an actress reading for a major part, and she knows she's right for the part, write it from the director's point of view that she's not right for the part. She's the wrong type, the wrong size, whatever, and your scene will have her convincing him that she *is* right for the part.

That's how you create conflict on the page and avoid it in your writing experience.

15

Act III: The Resolution

> Sarah (V.O.): "The unknown future rolls toward us. I face it for the first time with a sense of hope, because if a machine, a Terminator, can learn the value of a human life, maybe we can, too."
>
> —James Cameron and William Wisher
> *Terminator 2: Judgment Day*

Act III is approximately a thirty-page unit of dramatic action that begins at the end of Plot Point II and extends through to the end of your screenplay. It is held together by the dramatic context known as Resolution.

Resolution means "to find a solution; to explain or make clear; to break up into separate elements or parts." It is not the end of your story, it is the solution of your screenplay. Up until this point in the screenwriting process, the ending, that specific scene or sequence that you want to end the film with, may have changed.

Does your original resolution still work?

That's the first thing you'll have to decide as you approach the final act of your screenplay. In most cases, you'll find your initial impulse for the resolution, the very first creative decision you had to make when preparing your script, will probably be the same now as it was then. Think about it.

Way back in the beginning, we chose to start the creative

process with a simple choice: What happens at the end of your screenplay? What happens to your main character? Does he/she live or die? Succeed or fail? Marry or divorce? Win the race or not? Escape safely and bring the bad guys to justice? Destroy the Ring in the fires of Mount Doom? Be reunited with a loved one or not? Recover the stolen merchandise or not? Claim the heavyweight championship of the world or not? Be found guilty or innocent of the crime?

Good films are always resolved—one way or another.

Do you remember the endings of: *Match Point? Rushmore? Finding Nemo? Spider-Man 2? Bonnie and Clyde? Red River? Butch Cassidy and the Sundance Kid? The Treasure of the Sierra Madre? Casablanca? Annie Hall? Coming Home? Jaws? The Shawshank Redemption? American Beauty? The Searchers? Terminator 2: Judgment Day?*

What is the Resolution of your story? Has it changed since you began writing your screenplay? If so, what is the new Resolution—the new solution to your story? You do have a choice in the matter; you can choose to keep the resolution the same, or you can choose to change it. The choice is always yours. We're not talking about the ending here, that specific scene or sequence that ends the screenplay. We're talking about the solution to your story line.

The key thing to remember is that your story always moves forward—it follows a path, *a direction,* a line of progression from beginning to end, whether it's told in flashback or not. Whether it's told nonlinearly, like *The Bourne Supremacy, The Constant Gardener* (Jeffrey Caine), *The Usual Suspects,* or *Memento,* or linearly, like *Match Point, Walk the Line, Sideways,* or *Brokeback Mountain, direction* is defined as a line of development, the path along which something lies. And that is the story line.

Everything is related in the screenplay, as it is in life. You don't have to know the specific details of your ending when you are writing your screenplay, but you do have to know *what happens* and how it affects the characters. That's resolution.

Understanding the basic dynamics of your story's resolution is essential. That is the process that began at the very beginning of the screenwriting process. When you were laying out your story line, building it, putting it together, scene by scene, act by act, piece by piece, the first thing you did was determine the resolution, the *solution* of your story. You might have been working out the idea and shaping it into a dramatic story line, but you made a creative choice, a decision, about what the resolution was going to be.

As you stand at the edge of Act III and peer into the blank pages that lie ahead, you will see that there are usually a few story points that need to be resolved. You may have already determined the ending may need to change. If you want it to change, let it change. Structure is flexible, remember; like the tree that bends in the wind but does not break.

When you've completed Act II, stop writing and see where you are; what do you need to do in order to resolve your story? If you've already prepared your fourteen cards for Act III, go over them and see if they still work effectively. Most of the time they will be between 80 or 90 percent accurate, though sometimes I'll look at my cards and think I can do better so I'll redo the cards with new scenes and sometimes restructure the material. Sometimes, I'll forgo the cards and just do a new "beat sheet." For example, I'll write "the scene in the car," "planning the job," "the scene at the hospital," "the chase sequence," and so on. I don't need anything more specific than that. It usually works. If it doesn't, I'll go back and review the action, both physical and emotional, by writing a short essay on what happens in Act III.

Act III, the Resolution, is usually anchored by one or two, or sometimes three, dramatic (or comedic) elements that are needed resolve your story. When you approach Act III, the very first thing to do is define those specific scenes that you need. What is the resolution? Is it the same as it was when you began writing? Or has it changed? If it has changed, what do you have to do to keep the story line consistent? What is the ending, that specific scene or sequence that completes the screenplay? Can you begin to trace your narrative action line from the end of Plot Point II to the end of the story? Can you find a key scene or scenes that will lead you to the ending and dramatize the resolution?

Sometimes it helps to write a two-page essay about what happens in Act III. In my own experience, I find Act III the easiest part of the screenplay to write. By this time in the screenwriting process, I've straightened out and fixed the story line, found new dimensions in the characters, and reached a fluid source of creative energy that flows easily and smoothly. I also know that what I have to do to complete Act III, to complete this first words-on-paper draft, is simply put in the time in front of the computer—though I know that's easier said than done.

Before you start writing Act III, go over the cards or beat sheet until you feel comfortable with the story's progression. Make sure you understand what elements need to be resolved in Act III. You'll probably find you'll be on automatic, comfortable with the writing and discipline and story line. You still won't *know* whether it's working or not, because you'll lack objectivity, but it will usually *feel* like it's working, in spite of any doubts or insecurities. Just keep writing. Trust the process. Lay it down, shot by shot, scene by scene, page by page.

Act III is going to be driven by resolving your story. As mentioned earlier, either your action drives the character or your character drives the action. Many times, you can combine both. Woody Allen's *Match Point* is a good example, as is *Cinderella Man.*

There are times when the entire Third Act becomes a long action sequence that strengthens and reinforces the character as well. In *Cinderella Man,* James Braddock (Russell Crowe) is given the opportunity to fight Max Baer (Craig Bierko) for the Heavyweight Championship of the World. This is an extraordinary opportunity for James Braddock but it carries a heavy burden of potential injury and the possibility of death. By the time we reach Plot Point II, it's been established that Max Baer has already killed two fighters in the ring. Braddock, like so many others, has been a victim of the Great Depression and has undergone severe challenges just to care for his wife and three young children. It is an opportunity of a lifetime but the risks are high. That is the dramatic situation at the end of Plot Point II as many people think this fight will be a legitimate case of murder, while others want to be there to engage in the thrill of watching blood being spilt.

This is the dilemma that generates the major conflict within the family during Act III that must be resolved. Even though this is based on a true story, the filmmakers have taken the dramatic license to heighten the emotional situation that must be resolved. Before the fight, Mae (Renée Zellweger) tells James, "I stood by you until now. For all of it. But not for this, Jim. I just can't. So, you train, all you want. But you find a way to get out of that fight. Break your hand if you have to. But if you set foot out of this door to fight Max Baer I won't be behind you anymore."

That is the final ultimatum. How is it going to be resolved? "This is the only thing I know how to do," Braddock replies. "I have to believe I have some say over our lives. That sometimes, I can change things. If I don't, it's like I'm dead already." This struggle between family and fighting in the championship fight with the possibility of death or severe physical injury is the conflict that governs the entire Third Act. It is an internal as well as external conflict that must be resolved.

Act III begins on the morning of the fight. James says his goodbyes to his children and his wife and leaves for the stadium. There are a few scenes before we go into the dressing room to prepare for the fight. Mae comes into the locker room unexpectedly and unites husband and wife: she tells him, "I'm always behind you. So you just remember who you really are . . . you're the champion of my heart, James J. Braddock."

After that, the fight begins. The fifteen-round fight takes up the rest of the screenplay. And the final shot of the script, after he wins, says it all: "Jim stands in the center of the ring, his arm raised in victory, tears flowing from his eyes . . ."

So it ends; and what needed to be resolved in terms of story and character has been resolved. There are a few taglines superimposed over shots of the ring just before the final fade out, but the story line has been resolved in an exciting and compassionate way.

The resolution in *Cinderella Man* may seem easy, perhaps predictable. After all, the screenplay is based on a true story. So, even though we know what's going to happen, that Braddock wins to become the Heavyweight Champion of the World, the real issue is how it is done; the action is imbued with strong action and strong character. Even though the story is based on a true incident, *Cinderella Man,* like *Apollo 13,* captures the integrity of the story and remains true to its nature. Why it works so well is not simply a result of what the resolution is, but *how* it is executed. That's what makes a good screenplay stand out.

It's different in *Match Point.* This is a character study about the nature of luck—some people have it, some don't, as the narrator tells us in the opening shot. But the issue of "making your own luck," is more to the point here. At Plot Point II, Nola (Scarlett Johansson) is pregnant by Chris (Jonathan Rhys-Meyers), who is married to Chloe (Emily Mortimer). It's a very difficult situation, one which is weighing heavily on Chris. What's he going to do? Tell Chloe the truth about his infidelity or sacrifice "the good life" for a life of uncertainty and financial struggle? Neither is acceptable. And then, one night, he finds the solution. What does he do? And how is he going to resolve the issue? (I don't like to reveal endings so I won't say any more than this.) Needless to say, he is a person born to luck and on the surface, at least, holds the winning hand due to luck and circumstance. But what's going to happen, character-wise, after the movie has ended? Will he still be living "the good life"?

If you look at some of the classic American films of the last few decades—from the Sixties and *The Wild Bunch* where everybody dies, and *Hud* (Harriet Frank and Irving Ravetch) where the "hero" is still the same son of a bitch at the end of the script as he was at the beginning; to the Seventies with *The French Connection* (Ernest

Tidyman), *Apocalypse Now* (Francis Ford Coppola and John Milius), and *Coming Home* (Waldo Salt), where the endings are violent or bleak or thought-provoking; to the Eighties with *Ordinary People* (Alvin Sargent), *Witness, Terms of Endearment*, and *An Officer and a Gentleman* (Douglas Day Stewart); to the nineties with films like *Terminator 2: Judgment Day, Dances With Wolves* (Michael Blake), and *Magnolia* (Paul Thomas Anderson), you'll see that the resolution reflects the changing attitudes toward war, protest, racism, and social unrest. Some of the endings are positive or thought-provoking or feel-good endings, while others are bleak, negative, and in the end, everybody we care about dies.

Endings are tricky and they depend upon a lot of variables. I happened to be in Berlin a few months before the fall of the Berlin Wall, teaching a workshop for fifty German screenwriters. The course was held by one of the many universities where students were on strike. The corridors were empty and the hallways covered with slogans and sayings that reflected the attitude of the strike. It was a very exciting time and I was working with writers who wanted to comment and reflect upon the historical times in which they were living.

But when I read their stories, I was astonished; while the stories were good and interesting, there was a certain, uncomfortable consistency. Out of the fifty stories, forty-eight of them ended in death, suicide, destruction, or mayhem. I tried to explain that at this point in time they were living in an historical moment, and each writer had an unique opportunity to be focused on what kind of future they might want to create. But almost all of them had made a creative decision that their stories would be "true to life," meaning they would end unhappily and generally "despairing."

When I thought about it, I realized that they had come from a literary *Germanic* tradition that usually ends unhappily. And yet, they had the opportunity to bring forth something new that would reflect a future filled with new possibilities. I've always maintained that as screenwriters we have a certain responsibility to alter and impact our audience. I think of it as kind of a mission statement: by choosing the creative act of writing a screenplay, we have the opportunity of giving rise to a new possibility, based not on the past, or old patterns of behavior, but on a future built on hope and unity and self-worth, where we honor our uniqueness and individuality, our humanity, so we can achieve a higher state of consciousness.

That's my point of view. It's a choice for you to make regarding the resolution of your screenplay. So when you think about the ending of your screenplay, about the resolution of your stories, aim for the highest; it's not necessary to end your story line in a simplistic manner, meaning by death, destruction, suicide, and mayhem. I pointed that out to the German screenwriters, and while they come from that kind of historical and literary tradition, it reflects either an attachment to the past or a fear of the future. The future is what we make it.

I'm not saying to insert a false, optimistic, "up," "happily ever after" ending. What I am saying is to find a resolution and ending that fits and conforms to your story, a resolution that fits the times in which we live, and reflects our human values. Films like: *The Lord of the Rings, Whale Rider* (Niki Caro), *Erin Brockovich* (Susannah Grant), *Million Dollar Baby* (Paul Haggis), *Cinderella Man, The Shawshank Redemption,* and *Paradise Now* (Hany Abu-Assad, Bero Beyer, and Pierre Hodgson) all reflect this attitude.

In other films, like Woody Allen's *Match Point, The Constant Gardener, Walk the Line, Brokeback Mountain, Y Tu Mamá También* (Alfonso and Carlos Cuarón), *Capote* (Dan Futterman), and *Good Night, and Good Luck* (George Clooney and Grant Heslov), the resolutions are integrated into the story; they are real, believable, and true. But if you have a choice in the matter, and can project a positive, uplifting ending, then you have more of a chance of having your screenplay produced. And that's the name of the game. If you doubt this, and think an up, happy, or positive ending is simplistic or banal, simply look at all the fairy tales, myths, epics, and adventures that have formed the basis of literature since the beginning of the written word. You might reply that the ancient Greek tragedies or Shakespearian tragedies always end in death and mayhem, and I would agree. But on the highest emotional and spiritual level, these works of art ennoble and enrich the characters and the universality of the human spirit. In the eternal conflict between good and evil, does evil ever win?

Never.

That's just the way it is. In the long run, good always triumphs over evil. Just be aware of it.

What is the resolution of your story? When you establish that, you can decide on the specific ending. But first, does your ending still work? Is it still effective? Do you have to change the ending because of the changes you've made during the first two acts? Have you thought of another ending, a new one, more vital, more dramatic, more visual, than your original one?

Don't think too much about it. If you try to figure out the "correct," the "right" ending, you'll never do it. Choose an ending that works, that fits your story. You'll find out soon enough whether it's effective or not.

No matter what kind of screenplay you're writing, just focus on resolving your story and character. If you're writing a comedy, does your character change during your screenplay? If so, pay it off in Act III. Show it visually and dramatically to resolve your story.

In *Annie Hall,* Alvy Singer (Woody Allen) is a character who does not change—he is the same at the end of the screenplay as he was at the beginning. Cynical, filled with self-pity and doubt, he wants Annie Hall to fit into his expectations of what he *thinks* a relationship should be. Remember the lobster scene in the kitchen? Annie and Alvy are cooking lobsters and both are afraid to stick them into the boiling water. It's a beautiful scene, as memorable as a Marx Brothers scene from *A Night at the Opera* or *Duck Soup.* In Act III, after Annie has left Alvy to be with Tony Lacey (Paul Simon), he tries to recreate the lobster scene with a different woman. Same setting, same situation, same action, only now the result is different; it is forced, contrived, unfunny.

Alvy Singer's character is a key element in the success of the film. In the opening monologue, Alvy says, "I wouldn't want to belong to any club that would accept me as a member. That's the key joke of my adult life in terms of my relationships with women." It is prophetic, because it is paid off at the end. Annie changes, he doesn't.

The script ends with Alvy delivering a rambling monologue: "[Annie] had moved back to New York. She was living in SoHo with some guy. And when I met her she was, of all things, dragging him in to see *The Sorrow and the Pity.* [A four-and-a-half-hour documentary that Alvy had turned her on to.] Which I counted as a personal triumph . . . and I thought of an old joke, you know, this guy goes to a psychiatrist and says, 'Doc, my brother's crazy. He thinks he's a chicken.' And, uh, the doctor says, 'Well, why don't you turn him in?' And the guys says, 'I would, but I need the eggs.' Well, I guess that's pretty much how I feel about relationships. You know, they're totally irrational and crazy and absurd . . . but, I guess we keep goin' through it because, most of us need the eggs."

His character is consistent; at the end, he's alone, as cynical and resistant and set in his ways as he always was. His unwillingness to change, expand, and grow leads to this point. Sad, yet moving: a perceptive and universal comment about the human condition.

On the other hand, if you're writing an action film, or action-adventure, there are times when the resolution of the Third Act becomes one long action sequence. In *Witness,* John Book (Harrison Ford) has just acknowledged his feelings to Rachel (Kelly McGillis). But no sooner do they acknowledge their passions for each other than the bad cops show up at the farm where Book is hiding. They have come to kill him. The Third Act begins as the bad cops park the car, open the trunk, take out their guns, and start the long walk down to the farmhouse.

In *Witness,* an excellent film to study, three things need to be resolved. One, what's going to happen to John Book? Does he live or die? Two, does he bring the bad cops to justice? And three, what's going to happen between Rachel and John? How do they resolve their relationship? Those three things are resolved during the Third Act, which is an exciting action sequence and embraces the resolution of the screenplay.

An action film provides you with a number of ways to resolve your story line. One of my favorites is James Cameron's *Terminator 2: Judgment Day* (James Cameron and William Wisher). In my opinion, *Terminator 2* is one of the most influential films of our time. Not only does it revolutionize the technology of filmmaking through the use of computer-graphic imagery, but it incorporates a spiritual dimension into the action film unlike anything that has been seen before or since.

Terminator 2: Judgment Day reflects a certain ambiguity in the human condition. As technology becomes more advanced, human beings seem to become more withdrawn, inverted, some might even say, dehumanized. More like machines than humans. In *Terminator 2,* Sarah Connor (Linda Hamilton) is a woman possessed and driven to avenge the death of her lover and the father of her young son John. The man she is determined to kill is the scientist who created the computer chip that, according to the scenario of the existing future, takes us into the age of machines. Sarah knows that if she can kill this one man before that one little computer chip is created, she can change the future and humankind might stand a chance of survival.

"The future is not set," is what the ten-year-old John Connor (Edward Furlong), says at Mid-Point. "There is no fate but what we make." At this point there are still two things left to be resolved in the story line: first, how can they destroy the T-1000, the "bad" Terminator (Robert Patrick), who seems indestructible. Second, do they live or die in saving the future for humankind? What happens to The Terminator (Arnold Schwarzenegger), who is also a machine, a cyborg, and thus a product of the future? These things must be resolved by the end of the screenplay.

Act III in *Terminator 2: Judgment Day* is a fast-moving chase sequence that takes place inside a huge steel factory. Cameron sets up the demise of the T-1000 when the truck overturns, spilling liquid nitrogen everywhere. The T-1000 is engulfed in it and freezes solid. "*Hasta la vista,* baby," the Terminator says as he pulls the trigger and the T-1000 is blown into a million pieces.

It looks like it's the end and we think it's done, that it's finally over, until we see the shards of the T-1000 melting, liquefying, and the droplets start creeping together. Plip, plop, they merge into a sliding, slithering blob of mercury. Oh Jesus! The T-1000 is coming alive once more.

"Okay, buckle your seat belts, here it comes..." is the way it reads in the screenplay. And then we're in a massive shootout as the T-1000 is finally ripped apart as the force of the bullets thrusts the deadly cyborg into the flames of the molten steel. From ashes to ashes, dust to dust, steel to steel... this time it's really the end of the T-1000 machine. The three of them stare down at the molten steel: "Is it dead?" John asks. "Terminated," replies the Terminator. "Thank God it's over," Sarah says.

"No," the Terminator says. "There is another chip. And it must be destroyed also... It must end here... or I am the future," says the Terminator, as he slowly descends into the molten steel. The script reads: "There is a final thumbs-up. Then it is gone." We hold on this sea of flaming steel for a long moment, then dissolve into a little tag scene. We are racing down a dark highway at night and we hear Sarah's final voiceover: "The unknown future rolls toward us. I face it for the first time with a sense of hope, because if a machine, a Terminator, can learn the value of a human life, then maybe we can, too."

Words to think about.

As you sit down at the computer, writing pad, or typewriter, and engage in the creative process of resolving your story line, you may find that things will be going smoothly and easily until the last few pages of the script. Then you might feel strange, find yourself suddenly going "blank," not knowing what to write or feeling that you have no real desire or enthusiasm or ambition to complete the screenplay. You'll look for, and find, every excuse you can to avoid writing.

It's really very funny; after weeks and months of preparation, research, commitment, pain, toil, and trouble, after weeks of self-doubt, fears, and insecurities, after weeks of working your ass off, you may suddenly want to chuck it, with only a few pages to write.

It's absurd; you really can't take it too seriously.

What do you do?

First of all, this seems to be a somewhat common experience among writers. It originates below the level of awareness. Every writer I know, including myself, experiences this phenomenon. *Emotionally,* you don't want to end the screenplay. You want to hang on, not finish it. It's like a terrible relationship—no matter how bad it is, it's better than no relationship at all. The same principle applies to writing your screenplay. It's hard to end. It's been a great part of your life; you think about it every day, your characters are like friends, you talk about your story every chance you get. Writing it has kept you awake at night, caused you pain and suffering, and given you great satisfaction. Of course you don't want to give it up!

For what?

It's only natural to want "to hold on."

I hate to spoil your illusions, but there's a lot of work left to do on this screenplay. When you finish this first words-on-paper draft, you're only a third of the way through the screenwriting process. You're not done with anything; the ending of one thing is always the beginning of something else. You've got two more drafts to go before you complete this first-draft screenplay.

Just finish your script; resolve it. And once you write the final "Fade Out" give yourself a little pat on the back and celebrate with a glass of wine, or champagne, or whatever suits your disposition.

Put your screenplay on the desk in front of you and see how many pages you've written. Pick it up. Feel it.

You did it.

Then take a week off.

The first words-on-paper draft of the screenplay is now complete. Now the work really begins.

THE EXERCISE

Isolate the two or three dramatic elements of Act III that resolve your story line. Take a look at your cards for Act III. Do they still work? Do you need to change them? If need be, restructure Act III on fourteen new 3 × 5 cards. Then go over and over them.

When you feel comfortable with your material, start writing. You may begin to experience some resistance at this point. Many times, in my own experience, I come up with a new idea, so compelling and powerful that I want to stop what I'm doing and just jump into the new idea. Don't. Take out a notebook or a piece of paper and simply write it down in two or three pages. Write as much as you want about the idea, then put it away and go back to completing Act III.

If you experience any resistance, doubts, or judgments, or feel that you're "burnt out," just "bend with it" and acknowledge it. Continue writing. Always keep your resolution—the solution—firmly in mind.

If you want to change any of the details of the ending, do it. If your ending comes out different from what you want it to be, write it one way, put it away in a drawer somewhere, and then write it again; this time it will be the way you want it. If you're writing a comedy and it comes out serious and dramatic, write it down, stick it in a drawer, and then write it as a comedy. The same with a drama; if it comes out funny, continue to write, knowing it's only a form of resistance. When you've finished and it's out of your head and out of your system, stick it in a drawer somewhere and forget about it, then go back and write it the way you want to.

What's important is to create a resolution that is honest and entrenched in the integrity of your story line. If you try to figure out what "they" want, what you think the public would like, or what the production companies would like to see in order to sell your material, forget it; it'll never work. There's no way you can "figure" out what "they" want. Just write your screenplay from the position that this is your screenplay and this is how the story is resolved and this is the ending you have chosen for now.

It can always be changed later—when you do the rewrite.

16

The Rewrite

> Maya: So what's your novel about?
> Miles: Well, it's a little difficult to summarize. It begins as a first-person account of a guy taking care of his father after a stroke. It's kind of based on personal experience, but only loosely . . . It shifts around a lot . . . And some other stuff happens, some parallel narrative and then it evolves—or devolves—into a kind of a Robbe-Grillet mystery—you know, with no real resolution.
>
> —Alexander Payne and Jim Taylor
> *Sideways*

Many years ago, I was driving down Sunset Boulevard with a musician friend of mine visiting from London when we saw a huge billboard showing a gorgeous California blonde sunning herself at the beach. Standing on the sidewalk below the billboard was a young man who was holding a little girl, maybe two or three years old, by the hand. It was a beautiful scene. As we drove by, I heard my friend mutter, "I am a child."

I knew it was a line for a song. He reached into my glove compartment, pulled out an old envelope, grabbed a pen, wrote down the line, added a few more words, hummed a musical phrase, and in that moment the entire song came to him. It took him only a few minutes to write down the lyrics.

When we got back to my house, he sat down at the piano and began to play various phrases tying it all together. About 10 minutes later he said "listen to this" and he played the song's musical line for me. It sounded good, even though it was rough and somewhat sketchy.

Several days later he called and invited me to meet him at a recording studio in Hollywood. He was going to record the song, he told me. As I walked into the studio, I saw a huge orchestra on the stage, a number of backup singers, and a major recording artist. They started their rehearsals, and I heard the full song performed for the first time.

Needless to say, I was blown away. From a few scribbled lines on an old envelope to this intense musical experience within the space of a little more than a week! I couldn't believe it. I was jealous as hell; I wished I could write a screenplay or a book like that. I left the studio filled with a sense of wonder mingled with a layer of personal resentment and a lot of self-pity. When I think of the hours, the days, the weeks, the months, and in some cases, the years, of arduous and tedious work that goes into writing a screenplay or a book, it's no wonder I felt the way I did.

I wished I could write a screenplay that way, but it's not to be. Oh sure, I've heard stories of screenwriters who write a script in a week, or two, and they may all be true—but what you don't hear is how long they must have worked on the idea and characters and plot before they sat down to actually write the screenplay.

That musical experience with my friend haunted me because I was measuring his experience of writing that one particular song against my own experience of writing a screenplay or book. And I knew there was no way I could measure his songwriting experience against my own writing experience.

The more I thought about it, the more I saw that writing a screenplay is composed of many individual stages and they're all different. Each phase is totally separate and unique. You may get a flash of inspiration for a screenplay in a few moments, but executing it is a quite different story. Writing is a detailed, step-by-step process, a day-by-day progression, and you move through it in stages, making it better and more complete as you go along.

It's only natural. Science teaches us that. The scientific method since the time of Francis Bacon deals with measuring things or making tests which involve experimentation and measurable results. A scientist will try different things, exploring each possible alternative intelligently and systematically, always keeping a record of what works and discarding what doesn't.

So many people I talk to share with me that they don't like the idea of having to rewrite their material. After all, they've spent many months working on this first words-on-paper draft and feel that any changes that may need to be made should be authorized by someone who is going to buy or produce the script. In other words, they should be paid for rewriting the material.

Nothing could be farther from the truth. The old adage "writing is rewriting" is a truism, like it or not. Rewriting your screenplay is a necessary and essential part of the screenwriting process; it corrects the changes you might have made during the first words-on-paper draft, and clarifies and defines your story as well as sharpening your characters and situation. You want your screenplay to be the best that you can make it—otherwise why spend all this time writing it? It would be easier not to do it at all. Whether you like the idea of rewriting or not, at some point you're going to have to do it; you can't argue with it, you don't need to fight it. Just accept it because that's just the way it is. Nobody ever told you that writing a screenplay was going to be easy.

When you complete your first words-on-paper draft you know you're going to have to make changes. That's a given. Your screenplay is a living thing and it changes and grows from day to day. It is a *process,* and what you write today may be out of date tomorrow and what you write tomorrow may be out of date the day after the day after tomorrow. Don't expect creative inspiration to be your guide because you're going to be changing and correcting a lot of what you wrote the first time around.

Writing the first-draft screenplay is done in three distinct stages: the first stage is writing the words-on-paper draft, which you've just finished; the second stage is writing what I call the "mechanical" draft, where you correct any changes made during the writing; and finally, the third stage, which I term the "polish" draft, where you're polishing scenes and sequences until you've done the best job you can and the first draft is completed.

When you finish the first words-on-paper draft, you're ready to begin the process of rewriting. First, take a couple of days off to think about what you've done. What parts do you think work the best? What doesn't work? Are your characters fully fleshed out? Do you know already what changes you want to make? Just let these thoughts "cook" a little bit. You don't need to make any clear-cut or defined decisions at this point.

The first thing in the rewriting process is to see what you've actually got. At this stage, you may not even know or remember what you did in Act I. It's easy to forget that when you're in the paradigm, you can't see the paradigm; you have no sense of overview, no objective perspective about what you've done or not done.

You need some kind of an overview. You'll need to clarify your "take" on the material. You want to see what you've written with objective eyes and not be burdened with any subjective comments, likes or dislikes, judgments or evaluations. You need to "unplug" from your subjective view to gain an "objective" overview.

The way to do that is to read the entire first draft in one sitting from beginning to end. Lock up all pens, pencils, notes, and papers, shut the computer down, and just jump in and start reading. Resist the temptation to write notes in the margins about the changes you want to make. This exercise is for you just to read what you've got. It's the best way to gain objectivity.

As you're reading the screenplay you'll notice you're on a roller coaster of emotion. You'll read a scene and think to yourself how bad it really is, how could anybody write such drivel?; or, this is the worst thing I've ever read; or, the incidents and events of the story are so unbelievable and so predictable, nobody will believe it. You'll feel totally depressed. Just keep reading. Then, you'll read a scene you've written and think it's not too bad, and then you'll find another scene that works really well. Certain scenes you'll see are way too long and talky, but they can always be cut and trimmed. You'll be swinging on a pendulum of emotion, shifting between elation and despair. Just ride the roller coaster and don't get too plugged into your emotional response, whether it's despair, depression, or suicide. Just read the material.

It's easy to get distracted. One my students, a well-known actress, had completed her first words-on-paper draft. Late one night she called after she had read her script through for the first time. No sooner had I picked up the receiver than I heard her scream in my ear: "How could you let me write this... this piece of shit... it's awful!" and she burst into tears and banged the phone down forcefully. I looked at the phone, not sure how to react or what I should say or do. So I did nothing.

Later, she told me that after she read what she had written, she threw the script down in total despair, called me, then crawled into bed, turned the electric blanket up as high as it would go, and assumed the prenatal position with thumb in mouth. She stayed that way for two days.

She overreacted, of course, and often, when you read something you've written, it can be a devastating experience. If this happens to you, just ride it out. I waited about four days before I finally called her back because I knew she was going to have to deal with all those "unreal" expectations and emotions she had suffered. We talked at length about it and she shared that she was numb, she didn't feel anything at all. I suggested she wait a few days before she confronted her material again and "just do what you have to do to make it work."

When she finally did sit down to rework the material, she told me she felt like a machine, with no emotion at all. When she was able to move from a subjective view into an objective overview, when she didn't react to any of her judgments and expectations, and just concentrated on writing her story, it turned out very well. It took her about two weeks to regain her confidence. After all, she had taken her idea, formed it into a story line, then written and completed a first words-on-paper draft. That's quite an accomplishment.

So, when you finish this first reading, take some time to think about it. Contemplate your overall feelings about the story, the characters, and the action. As you begin to mentally "cruise" through the progression of the story line from beginning to end, you'll move into an overview position to balance the characters and the relationships that exist between them.

Is the story set up correctly? What about the relationships between the characters? Are they believable? Do they talk too much, or explain too much? Are the conflicts and obstacles your character confronts during Act II clearly defined? Do parts of the second act drag and sag? Does your ending work effectively?

Is there anything you would like to change?

Think about it.

After you read it, the next stage in the rewriting process is to sit down and write three essays, using free-association or automatic writing. Writing these essays allows you to unplug from the material and provides an effective overview. Each essay should be a couple of pages long; what's important is to let the ideas flow naturally and spontaneously. Don't try to force your story line to conform to your own expectations.

The First Essay. Answer this question: *What was it that originally attracted me to this idea?* What was the idea that attracted you to commit your time and energy to writing this screenplay? Was it the situation of the main character that appealed to you, or was it the dramatic premise, or the situation the character was in? Think about it. If you go back to that moment when you felt the first creative "tug," try to define what it was that attracted you to the material. If need be, close your eyes and see if you can recall that first moment you felt the urge to write this story. Let your thoughts roam freely and don't try to censor anything at this point. You're looking for that one moment of inspiration, that *aha!* feeling, that originally attracted you.

Then, in this first free-association essay, throw down all the thoughts, words, or ideas that you think attracted you to the idea. Don't worry about grammar, spelling, or punctuation; just throw down your thoughts on paper or in the computer. When I do this exercise, I write in longhand, in fragments, just as it comes to me, without any logical order. It is a process of free-association. Just try to capture what it was that attracted you to the idea. Do this in two or three pages. Do not censor what you write; just let it flow naturally and spontaneously. Write this up in a couple of pages and when you finish the first essay, go on to the next.

The Second Essay. Answer this question on a separate sheet of paper: *What kind of a story did I end up writing?* We usually start out to write one thing and during the process it often changes and we wind up writing something slightly different than what we originally intended. For example, you may start out to write a courtroom thriller but after you finish the first words-on-paper draft it actually turns out to be a strong romantic thriller set against a tense courtroom drama. Or you may start out to write a romantic comedy that ends up being more like a drama with comedic overtones. James L. Brooks, who wrote and directed *Terms of Endearment* and *Broadcast News,* wrote *I'll Do Anything* as a musical comedy, but the music didn't work, and when he removed the music it didn't work as a comedy either. During the process of writing it's very common to start out to do one kind of story and end up doing something slightly different. So go into the story you've written and see how it relates to your original idea. *What did you set out to write, and what did you end up writing?*

Again, write the essay in one or two pages in free-association. Just throw down your thoughts, words, and ideas in free-association.

The Third Essay. Take a new sheet of paper and answer this question: *What do I have to do to change what I did do, into what I wanted to do?* For example, you may have wanted to write a love story with a strong action-adventure theme, but you ended up writing a strong action-adventure played against the backdrop of a love story. Or vice versa. So, you have to change these elements. Look at *The Constant Gardener*—a thriller with a strong love interest; the female lead is killed early in the story. The screenwriter, Jeffrey Caine, had to create the love story through a series of complicated flashbacks; we see his wife through the husband's efforts to find out who was responsible for her death. In the same way, you may have to strengthen and set up more of the action-adventure elements, and tone down the love story.

In any case, you're going to have to change and rework what you originally set out to do. Sometimes, what you end up with is much better than what you started out to do. That's fine, but it still means you have to go back into Act I and the First Half of Act II, to set up and smooth out the story line so you have one fluid line of action.

In other words, *intention must equal the result.*

Again, this essay is written in free-association. Above all, you want to infuse your story with MDV, maximum dramatic value. So, what do you have to do to change what you did do into what you wanted to do? It may be that you need to add four or five new scenes in Act I, possibly remove a few scenes that don't add anything to the story or that simply don't work now, and set up the dramatic premise a little earlier. You may have to focus on your character, expand his or her characterization, perhaps even create a subplot with some of the minor characters. Now is the time to define what you want to do to implement these changes.

What's so important about these essays is to get clear on what you've written, so you can make it better. The best way to approach the rewrite process is by working in sections, or units, of dramatic action. That means working in Act I until you complete this unit of action. Then stop and work on the First Half of Act II. Define, change, add, or drop scenes, trim the dialogue until the Mid-Point. Then stop. Go into the Second Half of Act II and do the same thing. This way, the material does not become overwhelming and you can be more in control by working in sections, in units of dramatic action. Do the same in Act III.

Now, on this second, or "mechanical" draft, reread the material in Act I but this time you're going to be making notes in the margins: scenes you may want to change, dialogue you would like to add, or scenes you want to cut. Some scenes will be okay the way they are; some will not. Any dialogue changes, scene changes, or shifts in action, plot, or character, will need to be integrated into the script as a whole.

We had mentioned earlier that dialogue has two possible functions: either it moves the story forward, or it reveals character. Keep this in mind. When you're working with dialogue, it's interesting to note that the word itself comes from the Greeks and it means "a flow of meaning." Keep this in mind as you're writing; is your dialogue flowing smoothly, or is your script "too talky," or too explanatory? Are you sacrificing character for action, or action for character? You'll want to open up your story visually, utilizing both INT. and EXT. locations, telling your story with pictures and words.

Continue rewriting until you complete the Plot Point at the end of Act I. Always remember the context; you are *setting up your story,* setting up your characters and relationships, as well as establishing the dramatic premise and situation.

Each unit is a separate and complete unit of dramatic action. You'll find yourself doing more rewriting in Act I and the First Half of Act II. These two units of action are usually where you need to make the most changes, because that's where your story started to change. Check it out. See if that's accurate. In most cases, you'll be rewriting almost 80 percent, or more, of this First Act material. So what? Just do it.

You'll find rewriting Act I will be easier than you thought. Why? Because you've already established your writing discipline, and you know the story and the changes you want to make, so writing them should be natural and easy. Sometimes you might have difficulty deciding what to do, especially if Act I is too long. If that happens, you might need to cut a few scenes and move them from Act I into Act II. Structure is flexible, right? Or, you may want to enter each scene at a later point in the action and end it earlier. (If you would like more guidance, read Chapters 9–11 in *The Screenwriter's Problem Solver.*)

As mentioned, this second draft is what I call the mechanical draft, meaning this particular stage of the rewrite is more about getting it down on paper than being clever and original. It's "mechanical" because you just want to get the script in shape with a consistent narrative line, laying down scenes and dialogue which you know are not perfect but are used as a stepping-stone to the final, polish stage. This is where you are equalizing the story from what you started out to write and shaping it to fit what you did write. Usually, I just throw the scenes down to get them on paper, and don't worry about how good or bad they are. I'm just smoothing things out, mechanically. You'll correct any changes you made during the first words-on-paper stage, bring the script to the proper length, tighten up the dramatic tension, and sharpen the focus of your main character.

Even though you're going to possibly change a lot of things, perhaps rewriting 80 to 85 percent of Act I, maybe 50 to 60 percent of the First Half of Act II, 25 to 30 percent of the Second Half of Act II, and about 10 or 15 percent of Act III, don't think of this as a "creative" draft. This draft should not take the same time or effort required as when you were confronting the blank sheet of paper in the first-words-on-paper draft.

Concentrate on telling your story visually. You may find that you have the tendency to tell most of your story in dialogue. Maybe you're "talking" your story, explaining the character's thoughts, feelings, and emotions. For example, your character may be driving a car, see a jewelry store and say "I need a jade ring," and explain *why* she needs the ring. Then you might show her walking into the store and looking at the rings while she tells the salesperson exactly what she's looking for and why. She'll purchase the ring and then you might cut into the next scene, where she is showing off her new jade ring at a party. That's basically a scene of explanation. You don't want too many of those.

Instead, you can show the same thing visually: she sees the store, enters, and then cut into the next scene at the party where she is now showing off her new ring. Woody Allen did something like this in *Match Point.* We've seen Chris (Jonathan Rhys-Meyers) caught in his emotional dilemma; he doesn't know how or what to tell his wife, Chloe, (Emily Mortimer) about Nola (Scarlett Johansson) being pregnant with his child. Then, one night, he suddenly wakes up, eyes wide open as he realizes what he has to do to resolve the situation. He doesn't say anything and we don't know at this point what his plan may be. But at the moment he wakes up, he suddenly knows how he's going to get out of his predicament. That silent, unspoken moment is the Plot Point at the end of Act II. And in Act III, we then see how Chris solves his particular "problem."

Think visually, continually being aware of any cinematic transitions you might use as you move from one scene to the next and always looking for ways to enter and leave the scene. Enter late and get out early. Transitions are always a good way of cutting down the material, if that's something you need to do.

If you like, when you finish Act I of this mechanical draft, go back and clean it up. Polish a scene or retype some pages, cut out a few lines of dialogue to make it clearer and tighter. Don't spend too much time on it; it's important to move forward through the screenplay. Always work from beginning to end, beginning to end.

Move on to the First Half of Act II. Reread the material and make extensive notes in the margins on what you need to do to make it work, until you reach the Mid-Point. You'll find you might be changing about 60 percent of the First Half. Determine what changes you want to make. Then, if need be, lay out this section on 3 × 5 cards, just like you did with the Act I material.

Always keep in mind your sub-dramatic context and strive for conflict, either internal conflict or external, or both, whatever works most effectively. Make sure Pinch I is clean and tight and the Mid-Point clearly defined. Sometimes, you may find that you have too many characters and need to condense two characters into one character; or use the first part of one scene on page 40 with the last part of the scene on page 55. Whatever you need to do to make your story work, do it.

Does your Mid-Point still work effectively? Is it too long or too short? Too wordy? Or does it need exposition, action, or visual clarification? Do you need to redefine it visually? Again, just write it down. It doesn't have to be perfect at this point.

You'll probably spend a week or two rewriting the First Half of Act II. After you've completed the Mid-Point, you can stop and move on to the Second Half of Act II. Read it through. Make notes on any changes you want to make. If need be, and if you feel comfortable doing it, you may want to restructure the Second Half on fourteen 3 × 5 cards just like Act I and the First Half of Act II. Sometimes you'll feel like doing this and other times you won't. You be the judge. You're clarifying and redefining your story line so you want to make it as concise and visual as you can.

Once you know what you need to do, execute it simply, keeping the dramatic context and time frame clearly in mind. You probably won't have to change more than 25 to 30 percent of the Second Half of Act II. Just keep your story on track as you follow your main character through the action, setting up Pinch II and then moving on to Plot Point II. This section may only take you about a week or so to complete, depending on how much time you can devote and what you need to do.

When you finish Act II, don't spend too much time polishing the material. You're going to be doing this the next time around, in the third and final "polish" draft.

When you reach Act III, you'll really be home free. You know the resolution of your story, you're in a good creative flow, and any changes you've made earlier in the material should have already been paid off in this unit of action. Rewriting this part of the screenplay is usually the easiest and takes the shortest amount of time. You'll feel like you're almost done. In Act III, you'll be cleaning up and refocusing the resolution, and you'll want to look for ways to add any new visual dynamics to make your ending stronger and more effective. Here's where you may have a better idea for your ending, and if that's the case, change it. Now's the time. You may want to write a new dialogue scene or make it more visual, but first you'll want to make sure you have resolved your story line. The actual writing process itself at this time is pretty clear-cut and manageable and you'll probably know exactly what you need to do to finish this second draft of your screenplay.

You should be able to complete this "mechanical" draft of your screenplay in about four to five weeks, and it should end up being anywhere from one hundred ten to one hundred twenty pages, no longer. Bringing it to the proper length should be one of your first priorities. If you're a first-time screenwriter, defined as someone who has never had a screenplay produced or purchased, they (whoever "they" are) are not going to accept a screenplay from you that is longer than one hundred twenty to one hundred twenty-five pages long.

Sorry to be the one to tell you this. Your story line needs to be clear, with all the necessary changes fused into an organic story line from beginning to end, within one hundred twenty pages. The average screenplay today is approximately one hundred twelve to one hundred twenty pages long.

When you complete this mechanical draft, take a few days off. Do what you want, but give yourself some time to digest the changes you've made. And then, you'll be ready to move into the third stage, the "polish draft" of your screenplay.

This is where you'll really be writing the first draft screenplay. You'll be polishing, accenting, and texturing each scene, changing a word here, a word there, a sentence here, a scene there, sometimes rewriting a scene up to ten or fifteen times to make it right.

You'll still be working in units of dramatic action, Act I, First Half and Second Half of Act II and Act III, but you'll be approaching each scene with the lens of a microscope. You'll go into each scene, analyze it, maybe cut this line, or move that line from the beginning of the scene to the end, lift one or two lines from the middle of the scene and tighten, condense, and polish the scene, word by word and line by line. You may be removing or tweaking lines of description as well. You want to make this "the best read" you can.

One of the rules I created for myself when I was writing screenplays is that no descriptive paragraph should be more than four sentences long. I know that's an arbitrary statement, but I've read so many scripts that had "thick," "dense," "bulky" descriptive paragraphs of half or three-quarters of a page. You want lots of white space on the page because that's what a professional screenplay looks like. If you want to see what a professional screenplay looks like, get any screenplay, and read it. Just Google *screenplays* online and it will guide you to a number of sites where you can download scripts. You'll notice how the descriptive paragraphs are lean, tight, and visual without too much explanation.

Sometimes, you'll find you may want to remove an entire character and give his or her lines to another character, so you don't have so many people on the page that the text becomes confusing. Oliver Stone told me once that when he wrote the first draft of *Platoon*, he had twenty-six characters in the first ten pages. You can't do that. You want to keep the action and character lines flowing simply and smoothly.

In this polish stage, after going over a scene five or ten times to make it right, you may find that it still doesn't work. As you ponder this dilemma, you'll realize that you might have to move three lines from a scene in Act I into another scene in the First Half of Act II. Or, you might bridge one scene with another scene, and drop a nice transition because it doesn't really work that well. You may telescope scenes, meaning you take one scene from the First Half of Act II, and combine it with another scene in the Second Half of Act II, thus establishing an entirely new scene that says the same thing in a shorter time. Remember the purpose of the scene: either it moves the story forward or it reveals information about the main character. If your scenes do not satisfy at least one of these two requirements, then cut the scene. You don't need it.

You'll be noticing certain rhythms of action, and possibly see places where a simple "pause," or "beat," before a character speaks will strengthen the dramatic tension of the scene. You'll change: "he glances at the woman sitting across from him" to "he regards her questioningly." You'll sharpen visual images by adding adjectives, tightening and condensing dialogue by cutting words from speeches, sometimes whole sentences, occasionally chunks of dialogue.

Again, work in units of action. First, complete Act I, then the First Half of Act II, the Second Half of Act II, then Act III. Working in units like this allows you to control your story and move forward, step-by-step, toward the resolution.

Good structure, remember, is like the relationship between an ice cube and water, or fire and its heat. As you're polishing your screenplay, you'll smooth the structural line until the incidents, episodes, or events that anchor the story line won't even be noticeable.

The key words are: tighten, trim, condense, polish, cut, cut, then cut some more. Most new writers don't like to cut words—or paragraphs—but you have to be ruthless. If you're wondering whether you should keep a scene, a specific line of dialogue, a descriptive paragraph, or a sequence, chances are that you'll cut it.

There is only one purpose in this third, or polish draft, and that is to make what you've written into the best screenplay you can.

How do you know when your rewrite's done?

It's a difficult question, a hard call. You'll never really know for sure, of course, but there are certain signs to look for. First of all, understand that your script will never be perfect. There will always be a few scenes that don't work. No matter how many times you write or rewrite a certain scene, it may never be the way you want it to be. Sometimes, you'll just have to let those scenes go. No one will ever notice that they don't work or measure up to *your* expectations.

You might also find that you're spending a lot of time on minor changes. You may change "but there are signs," to "and there are signs." That's a sure sign that you're ready to stop. That's when you can lay down your pages and say, "It's done. I've completed the first draft of my screenplay." That's when you can let it go. It will either stand or fall on its own.

At this point, I might suggest that you give your first draft to one or two people *you trust*. Personally, I would not suggest giving your script to your loved ones, or significant other. Why? Because out of their love, kindness, and friendship for you, they'll want to be as "honest" as they can; after all, you're putting your trust in them to let them read and evaluate your material. So, out of their love for you, they'll be ruthless; they'll tell you that this character is dull, flat, or the premise doesn't work and the dialogue is thin and weak. All your worst fears will be realized when you ask your loved ones to comment and critique your material. You've got to trust me on this one.

For example, in one of my screenwriting classes, I had a woman who was blessed with a wonderful sense of humor and a naturally wacky and unique style. She had never written a screenplay before but had an idea she wanted to write into a comedy. So, she came to class and went through the process. She laid out her subject line, developed her characters, and then wrote the four-page treatment. Then, feeling insecure about what she had written, she gave it to her husband to read. Now, her husband happened to be a very gifted film composer who had worked in Hollywood for years. He read her treatment and out of the "goodness of his heart, out of love for his wife," he wanted to be totally honest with her.

And guess what happened. In the name of love, he literally crucified her. Your characters are weak, he told her; the plot is mundane; no one would ever believe the situation. And you know, in his mind, he thought he was doing the right thing. He really wanted to protect her from the harsh realities of Hollywood and didn't want her to get hurt. She listened politely to what he had to say, then took the treatment, put it in a drawer somewhere and never looked at it again. To this day, she has never picked up that story line or sat down at the computer to make another attempt at writing the screenplay. And, it was a good story that had a lot of potential.

From that experience, I tell people not to give their material to a loved one, or spouse, or significant other for feedback; just know that out of their love and affection for you, they'll confirm your worst fears. Or, they'll tell you how much they like it and you don't know whether it's the truth or a lie. We're all so insecure anyway we never really, truly know whether what we wrote is working or not. And you don't want anybody telling you what you already know.

Especially in Hollywood. Most of the time nobody tells you the truth anyway. They might say something like, "I like it but it's not really something we want to do at the present time," or, "we have something like this in development," or "we've already done that movie."

That's not going to help you. You want some feedback; you want someone to tell you what he or she really thinks about your script, in terms of what's working or not, so choose the people you give this first draft to very carefully.

After they've read it, listen to what they say. Don't defend what you've written, don't *pretend* to listen to what they say and then leave feeling righteous, indignant, or hurt.

See whether they've caught the "intention" of what you wanted to write about. Listen to their observations from the point of view that they just *might be right,* not that they *are* right. They'll have observations, criticisms, suggestions, opinions, and judgments. *Are* they right? Question them; press them on it. Do their suggestions or ideas make sense? Do they add to your screenplay? Enhance it? Or, didn't they get it?

Go over the story with them. Find out what they like and dislike, what works for them and what doesn't. At this point, you still can't see your screenplay objectively. If you want another opinion, "just in case," be prepared to get confused. If you give it to four people for example, they'll all disagree. One person will like the relationship, another won't. One person will say they like the robbery, but not the *result* of the holdup (they either get away or they don't); and the other one wonders whether you couldn't strengthen the relationship between the other characters.

Having too many people read your material just doesn't work—at least, not at this stage. You want initial feedback from two people you know you can trust, who will be totally honest with you. When you've made all the changes you think will make the screenplay better, then you can send it out into the world through a literary agent, or producer, or production company, or attorney, or anyone you can get it to.

It's either going to stand or fall on its own. It's not going to be "perfect."

"Perfection is an ideal; it exists only in the mind, not in reality," Jean Renoir said.

Believe it.

THE EXERCISE

Are you ready? Let's do it.

First, sit down and read the words-on-paper draft from beginning to end in one sitting; take no notes, just sit down and read. You'll be on a roller coaster of emotion. Don't fight it, don't deny it, and don't try to "reason" things out. Just keep reading. You'll be making changes in your head, and that's okay. You'll swing between despair and elation, so enjoy the ride. When you've finished reading, take a day or two to digest your experience.

Then, using free-association, write the three essays in a couple of pages each. The first essay you're writing answers the question: *What was it that originally attracted you to the idea?* Just throw down words, thoughts, and feelings as you recall your first spark of inspiration and why you wanted to write the screenplay. Don't judge or evaluate your answer; just throw it down. You want clarity and insight here, so you don't have to worry about grammar, spelling, or the correct sentence structure. This is only an exercise for you, no one else.

When you've completed this first essay, write the second essay: *What kind of story did you end up writing?* You may have wanted to write an action-thriller but you ended up writing a romantic thriller. Define and articulate *what kind of a story you ended up writing.* Do this in a couple of pages of free-association. Just throw down your thoughts, words and ideas. Don't limit or censor yourself.

When you've completed the second essay, write the third essay. Answer the third question in a couple of pages: *What do I have to do to change what I did do, into what I originally wanted to do?* As mentioned, what you ended up doing may be a better script than what you originally wanted to do. So what do you have to do to change it? You may need to set up the characters more forcefully, or strengthen the relationships, or open it up visually. This is an exercise that clarifies what you need to do make your script a good read.

After you've answered the three questions you're ready to move into the actual writing.

Start with Act I. Read it as a unit of dramatic action and take notes, either in the margin or on a separate piece of paper. Structure and correlate any new scenes with the old scenes written, and then, if need be, lay out your new Act I structure on fourteen 3 × 5 cards. Go over the cards until the flow of action feels comfortable to you, then begin writing. Your first few pages may be stilted and awkward; it's okay, don't worry about it. This is only the "mechanical draft." You may be changing anywhere from 80 to 85 percent of your material. Don't worry about it. Just do it.

Work in units of action. The whole process of rewriting this first act could take a week or two. Don't worry if your work feels stilted, or episodic; just lay out your story line focusing on the threads of your story.

Then move into the First Half of Act II. Read this unit of dramatic action, make notes in the margins, and, if need be, restructure it on 3 × 5 cards. Then, start rewriting, one scene at a time, one page at a time, through Pinch I to the Mid-Point. You may be changing 50 to 60 percent of the material in this unit. Be clear on your sub-dramatic context, and what you need to do to smooth out the story line.

As you write the Mid-Point, be sure the focus of your story is clear and defined. Then move into the Second Half of Act II. Use the same process; read the material, take notes, structure it on 3 × 5 cards if needed, then start writing. In this unit of action, you'll only need to change about 40 to 50 percent of the material. Just change what you need to change; don't worry about rhythm, tension, or transitions in this "mechanical" stage.

Move into Act III. Bring it to length, and make all the changes needed for a consistent story line. Check your ending. Does it work as effectively as you want it to? Or, do you need to modify it somewhat, perhaps even change it radically? What's important is that it works; do what you need to do to make it the best ending you can.

When you've completed this "mechanical" stage of the screenplay, move into the "polish" stage. Again, work in thirty-page units of dramatic action; polish, hone, clean, tighten, accent, cut, and shade your material.

Your name is on the title page, so do the best job you can.

Remember, a screenplay is a reading experience before it becomes a film experience.

17

The "Good Read"

> Red: "I find I am so excited I can barely sit still or hold a thought in my head. I think it is the excitement only a free man can feel, a free man at the start of a long journey whose conclusion is uncertain... I hope I can make it across the border. I hope to see my friend and shake his hand. I hope the Pacific is as blue as it has been in my dreams... I *hope*."
>
> —Frank Darabont
> *The Shawshank Redemption*

During my time as the head of the story department at Cinemobile Systems and Cine Artists, our film production company, I read more than two thousand screenplays and at least one hundred novels in my search for material. Since that time, some twenty-five years ago, I have read and evaluated thousands and thousands of screenplays. And in all that time, I have found only a few that were worthy of film production. And yet, in spite of my newly acquired cynicism, I pick up every new screenplay with *the hope* that this is going to be *the one* that will knock me on my ass. Believe it or not, I want that to happen—badly. Talk to any reader in Hollywood and he or she will probably tell you the same thing.

I am always looking for the "good read."

What is a "good read"? I don't know how to define it exactly, I can only say that it is a dynamic reading experience that hits me with a *visual style* that unfolds in pictures. It "looks" a certain way, it "reads" a certain way, and it "feels" a certain way. A good screenplay works from page one, word one. *Chinatown* is a good read; so are *The Shawshank Redemption, The Bourne Supremacy,* and *The Lord of the Rings.*

What attracts me immediately is the way the words are put down on paper: crisp, sparse, and visual. I can tell whether the story is set up in the first few paragraphs. Does it open with a dynamic inciting incident? Does it grab my attention? Are the characters appealing, well-rounded, and three-dimensional? Is the premise and situation set up with insight and clarity in the first ten pages? Is there enough information presented to captivate me so I want to continue reading? Or is the story cluttered with too many characters, dense plots, and subplots?

When I find a "good read," I know it; there's a certain excitement and energy that grabs me immediately, from page one, word one. What I'm looking for is a writing style that moves the action across the page like lightning. Where I can't help but keep turning pages, which, of course, is the screenwriter's function—to keep the reader turning pages.

And this, believe it or not, is the contradiction: *nobody likes to read in Hollywood, yet everybody loves to read a good screenplay.*

That's just the way it is. Things never change in that respect.

Why? Because there are so many poorly written screenplays; perhaps one out of a thousand is worthy of moving up to the next level of the executive chain. And when you find a "good read" everyone wants to read it, so it is faxed and emailed to development executives all over Hollywood.

So, what does the reader look for when he or she is evaluating the material? Several things. I thought it would be interesting to illustrate the reader's process when he or she is given a script to read. Every screenplay submitted goes through this same journey. If you are submitting a script to a studio or production company, this is what most likely will happen.

When the material is submitted, either by an authorized literary agent, or attorney, or producer, or director, it's given to a reader to read. (Unsolicited material is usually returned unread due to various legal issues.) The reader reads the script, then he or she writes up a short, detailed synopsis and offers his or her personal opinion of the material in a couple of pages. This is referred to as *coverage*. Coverage is a tool for the film executive who doesn't read the material but has to respond to the person who submitted it, either agents or producers or directors. Coverage includes the name of the writer, the particular genre, a logline (a brief, one-sentence description of the story), and various checkpoints on a chart which indicate the reader's judgment regarding the quality of material in terms of structure, character, story, dialogue, and overall writing ability. It is broken down in terms of: excellent, good, fair, and poor. I've taken the liberty of summarizing a reader's evaluation from a major film company and it's a pretty good reflection of what the reader looks for when assessing the material.

In this example, I've avoided using any names and titles. First, in the upper left-hand corner, there is the *title*, the *author*, and the *genre*, a one-word description of the type of story: action-adventure, love story, western, comedy, romantic comedy, farce, romance, drama, science fiction, animated, or futuristic. In this particular example, the genre is a *romance with sad ending*.

Second, there is a brief summary of the story, a logline, a four- or five-line description of *what* the story is about; in this instance the synopsis reads: "A beautiful, ambitious young attorney schemes to get ahead in a Chicago-based law firm. Her boss, married with three kids, falls in love with her. She subtly demands to be made a full partner, which ruins him politically. His marriage on the rocks, he leaves to start his own firm, making her a partner. Within weeks, he's begging his wife to take him back. Our girl steams ahead."

That's what the story is about; it is the *subject* of the screenplay. (If you want to read good loglines, read the movie synopses in *TV Guide*. It's a good example of the way you need to "pitch" your story line.)

Third, after the logline, there is a one-and-a-half page detailed synopsis of the story, in depth and detail, which I have omitted.

Fourth, there is the reader's *analysis*, with structure and character emphasized. In this particular evaluation, the analysis is broken down into specific categories:

I—Character

a) Design: A ruthless young career woman takes advantage of a middle-aged husband and father, and he abandons his family for her.

b) Development: Almost good. The author must have it in for women. This is one of the bitchiest portrayals since *Fatal Attraction, All About Eve,* or *Body Heat.* The characters just don't ring true. They're not full enough.

II—Dialogue

Fair. This may be Chicago but it's very small time. The dialogue here makes the cardinal sin of making *everything* obvious. The story is all told in dialogue.

III—Structure

a) Design: A Lolita with brains works her way up the ladder in the legal world by manipulating her boss, a family man, and then dumping him once she's accomplished her primary goals.

b) Development: Fair. Because it's all so obvious and soap-opera–oriented. The main character has no depth, and she's an unsympathetic character.

c) Pacing: Good. Though there's no doubt about what's going to happen next, and very little dramatic tension. But it doesn't drag either.

d) Resolution: Poor. The script suddenly ends. We are left up in the air. The poor husband goes crawling home and we never see the main character again.

That's a brief summary of the analysis and evaluation of the reader's coverage of this particular screenplay. Then there is a *Reader's recommendation,* where the reader adds his or her impressions in a few sentences. In this case, the screenplay is: "Not recommended. A mediocre romantic drama in every respect. It's the unsympathetic portrait of a pushy, midwestern career woman. The ultimate point of the whole thing remains a mystery. It's downbeat, and totally without the black comedy textures one associates with others of the type. It's a cornbelt soap opera, not a feature film."

As short and curt as this coverage is, it is what every studio executive, agent, and movie producer reads to form their opinion.

You might ask yourself what the reader is going to say about your screenplay. If you look at it from the reader's point of view, there's always another script to read; usually the pile on the desk is about two feet high.

Today, more people are writing screenplays than ever before and the popularity of screenwriting and filmmaking has become an integral part of our society and culture. Last year some seventy-five thousand screenplays and teleplays were registered at the Writers Guild of America, West and East. Out of all these, some four hundred and fifty films were produced, either in Hollywood as major studio productions, or by various independent film companies. You do the math.

Within the next few years, the number of people writing for the visual media will probably double and triple in size. And it's only going to expand exponentially as the evolution/revolution of technology impacts the world and the way we see things. It seems this is the only time in human history where we have created a technology which our children are teaching *us* how to use.

Today, we are entering a new phase of visual storytelling. The two most popular majors on college campuses are business and film. And the dramatic rise of computer technology and computer-graphic imagery, along with the expanded influence of MTV, reality TV, iPods, Xbox, PlayStation, new wireless LAN technology, and more, are shaping an international cinematic revolution. Already, we are making short films on our cell phones, so we can email them to friends and family, then project them on plasma TV monitors. Clearly, we have evolved in the way we *see* things.

My two nephews, aged ten and eight respectively, made a surprise birthday video on their computers for their father that displayed an incredible understanding of storytelling with pictures. Needless to say, I was knocked out. They were thinking visually in new ways, fusing an understanding of their source material into a little six-minute film that utilized photographs, video, computer graphics (self-made), live interviews, music cues, and old family footage, and integrated them all into a remarkable visual experience.

The marketplace for the screenwriter is changing drastically and the need for new directions in terms of visual storytelling is in its infancy. Right now, television programming is being made and distributed specifically for our cell phones and iPods. Already, companies are looking to produce specialized material for the vast number of markets that will be available.

The vast constellation of Hollywood production companies is also changing to fit the needs of these new technologies. It won't be too long before the entire motion picture and television market will be something other than what it is today. No one knows exactly what this market will be, domestic or international, but one thing is certain: the opportunities for the screenwriter and visual storytelling will be enormous.

If you're serious about writing a screenplay, now is the time to sharpen your skills and perfect your craft.

The future is *now.*

A lot of people tell me they want to write screenplays. They call me, write me, badger me, finally join a workshop, then two or three weeks later drop out without a word. Their commitment, to themselves and their writing, is zero. Action is character; who a person is is what he does, not what he says.

If you're going to do it, do it.

That's what this book is about. It is both a guide and a tool. You may read this book a hundred times, but until you put it down and do the exercises and deal with the blank sheet of paper, you're only going to be *thinking* about writing a screenplay and not actually writing it.

It takes time, patience, effort, and commitment to write a screenplay. Are you willing to make that commitment to yourself? Are you willing to learn and make mistakes? To do some terrible writing? Are you willing to do the best job you can even if it doesn't work? The things you try that *don't* work will always show you what *does* work.

What's really important about writing a screenplay is doing it. First, set yourself a goal, then create an intention about what kind of writing experience you intend to create for yourself. Then do the exercises at the end of each chapter, one at a time, and soon you'll achieve what you set out to do. That's what this is all about.

In my workshops, after people complete their first-draft screenplay, everybody applauds. It is our acknowledgment of the time, dedication, and commitment to the work they have done, along with the toil, effort, pain, and joy that goes into the writing experience.

The Screenwriter's Workbook is a guide that leads you through the screenwriting process. The more you put in, the more you're going to get out. That's a natural law.

"True art," Jean Renoir once told me, "is in the *doing* of it."

Writing is a personal responsibility; either you do it, or you don't.

It's your choice.

Index

A

I

J

K

L

R

Y

Z